Teaching and Learning

A Model for Academic and Social Cognition

Marjorie S. Schiering, Drew Bogner, and Jorun Buli-Holmberg

Rowman & Littlefield Education
A Division of
Rowman & Littlefield Publishers, Inc.
Lanham • New York • Toronto • Plymouth, UK

Published by Rowman & Littlefield Education
A division of Rowman & Littlefield Publishers, Inc.
A wholly owned subsidiary of The Rowman & Littlefield Publishing Group, Inc.
4501 Forbes Boulevard, Suite 200, Lanham, Maryland 20706
http://www.rowmaneducation.com

Estover Road, Plymouth PL6 7PY, United Kingdom

British Library Cataloguing in Publication Information Available

Library of Congress Cataloging-in-Publication Data

Schiering, Marjorie S., 1943–
Teaching and learning : a model for academic and social cognition / Marjorie S. Schiering, Drew Bogner, and Jorun Buli-Holmberg.
p. cm.
ISBN 978-1-61048-426-8 (cloth : alk. paper) — ISBN 978-1-61048-427-5 (pbk. : alk. paper) — ISBN 978-1-61048-428-2 (electronic)
1. Educational sociology. 2. Progressive education. 3. School management and organization—Social aspects. 4. School improvement programs. I. Bogner, Drew, 1957– II. Buli-Holmberg, Jorun, 1951– III. Title.
LC199.S54 2011
371.2'07—dc22
2011004005

∞™ The paper used in this publication meets the minimum requirements of American National Standard for Information Sciences—Permanence of Paper for Printed Library Materials, ANSI/NISO Z39.48-1992.

Printed in the United States of America

CONTENTS

PREFACE

What led you to want to be a teacher? Do you remember elementary, middle, and high school? Is what you remember mostly positive or negative? Perhaps there is a mixture of feelings and emotions attached to those years. While some teachers excited us about learning, others did not. Some classes were enjoyed and some just had to be gotten through, taking in curriculum that was required by our state government's educational standards.

Something led you to want to teach. Was it an interest in children's success, both academically and socially? Was it a desire to facilitate students, at whatever age, in knowing themselves—impacting their future in a positive manner? This may have served as the impetus for going into the educational field. You're invited to take a moment and reflect on what led you to want to be a teacher.

To be good at this craft of teaching, we understand that those recipients of information are not just thinkers, but feeling human beings. Subsequently, in order to teach the whole child, there needs to be an acknowledgment of differences and similarities of students in our charge. *Teaching and Learning: A Model for Academic and Social Cognition* was created to stimulate this awareness and bring it to realization.

This model presents the things that influence our lives both internally and externally. Just recognizing this presents a broad picture of what impacts learning—our own and that of our students. Subsequently, the first part of this book examines who we are as educators and who our students are as learners. The second portion provides means for implementing and applying the model, whether that is in the school, home, or community.

This book is designed to hold a conversation with you, the teacher candidate, practicing teacher, or interested parent or person. There is information presented that addresses you directly, and at other times there's material for your reflection that may be addressed with a friend or in groups. Much of the text is from our personal experiences as educators, and some is from those of other known authors.

As the famous animation artist and visionary Walt Disney said, "We keep moving forward, opening new doors, and doing new things, because we're curious and curiosity keeps leading us down new paths." "Go forward," we say. "Go forward and enjoy the read! Learn and teach effectively!"

Authors' Philosophy

The philosophies presented in *Teaching and Learning: A Model for Academic and Social Cognition* are based on concepts relating to the model's theoretical constructs. The core perspective is that there's an interrelationship between thinking and feelings that's reciprocal. Reflection on past experiences effect behaviors in the present and influence one's future actions. Thinking and feeling are seen as major influences for behaviors and actions in academic and social settings.

The concept of holons—everything being connected to something (Koestler, 1978), or nothing being separate from anything else, with an interdependence being realized—is part of the model's philosophy. Common social and societal realities experienced in all settings impact on individual and whole groups' belief and value systems. These, in turn, are affected by external factors of religion, economics, academics, and politics to form a world sociology. These philosophies serve as the underpinning and overriding components for knowing who one is as a learner and teacher. They collectively rely on awareness of academic and social thinking and feelings/emotions.

ACKNOWLEDGMENTS

We would like to give special acknowledgment to Drs. Rita and Kenneth Dunn for their learning style model. In many ways, their model served as a philosophical antecedent to *Teaching and Learning: A Model for Academic and Social Cognition* and continues to inform best practice in teaching. Their model involves the active engagement of children learning new and difficult material by knowing their learning preferences within the five strands of environmental, emotional, sociological, physiological, and psychological factors.

These educators have several hundred publications addressing best practice for children's learning, and how to implement learning-style teaching strategies in the K–16+ classroom. They have worked tirelessly for the benefit of student learners' academic success and to this, we are indebted.

Additional recognition is offered to those teachers who read the first version of this manuscript and offered comments regarding its contents. These people are Drs. Robert Kinpoitner, Audrey Cohan, Arthur Morgan, and Larry Honigman, as well as colleagues Ida Ayres and James Million. Sharing of their learning and teaching expertise facilitated our continuance of this book. This led to a reconfiguration of portions of the manuscript and additions. Subsequently, it led to a second reading of the manuscript by additional individuals who were either in education or related fields, or were parents of students presently at the K–16 level in school. These people include Drs. Audra Cerruto and Barbara Hayes, Rev. Susan Lunning, Joan Byrne, Tony and Sue Warner.

Further Acknowledgments

Marjorie Schiering: Special appreciation is extended to my husband, George, who has listened to and commented on the model's content, before and after its initial conference presentation and publication in 2003. As one is his/her experiential past that affects the present and future, the following persons are acknowledged: my children, Matthew, Alyssha, Joshua, Jolie, Mara, and Seth; siblings Judy Borkum and Edward After; parents Mollie and Red; Daisy Schneider; and Roy Pellicano for a comment on a world sociology.

Also recognized are Mr. Bailent, principal of the first elementary school in which I taught in Columbus, Ohio, and all the students who, during my forty-five-year career, showed me that learning and teaching are infinitely interconnected and we never stop learning and teaching, simultaneously. Lastly, there is appreciation for Miss Carragher, who taught me in a tenth-grade social studies class that telling someone "I believe in you" may well serve as the catalyst for their self-respect, and for their coming to the point of realizing "I am enough."

Drew Bogner and Jorun Buli-Holmberg: We acknowledge our spouses, Karen Bogner and Jon Eric Holmberg, for their support and willingness to make available even more time from our personal lives to pursue this academic endeavor.

Combined Special Acknowledgment

The authors of this book collectively offer their special acknowledgment, gratitude, and appreciation to Mrs. Diane Fornieri, assistant to Dr. Drew Bogner. The transcribing of the book's content, addressing photocopying, mailings, corrections to text structure, and a myriad of other activities involved in compiling this manuscript, over a three-year time period, would not have been a reality without her dedication to the overall endeavor. A thank you hardly seems adequate considering Diane's expertise applications, as well as her attention and allegiance to our project.

PART ONE
A NEW LEARNING AND TEACHING MODEL

The Teacher's Hands

For six and more hours --five days a week from kindergarten through grade twelve, and sometimes before and after that, parents put their most precious gifts, their children, into the teacher's hands.

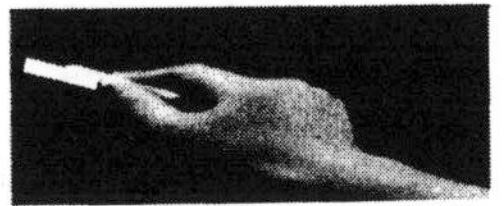

You're becoming a teacher, or you are a teacher, and in either instance you know, whether overtly or subliminally, that the responsibilities of educators encompass a great deal of information presentation and processing. You may see this as the academics of education, as it deals with "what" you're teaching. However, underscoring that, there's the classroom environment, which takes into consideration emotional factors. You would think of this as being "how" the class interacts when learning and as the social part of education. Together they form a whole classroom.

You probably recognize each classroom as being unique because of those occupying that space having different abilities and personalities.

And it is the demonstration of these that come to form the concept of schooling being a diverse situation. So, there are differences, that's a given. What may not be a given is the teacher's role to balance these differences in a way that promotes learning being enjoyable and a process that's worth one's involvement.

During the years of teacher training and later, as educators experience the dynamics of their classrooms, having this mixed academic and social environment becomes clearly evident. Methods courses and those involving professional development are based on "how to" use varied means for disseminating information that needs to be learned. Underneath, or in conjunction with these, are the socialization issues.

Clearly, these impact the shared environment of the formal school setting. In that vein, just one responsibility of teachers is to promote self-awareness and high self-esteem by providing information that will create amicable relationships. Then teaching is not just having what's in a textbook being learned. Teaching also involves the communal interactions of a classroom influencing and being conducive to an environment that promotes, through discussion, definition and modeling, the ability to interact with others.

For six and more hours—five days a week from kindergarten through grade 12, and sometimes before and after that—parents put their most precious gifts, their children, into the teacher's hands. What happens in that classroom shapes those in that space. This develops a desire to gain knowledge and the formation of attitudes, belief and value systems, and dispositions and demeanors.

What happens in the classroom serves as the catalyst regarding a desire to learn. The combination of individual's and the whole group's academic and social cognition, the thinking and feeling in the classroom, and the interrelationship of learning and teaching, as well as the internal and external factors that influence *who* one is as a learner and teacher, are the topics presented in part I of this book.

How would one define teachers? Fundamentally, they are present and future caretakers of learning and teaching. How this happens will influence the very core of who we are as individuals, and what come to be the thinking and feeling realities by which we live—wherever this may be. Because of the academic and social cognition that "is" the classroom, educators/teachers are major "memory creators" for one's lifetime reference and reflection.

CHAPTER ONE

ACQUIRING MEMORY, REALIZING COGNITION, AND COMPREHENSION

We are in a state of becoming: the child, the adolescent, and the adult. All of us, each day, are going about the task of living, learning, thinking, framing, and reframing reality. These phenomena are natural, identifiable, and capable of being described. The person who is aware of memory acquisition, how cognitive and metacognitive processes work, and how comprehension is formed and occurs, is most able to take responsibility for learning—while being best prepared to learn and teach.

The memories we have of past experiences shape the personality we, as learners and teachers, exhibit on a daily basis in the present. And we all have different memories, because we've had different experiences, although shared memories may evoke the same feelings, or ones quite dissimilar. What's important to realize is that we are influenced by our past experiences. We bring them with us every day at any given moment, and since we do this, so do we realize that the children we teach do this as well.

That past influences future endeavors, which rely on individual and collaborative sharing of collective memories. For this reason, this book commences with understanding of how memory works with respect to being a reflective practitioner, realizing what cognition and metacognition are, and then recognizing comprehension in relation to these. The teacher's role in education is that of being "memory creators."

Teachers present lessons that effect and affect learner's cognitive functions, creating and delivering information that will be referenced and reflected upon throughout one's lifetime.

Key words: memory, comprehension, orientation, attention, problem-solving, rites of passage, cognition, metacognition, memorizing

Memory and the Thinking Connection

"What is memory?" you might ask. Memory is the ability to recall information or experiences from the past and bring them to the present. For example, when driving, one passes a diner whose sign and place hold a special recognition. Recalling the pleasant meal had there, and reflecting upon it, a decision is made to go inside and get some supper.

Memories are recalled all the time based on recognition of connected and similar events—this happens in daily life with each of us and certainly the students in our classrooms, framing what they will learn and how they will learn. Various students hold different memories (McNamara and Wong, 2003). The context of how content or classroom material is presented and the classroom environment may trigger different memories in different students, leading to varied reflections that may positively or negatively impact the students' learning.

Cognitively, memory involves recognition, recalling, and reflection. Did you know that memory may be initialized prior to birth? It is! Numerous studies evidence a recalling of smells and sounds initially introduced during a mother's pregnancy. Later these are evidenced as recognized in newborns when they are "experimentally" presented with these sounds and smells.

Developmentally, a baby coos and the parent interprets what is meant by this sound. As the baby matures to being a toddler the cooing is replaced with language that expresses what is wanted, or needed. The comprehension is then less interpretive and more established. Memory has been utilized with cognitive awareness through recognition, recalling, and reflection.

Transition years, referred to as rites of passage, bring specific memories to the fore. These are the years between five and six, emergence into adolescence, then young adulthood. Middle to later years may be seen as additional rites of passage times, as viewpoints and/or perspectives are modified, due to memory of past experiences. Memories are powerful drivers to learning and often frame how a person acts in a given situation. For us as teachers, the same is true: memories both positive and negative can influence how we act and how we approach a given set of content. We love to teach what we love.

For you to personally realize memory, you're invited to look back for a moment and try to recall your earliest memories. This may be difficult, because often memories are most frequently triggered by a present experience, but let's give it a try. Recalling as best you can, you're asked to think about the answers to these following questions.

Where did you live when you were growing up? What was the neighborhood like, and did it change over time? Why do you suppose it did or didn't do that? Who were significant people in your life? With whom were you friends when you first went to school? Are these people still in contact with you? When did you learn to read and write? What were your experiences with these? How did that change over time? Did you like school, and if so, when were the best years? As you matured did you learn to ride a bicycle, or were you walking here and there? What was something/an event funny to you then, and what's funny now? Did you think about driving a car . . . what kind and what was your first experience as a driver?

What about relationships? How did and do you form them? What are things that brought and now bring others to your attention in a negative and/or pleasant way? What do you think about the future based on your past? What are some dreams and desires you've had? What places have you visited near or far from where you live?

When it comes to teaching you might think about these questions involving memory: What style and manner of interaction with a teacher gave you a positive self-image and motivated you to learn? What made a person a good teacher; a master teacher—how do you emulate this? Based on your own personal experiences of learning, what are your three top "to dos" and three "don't dos"? Finally, did you ever wonder how your memory is formed?

Brandt (1999, p. 238) states, "The most fundamental thing scientists have learned about memory is that we do not store memories whole and therefore do not retrieve them that way either. When we remember something we actually reconstruct it by combining elements of the original experience." Neuroscientist Antonio Damasio (1994) explains that a memory is recalled in the form of images at many brain sites rather than at a single site. Additionally, in 2008 he related, "Brain research indicates that multiple usages of neural pathways lead to the laying down of memory traces."

How memory works or the question of why one remembers has been addressed by asking these questions: What causes one to remember some things and not others? Is this due to the personal involvement of an individual in what's happening? Do the spoken or gestured style of delivery and the listener's, viewer's, or participant's interest in the content material affect recollection?

Does one of these take precedence over the others? Gazzaniga (1998, p. 10) stated, "Evolutionary theory has generated the notion that we are a collection of adaptations—brain devices that allow us to do specific things. . . . Many systems throughout the brain contribute to a single cognitive function." Subsequently, each of those aforementioned questions would receive a "yes" answer in that each circumstance influences what we remember.

Then, understanding how the memory works imposes a major dynamic when referencing the connections between experiencing things through our senses (hearing, seeing, touching, tasting, or smelling) and each of these serving as a means for beginning cognitive skill development. What we recall/remember through reflection (feeling-, thinking-, and emotionally wise) influences our memory acquisition (remembering).

In addition, biologically, neurons, which are the functional and structural components of the nervous system, form patterns called "engrams," and simultaneously these activate memory (Shenk, 2000; Yount, 1996). Memory formation is part of cognition, because memory influences the joining of thoughts, ideas, opinions, and judgments with feelings, through recognition, recalling, and reflection. So, what is cognition?

Cognition

There have been a multitude of conversations and perhaps as many articles written regarding the topic of cognition. One questions, "Is cognition thinking?" We respond, "Yes, it is. The words are synonymous." An overall definition states that cognition is the process and/or processes that occur and are labeled, "thinking." However, in a finite sense, cognition refers to the ability of the brain to process, store, retrieve, and retain information.

An example of this procedure may be you receiving an invitation to a party of former schoolmates. You process the contents of the invitation with its given date, time, and directions, as well as the enclosed list of those who've been invited, and you store this information until the date for responding is at hand. At that time you retrieve the invitation's content information and make a decision as to whether to attend or not, resulting from what you've retained about this upcoming get-together—you processed, stored, and retrieved the retained information.

Since cognition relies on the use of memory based on past experiences, ask yourself whether it was easy or difficult to answer all those questions at the start of this chapter. Were some questions easier to address than others, and if so, why do you suppose that was the case? In realizing cognition, the act of remembering occurs in three ways:

1. Attention: the ability to focus on a specific stimulus without being distracted.
2. Orientation: the ability to be aware of self and certain realities and facts while manipulating the information. This addresses the ability of a person to respond to stimuli and align with everyday life experiences.
3. Decision-making and problem-solving: the ability to understand a problem, generate solutions, and evaluate these.

These three areas of thinking/cognition move from and between levels of difficulty. Whether this starts with beginning awareness through the use of one's senses with recognizing and acknowledging the sound of a voice or the touch of a mother, or involves examination of stimuli, prioritizing, synthesizing events, or evaluation—thought is involved. The degree of thinking one does separates cognition from metacognition.

The transference from and between lower-order and higher-order thinking, going from and between cognition and metacognition, occurs thousands of times every day. And we're hardly aware, as we mature, that this is happening. But it does, and the advanced thinking is referred to as metacognition.

Metacognition

Metacognition is thinking processes at the highest levels. It involves the intricacy with which one processes, stores, retrieves, and retains information. The movement from and between one concept to another represents both cognition and metacognition. However, the latter of these focuses on "strategies for planning, monitoring, or self-checking cognitive/affective strategies, and self-awareness when making a decision or solving a problem" (Abedi and O'Neil, 1996).

Some of the thinking processes incorporated for problem-solving, as explained by Fine (1997), subdivide into the following categories: (a) evaluation, (b) explanations, (c) intent assessment, (d) communication, (e) actualizing, (f) judgment, and (g) summarizing, past personal, read, or shared experiences. Using these seven metacognitive terms, examples are provided in statement and then question format to ascertain the meaningfulness of metacognition.

Statement and Question for Meaningfulness (QFM)

(a) Evaluation: Wow, what a great test score! QFM: What made you think your test score was favorable?

(b) Explanations: My thinking is that physical exercise is good. QFM: What are three personal advantages you envision for exercising?

(c) Intent assessment: The activities I observed matched the lesson objectives. QFM: In what ways might you determine a test result other than observation?

(d) Communication: "I saw the deer scale the fence," said Tom. QFM: What was this like for you when you saw it happen?

(e) Actualizing: I'm washing clothes now. QFM: What made you do this now instead of tomorrow?

(f) Judgment: My thoughts about not eating before sunrise are concretized. QFM: What's your strongest thought on eating before sunrise, and how do you suppose you developed that idea?

(g) Summarizing: At the end of each chapter there's information about its contents. QFM: What were three things related at this chapter's closing?

(What are some examples you might give for each of the metacognitive skills listed above?)

Metacognition may also be explained as a set of skills and strategies one uses in monitoring and modifying how one learns, or as the knowledge and control people have over their own thinking and learning activities (Cates, 1992). Examining this idea of decision-making and problem-solving as part of the metacognitive process, it should be noted, requires generative knowledge, which is awareness of material to solve problems (Ennis, 1985).

Also, Blank (1997) relates that it's knowledge being constructed when students restructure or replace existing conceptions. Revealing and reflecting upon the status of one's conceptions and problem-solving techniques, how one knows what one knows, is a metacognitive element. As Bruer (1993) states, "The cognitive process as it relates to metacognition involves patterns and relationships, emotions, the need to make sense, intrinsic interest, formal and informal learning, history dates, and even mathematical formulas. One's way of enacting these processes defines logical structure since so much is based on individual perception" (p. 36).

Another example would be that cited by Bogner (1990) when presenting the concept of solving a problem being part of metacognition, when he states, "Thinking begins as soon as the baby who has lost the ball that he is playing with begins to foresee the possibility of something not yet existing—its recovery—and begins to forecast steps towards the realization of this possibility, and by experimentation to guide his acts by his ideas and thereby also test the ideas" (p. 185).

Therefore, making connections from recalling past experience (memory implementation) is a progressive orientation that results in metacognition (McTighe and Lyman, 1988). This is an awareness and action through thinking and occurs as the equivalent to going back and then forward to examine assumptions or structures in a person's life (Fogarty and McTighe, 1993). With this understanding there are continual connections made between what was and what is and/or may be in the future.

One envisions that "there is not a separation in cognitive and metacognitive reality, but a melding of doing and being, a simultaneous or reciprocity of thinking and feeling for the formation of comprehension/understanding. Comprehension is, ultimately:

- A result of cognition and metacognition with metacognition exhibiting the ability of one to examine a situation;
- Reflecting on past similar or dissimilar situations that have relevance to the one being questioned; and
- Bringing that information forward to solve a problem or address the circumstance in the present or near future" (Honigsfeld and Schiering, 2004).

Comprehension

Comprehension involves memory, cognition, and metacognition. Memory is the storing and then recalling and retrieving of thoughts and feelings. Cognition and metacognition are recognized as being lower- and higher-level thinking. Comprehension is the use of one's memory and these leveled thinking processes with the ability to understand or have knowledge about something. It is the main goal of education.

We want students to gain an understanding of things. As such, school is not the simple acquisition of facts, but rather a place where students come to understand something in connection to how it works, can be used, or the association/correlation to other things. "Thinking/cognition is recognized through 'comprehension' to produce understanding" (Allport, 1937). Comprehension may or may not be verbalized, but regardless of this, it's demonstrated through things said, and/or actions and behaviors in three applications, which include the following:

1. Literal: Fact-based evidence of comprehension.

   Example: The first U.S. president was George Washington.

2. Applied: Comparison and contrast comprehension, resulting from making connections to one's own experience, or read or heard material.

   Example: Reading about Washington's presidency and that of Abraham Lincoln, I think I experience liberty and justice for all, because of their contributions to democracy.

3. Implied: Inferential comprehension, based on context or illustrative material being presented in oral, visual, tactile, or kinesthetic formats.

   Example: Talking with others and reading about several of the U.S. presidents, it seems to me that one of their major responsibilities was setting policies that we use today.

Schiering (1999, p. 30) and Schiering and K. Dunn (2001, p. 45) explain, "These three applications define comprehension as, ' . . . relating to cognition and the orders of thinking, because in making a decision and solving a problem there's a receptive, meaning-making, and active orientation' (Li, 1996; Olsen, 1995). And as Abbott, 1994 relates, 'This active orientation results in learning, which involves conceptual change—a modifying of one's previous understanding of concepts so that they become increasingly complex and valid.'"

Comprehension and Memorizing

If one memorizes information, is that indicative of one experiencing an understanding of it? Actually, memorization oftentimes demonstrates the lack of cognitive interplay that happens when comprehension occurs. This type of memorization is seen as one repetitively receiving the same information. As Freire (1998, p. 34) states in *Pedagogy of Freedom*: "Intellectuals who memorize everything, reading for hours on end, slaves to the text, fearful of taking a risk, speaking as if they were reciting from memory, fail to make any concrete connections between what they have read and what is happening in the world, the country, or the local community. They repeat what has been read with precision, but rarely teach anything of personal value. They speak correctly about dialectical thought, but think mechanistically. Memorizers inhabit an idealized world, a world of mere data, disconnected from the one in which most people live." Subsequently, repetition of material does not result in comprehension, but rather retention of information as a result of this repetition. Would you agree? Why or why not?

Memorization may result in comprehension resulting from cognitive awareness, as opposed to rote memorization—repetition so something is committed to memory. This is done by one realizing, recognizing, acknowledging, classifying, comparing and contrasting, evaluating, synthesizing, decision-making, and problem-solving. This requires acknowledging that there needs to be the reality of cognition, metacognition, and memory being present, simultaneously, or with one affecting, and having effects on the other for understanding, which results in comprehension.

Memorization Effecting Comprehension: An Example

For this writing, Bogner (2007) examines the idea of memorizing being part of comprehension by making connections through referencing and recalling past experiences by using a memory technique. When his daughter was going through a difficult learning task, she related that if she could just memorize the material then she'd know it and comprehend it. He assisted her by making varying connections that served as the memory traces that led to a recollection of each of the United States.

"For memorization of some of these geographical locations it was the states' mere physical shape. Ohio looks like an 'O,' or the 'V' shape of Vermont. For others it was a reliance on other collective memories that was recalled and compared and contrasted in more complex cognitive ways. The comprehension occurred when he made connections to past events in his daughter's life. 'Remember when we traveled to Colorado? It's right next to Kansas, (where we were living in 1995)'" (Bogner, 2007, p. 1).

The simple task of memorization of the fifty American states depicts the variation of richness between the complexity of memory traces (engrams) and the varying levels of cognitive processes that lead to their formation, much more than what we would expect in the classic perceived rote task of memorization through repetition.

Bogner continues, "The standard trick of a 19th Century memorization genius was to place each thought (such as a list of 100 names) in a room associated with an object. For example, the name, Beard, would be associated with the bureau with a shaving cup on it for Beard. This type of memorization wasn't based on *repetition*, but the complex cognitive process of identification of patterns, comparisons and contrasts, and development of a sorting mechanism" (2007, p. 1)

This is much the same as creating memory from a heard story in that one's mind creates associations to assist in retaining the information. Hence, when recalling past experiences, or making connections to the present, thinking happens, and cognition and metacognition are employed, and memorization may well result in comprehension which is, in fact, one form of learning.

(Do you remember memorizing things? If so, to what did you apply the memorization technique? How long do you recall retaining that information?)

Learning

Learning is the process of linking comprehension to cognitive processes by developing skills that are genuinely transferable to everyday situations. "Learning is connected to reflective intelligence and affected by self-awareness, beliefs about one's abilities, clarity and strength of learning goals, personal expectations, and motivation to know about things" (Abbott, 1994). Additionally, learning is a social experience.

As such, learning involves interaction between and among learners as meanings are shared. Information is exchanged and problems are solved in a cooperative manner (Glatthorn, 1995). "The ability to learn requires thinking about one's own thinking" (Olsen, 1995, p. 134). Learning is a reflective process that is colored by individual perspectives including perspectives about self, and it is the subject of chapter 2.

Before we begin the next chapter, there are some questions for you to answer from this one. These serve as a review of the chapter's material. And at this point we ask you to keep a journal for answering these questions. Also, this journal is for writing down anything you may have learned from the information presented, whether here or in future chapters. Or, if you prefer, keep an audiotape around and record your answers, as well as any thoughts, ideas, opinions, judgments, and feelings stimulated by your reading and sharing.

Chapter Discussion and/or Journal Questions

1. What are definitions of memory, cognition, and comprehension?
2. What are some things you remember from elementary, middle, and high school years?
3. What are the three areas of thinking regarding memory and their definitions?
4. With examples, how might these three areas apply in a classroom?
5. How might you explain metacognition and, in written sentence format, what are a few examples of metacognition?
6. According to Bruer (1993), how does metacognition relate to the cognitive processes?
7. What is the connection between cognition and comprehension?
8. What is the definition of conceptual change?
9. What is the connection between comprehension and memorizing?
10. What are three types of comprehension, and how do these differ from one another? Provide one example of each type.
11. What's one definition of learning?

CHAPTER TWO
VARIED LEARNING AND TEACHING PERSPECTIVES

A Question
(M. Schiering)

Born from a thought
On a day of rumination
In solitude amidst a crowd
There emerged, within myself,
pervading questions.
They tickled the cortex of this brain and then . . .
Spread slowly to block out any surrounding or extraneous interferences.
These questions grew with an insistence and intensity,
which could not be ignored.
The questions were:
Who am I as a learner and teacher?
How do I best learn and teach?

There are different types of learning as much as there are diverse ways to teach. What happens when learning occurs? What explains being a teacher? What exactly is learning? What is involved in the act of learning and teaching? Why is teaching sometimes effective and other times not that way? These two processes of learning and teaching seem to go hand in hand. Each complements the other and is necessary for the other to take place.

Because of the complexity and multilayered components of these questions, it's not a simple task to provide one concrete answer to how one learns and teaches. However, understanding the definition of the learner and teacher, one first might examine the varied perspectives of theorists on learning and teaching.

Definitions and explanations of varied theoretical models for learning and teaching, with the baseline perspectives of these two, are presented. The differences between thoughts, ideas, opinions, judgments, and feelings are provided. Attention is given to behavioral, emotional, cognitive, developmental, experiential, sociocultural, and collaborative, as well as several other learning and teaching perspectives.

Each author's perspective is then addressed regarding how their learning theory is *applied to teaching* and the *practitioner's use of the teaching method.* The close of this chapter connects these theorists' learning and teaching perspectives and also provides the theoretical framework for the comprehensive model for academic and social cognition, which is presented in chapters 3–8.

Key words: Learning, teaching, thoughts, ideas, opinions, judgments, feelings, theoretical perspectives

> As I teach I learn and as I learn I teach.
> What I learn and teach varies every day. My present and future learning and teaching are dependent on my experiential past, and how events in my life have been perceived and interpreted.

Defining Learning

Learning, as we realize from information presented in the previous chapter, is a result of memory, cognition, and metacognition impacting comprehension. That is what happens when one learns, and it happens in all daily life situations, since it is a natural process for everyone. As Wenger (1998, p. 227; 2006, p. 1) maintains, "Learning is not an activity, something a person does when they don't do something else. It is not something individuals stop to do, but rather the process of learning happens everywhere and at different levels, individually, collectively and socially."

What are a few things you learned today? What are a few things you learned or revisited, topic-wise, from chapter 1?

The Act of Learning: Information Processing and Modifications

One form of learning is called information processing. This is likened to the mind being like a computer where there is input and storage of information. What happens next, like with the computer, is retrieval of this material, whether words or images. This involves reflection and use of one's memory for what needs to be entered, what is to be stored in some fashion, and means for accessing this information at a later time (Glass and Holyoak, 1986).

Another form of learning involves modification; it involves change, but change in what? Strict behaviorists regard learning as a change in the way one acts. For example, there is an observable change in the performance of a person when he or she has achieved the fine art of the brushstroke when painting a picture, or the proper use of a microscope during a science experiment.

Successes cause change in one's approach to learning. The opposite of success may also be seen as the reason for modifications. For example, one's conduct changes when the aforementioned brushstroke application is not achieved, or the microscope doesn't focus properly. Or success may cause one to alter one's approach by focusing on a specific discipline for additional achievement.

Learning may alternately be defined as a modification in human disposition or capability, which can be retained (Gagne, 1977). During this process a person may learn, but his or her conduct need not change while his or her attitude does evidence this. The appeal of defining learning as a change in behavior, performance, actions, manner, or an observable change in human disposition is obvious. Recognizing learning as observable change allows it to be measured and, therefore, verified.

If learning is defined with no reference to changes in behavior, it is difficult to determine whether learning has actually occurred or not. Linking learning to changes in behavior solves the scientific dilemma of how to measure when and if learning occurs in response to certain interactions with the environment, or methods applied when giving instruction. However, some theorists see the definition of learning as changes in behavior as being too restrictive, failing to adequately explain the subtleties of learning. Varied accounts tend to focus on learning as changes in human disposition or capability.

Hilgard and Bower (1975) suggest that the controversy over learning is really about facts and interpretation of facts and not over the definition of the term *learning*. However, in chapter 1, learning was related to comprehension and its various forms. So, learning involves not just literal/fact-based interpretations, but applied and implied comprehension as well. Most simplistically, learning is a loose, open-textured concept. In the struggle to understand the complex operations of the learning process, the act of learning has been defined in various ways.

There are two definitions that may seem to encompass most learning theorists' perspectives regarding the act of learning:

1. Learning as change in behavior. One example of behavioral change would be a learner moving from not paying attention in class to being attentive.
2. Learning as change in capability. One capability modification would find the learner doing well not just on this assignment, but all others as well, when previously the learner was doing poorly. Another capability change would be a learner approaching an assignment with confidence when previously the learner feared what was to be accomplished.

Depending on the learning theory that one consults, these changes may be demonstrated by a modification in general actions of a person, or by a change in neural pathways and/or consciousness affecting one's dispositions and resulting behavior. Another agreed-upon facet is that the learning process is the result of the individual interacting with the environment. Once again the nature of this interaction is highly variable; it may be a "stimulus-response" situation, or a more conscious and intentional interaction with the environment.

We ask, "How does learning occur? What factors influence learning, allowing it to happen more or less effectively?"

Illeris (1978) was mentioned in an article by Hausstatter and Nordkvelle (2007) concerning group work of students. He claimed that learning evidences conceptual knowledge that's widely used and has many different meanings. We relate the following concepts about learning from our extended research and personal practice:

1. Learning is psychological. This is where learning is perceived as and describes what's going on in each individual. It happens while being characterized by a stable behavioral pattern, as a result of experiences and training.
2. Learning is the interaction processes (direction) between the individual and the surroundings, where the psychological processes are more or less involved.
3. Learning is a by-product of one's experiential environment in accordance with how one responds to it. And it is synonymous with teaching, as imagined that the learner has learned what has been taught.

In summation, learning is a complex phenomenon that is influenced by many factors. At its foundation, it's a reconstruction of past experience that influences individuals' and whole groups' behavior and dispositions.

Defining Teaching

Teaching is the act of passing on information for learning. This may be accomplished in a variety of ways, and these are addressed in the concluding chapters of this book. Most importantly, teaching is defined by the style of delivery and attention to learners' needs that one uses on a regular basis in the classroom or other settings where learning occurs. Haugsbakk and Nordkvelle (2007, n.p.), referencing the new language of learning, related that "teaching is the facilitation of learning."

For teaching to be effective and affective the learner is understood to be more than a passive recipient of knowledge, but rather one who is actively engaged in the learning process by being involved through teacher attention to, as Dunn and Dunn (1978; 1992) relate, the classroom's environment and emotional, sociological, physiological, and psychological factors.

What makes teaching effective is teacher modeling with respect to demonstrating a teacher's personality and attitude being positive and uplifting, experience in instruction, aptitude that connotes an underlying ability to disseminate information while being a reflective practitioner (Borish, 2007), providing motivation, and an overall desire to have learners learn.

Then, whether the learner learns what has been taught is dependent on *who* the teacher is, by understanding what thoughts, ideas, opinions, judgments, and feelings are being conveyed. To better understand that, the following definitions are given concerning differences between these cognitive terms (Schiering and Bogner, 2007). (In chapter 5, these are given specific attention in a narrative scenario.)

1. Thoughts: Immediate conscious responses to reflection, which involve memory. Reflection is further defined by Schon (1997) as having two forms, which are reflection "in" action, or thoughts occurring now in the present, and reflection "on" action, as referencing something that happened in the past. Example: From my experience, I have thoughts that focus on learning being multidimensional.

2. Ideas: A prediction of future responses or speculation based on one's perspective as a result of reflection. Example: She got the idea about good teaching practices from the book on educational theory.

3. Opinions: A combination of thoughts and ideas in that a formulated concept results. Example: The teachers were asked their opinions of the curriculum.

4. Judgments: Concretized thoughts, ideas, and opinions which are impacted by memory, while being based on reflection concerning past experiences. Oftentimes based on one's level of attachment to a situation. Judgments are not easily changed, but they may well change. If easily modified, then you've ex-

pressed a thought, idea, or opinion, as opposed to a judgment. Example: My judgment is that many teachers are facilitators of learning. Until evidence of this is demonstrated on a continual basis not to be true for you, the judgment will remain a judgment—solidified thought.

5. Feelings: A sensory and/or emotional response to stimuli that may be descriptive or classificatory. Example: The water felt soft as it slid through my open fingers.

   Feelings are also defined as being the quality that something has in that one responds in a manner that connotes feeling of an emotional or intuitive nature and/or reflects on something to establish a formed response that is grounded in thought, ideas, opinions, and judgments. Example: The music collectively evoked the audience's strong sense of joy as the symphony began.

   Subsequently, feelings and emotions are one and the same and can be observed or defined as being joined. These then are transrational responses to stimuli in that a sensory response to situations occurs at the same juncture as deeply held thoughts, ideas, opinions, and judgments. Feelings/emotions may be seen as "root responses" to stimuli.

Combining Learning and Teaching: Theoretical Perspectives

Educators enter the classroom or approach the learning situation with a set of assumptions; assumptions about themselves and assumptions about the learner and his or her capabilities and interests, as well as assumptions about how learning occurs. These assumptions, whether conscious or subconscious, help the teacher frame how he or she will approach, design, and structure the process of learning for the student. It is important to note that most educators borrow from more than one theory, using various ones to gain perspective on different aspects of the learning process.

This is understandable, as most theories are attempts to elucidate/illuminate precise aspects of complex natural phenomena. So, in practice, most educators respond to the process of learning and teaching, as they draw from bits and pieces of various theories and social assumptions. Some may be well thought out and nameable while others are less discernable. But what an individual believes and assumes will surely impact how the teacher teaches and how he or she will approach the learner and the learning process. From what you've read thus far, ask yourself how you think learning occurs and teaching is best conducted.

Experiential Learning: Dewey and Kolb

Bogner (2008, p. 1) synthesizes Dewey's thoughts on learning by relating, "Learning may be defined as a reconstruction or reorganization of experience which adds to the meaning of experience and increases ability to direct the course of subsequent experience." He continues with this synthesis in the bulleted areas that follow:

- "Learning is a natural process. Throughout life, it is evident that individuals engage in learning, striving to connect life's events to meaning" (Bogner, 1990, p. 110).
- Learning is stimulated by problematic situations. "Learning, by being a natural event results from an equally natural situation, namely controversy or discrepancy. To learn, individuals must be actively engaged in a mental process of connecting events to meanings" (Bogner, 2008, p. 1).
- Learning is an active process. Learning results from the active involvement of the individual in reflecting upon an experience and an action he or she performs in an environment. For example, the learner pounds a nail into the wall and hangs a painting on the nail, only to see the painting crash to the floor as its weight pulls the nail from the wall.
- Learning occurs next when the individual reflects on the results of his or her action. In this case, the learner refers back to the directions that came with the painting, noting now the paragraph directing the individual to sink anchors into the wall to hold the weight of the painting. This reflection on the ac-

tion and the conclusions drawn from that reflection represent the learning. One may learn from the above example that it is important to drill a hole in the wall and insert an anchor prior to hanging the painting.

- Another may reflect on the same experience and draw the conclusion that he or she is simply "not handy" and "learned" from the experience that, in the future, he or she needs to hire someone else to hang works of art. Subsequently, learning from the experience may well result in two people drawing two entirely different conclusions from the same experience.
- Learning involves the formation of connections between various ideas, meanings, and events. Learning is experientially based and is essentially a process of detecting connections or relationships between one's environment (termed *experience*), and the mind and the action (termed *reflection*). Simply stated, "Learning results from reflections on an individual's experiences" (Bogner, 2008, p. 1).
- Learning is a directed mental activity. The processes of learning and thinking are intricately connected, with neither being a random process, but seen as being linked to specific needs or goals. According to Dewey (1938), all knowledge, thinking, and learning grow out of experience. One must do, but in order for learning to occur, one must also reflect on the doing. The act of learning involves both a sensory or experiential component and a mental or cognitive component.

Bogner (2008, p. 2) explains that Kolb (1984) concurs with Dewey in that new knowledge is born out of "observations and reflections" made in association with the individual's current stock of meanings, concepts, and knowledge. The new knowledge is, therefore, developed out of the old knowledge. The new knowledge is a *reconstruction* of the old knowledge. Observation and reflective inquiry lead to thoughts on the applicability of currently held beliefs or meanings about the ways certain things operate in the world. These new thoughts lead to a reconfiguration of meaning.

Experiential Learning Applied to Teaching

The teacher subscribing to the experiential theory of learning will construct lessons that give the opportunity for the student to learn by experiment, by doing, or by constructing something; in short, by being active in the process of learning. This theory of learning is antithetical to the theory of learning that presupposes that the learner is just taking in information "that comes to the person in an already prepackaged way" (Schiering, Buli-Holmberg, and Bogner, 2008, p. 12).

According to the experiential theorists such as Dewey and Kolb, learning only occurs when an individual has the opportunity to perform an act, either mentally or physically, and then reflect on the meaning of this action. During the process of reflection, the individual forms new connections between this act or piece of information and others, which are a part of the individual's previous experience.

The process of teaching serves to improve upon the natural course of learning. It formalizes what is often a random and haphazard activity. It encourages the individual to do and to reflect on the consequences of his or her actions, to form connections between previously unrelated events or actions.

Practitioners' Use of Dewey's Method of Teaching

- Structure the subject matter of education so that it is consistent with the experience of the learner;
- choose content for learning that is useful, consistent, and applicable to the present experience of the learner and not just useful in a distant future;
- individualize the subject matter or content to the experience of each student;
- accentuate learning by emphasizing both doing (experience) and reflection; and
- extend one's learning situation into another field or to further the experience of the learner into new situations ripe for continued learning.

In a traditional educational setting, when things have to "be made interesting," it is because the interest itself is wanting. In Dewey's method of teaching, if a teacher wants to be truly concerned with lessons being interesting, relevant, effective, and productive, then the teacher should carefully select subject matter which relates to the learners' current or past experiences. If the teacher is successful in this structuring of subject matter, then the student will learn and enjoy the process of learning. It will seem natural. Indeed, it is natural (Bogner, 1990).

Developmental or Hierarchical Learning: Piaget

Piaget (1936/1963) focuses on how the development of language influences the process of thinking. His theory focuses on maturation and cognitive development in age-related sequential stages. The basic principle in his theory is that children construct their own understanding. Knowledge is not a copy of the reality. Therefore, learning is a process in which the child, through assimilation and accommodation, develops meaningful structures of knowledge.

This happens when children have their own experiences and interpret these based on an already established structure of knowledge, which relates to Dewey and Kolb's perspective. However, it differs with respect to the knowledge only being provided, with one acquiring the first stage of development before being able to move to the next.

According to Piaget, the child seeks equilibrium between an established structure of knowledge and new knowledge through the aforementioned assimilation and accommodation. The former occurs when a new impression fits into an already established cognitive scheme. The latter occurs when one changes an already established cognitive scheme and learning on a higher level happens. Therefore, new learning results from an expanded thinking pattern by the adaptation of the new and adjustment of the old.

Developmental or Hierarchical Learning Applied to Teaching

Educators who follow this model are likely to construct lesson plans that are considered to be "age appropriate." This is accomplished by making sure that the tasks and the subject matter match the cognitive level that is considered "normal" for the age group. The teacher addresses assignments with the assumption that one must master certain lower-level cognitive skills before one can access and use higher-level cognitive skills. Young children and prelanguage children are not capable of higher-level, more complex thinking; subsequently teachers will presuppose certain outcomes as being possible and others not, without testing whether higher-order thinking is actually being experienced by the learner.

Practitioners' Use of Piaget's Method of Teaching

Educators at the preschool level would focus on such tasks as classification, understanding of time, and numbers. Avoidance of experimentation and hypothesis formation would occur, as these are higher cognitive skills not believed present until later ages. Movement between age groups is not realized in the classroom and moving between lower-level and higher-level cognitive functions is discouraged.

Fundamentally, children learn by exploring their environment and learn best when given a chance to manipulate it. However, the processing of these interactions varies by age and the cognitive developmental level. As one develops greater cognitive abilities, one's understanding of subject matter becomes richer and more complex. Therefore, the acquisition of cognitive skills and knowledge may be planned from grade level to grade level, moving from lower to higher levels of difficulty.

Sociocultural Learning: Vygotsky

This theoretical perspective is based on learning as a construction of knowledge between the individual and the society. As social beings, much of our learning occurs within some type of social setting, happening within groups or as a result of interactions with others. Vygotsky (1978) was concerned with the process of developing the higher levels of thinking such as memory, attention, decision-making, and concept formation.

According to his theory, each of these results from culturally required development by scaffolding or building knowledge. He maintains that the individual, already from his or her birth, is a social and collective human being. The person's development is dependent on surrounding conditions such as home conditions and the learning environment in schools. While Vygotsky agrees with Piaget that language is an important tool for thought and problem-solving, he relates that the child's competence has to be understood from three aspects:

1. The "actual zone," which refers to what the child can do by himself or herself;
2. the "potential zone," referring to what the child can manage with help from others; and
3. the "proximal zone of development," defined as occurring between the actual and potential zone (Vygotsky, 1978; 1986) as "the distance between the actual developmental level, as determined by independent problem solving and the level of potential development, as determined through problem solving under adult guidance or in collaboration with more capable peers" (1978, p. 86).

Sociocultural Learning Applied to Teaching

Individuals seek out and are seen as often being aided in learning by persons who have more knowledge and understanding of the subject matter. This person is referred to as "the competent other." Teachers who follow this theory will structure learning to take advantage of this natural process of learning from others with more knowledge.

Practitioners' Use of Vygotsky's Method of Teaching

Teaching assignments and information reception will focus on tasks the learner can do without assistance and also may manage with help from others. The teacher will assemble groups where individuals who are more competent will be in a position to assist those with less knowledge or competence. Likewise, the teacher or the school may assign mentors or establish tutor relationships.

Assignments can also be constructed that will push the student into conversations with more competent individuals—for example, interviewing a person who has expertise on an issue or can share another perspective. The practitioner applying Vygotsky's theory would be likely to incorporate differentiated instructional techniques when teaching.

Ecological Learning: Bronfenbrenner

The ecological components of Bronfenbrenner (1979) include various aspects that impact the human development processes, as well as learning. Special emphasis is placed on the social settings where learning occurs. His learning theory gives possibilities for analyzing complex and dynamic development processes. Bronfenbrenner defines the method of this ecological process as being progressive, a reciprocal adaptation between an individual's development and the changeable environment that surrounds him or her.

As a result, learning occurs when one's development is influenced by the social relations that arise in and between the different settings where one is a participant. Transition is a central component in ecological theory and occurs "whenever a person's position in the ecological environment is altered as the result of a change in role, setting, or both" (Bronfenbrenner, 1979, p. 26).

Ecological Learning Applied to Teaching

A learner's development is a direct consequence of the number of different groups, settings, and roles in which the person interacts and is engaged. Following this theory, teachers will structure the learning environment to place students in a variety of roles and settings, challenging them to be team leaders, writers, scientists, artists, and/or collaborators.

Practitioners' Use of Bronfenbrenner's Method of Teaching

The teacher must be inviting to students, encouraging them to take some risks in their new and varied social settings and roles. It is the dynamism of risk-taking that is critical to development. In a holistic way, this practiced theory gives support to the importance of the arts and music in the curriculum and the equal appropriateness of the presence of extracurricular activities, such as athletics, in the school. This is because all of these activities allow the student to assume different roles with varying social groupings, leading to greater personal development.

Collaborative Learning: Wenger

Wenger (1998) relates that interactions with others help each individual to bring more out of the learning process than he or she could if he or she had not acted together with others. Therefore, thoughts, ideas, and understanding develop within the individual but not independent of others or outside of society. It is through interaction with one's environment that one can develop extended knowledge. In this perspective, Wenger presents the concept of learning conditions as a way to explain the interplay of human relations where learning happens. Learning conditions are always a part of a social relation.

Wenger (2006) explains that the individual is the focus, and as a person in the world, he or she is a member of a sociocultural community and signals that learning happens in a context. "Communities of Practice are groups of people who share a concern or a passion for something they do and learn how to do it better as they interact regularly" (p. 1). Learning that happens in one specific, practical, and social context is not automatically transferred to another context. Knowledge and skills will be situated to specific types of practice, as certain group setting and interactions enhance learning, while others detract from it.

Collaborative Learning Applied to Teaching

Because learning happens in social settings, teaching is often culturally bound, with the learning being connected to a specific situation. Transference of thoughts and context are not harmonious between varied social settings. However, the collaboration within a group enhances comprehension of presented material.

Practitioners' Use of Wenger's Method of Teaching

Teachers will structure group settings, such as classroom interactions, so that these situations assist the individual learner through the group's usefulness or overall effectiveness. Educators who follow this theory will not assume that learning in one setting can automatically be transferred to another setting. Instead, the teacher will need to assist the students in making connections between one situation and another, helping the students to see how an already acquired skill or set of knowledge is pertinent to the new setting.

amental component of this type of teaching is that there is action within groups. Also, the students have a sense of com- in their group. Roles within the group are not assigned, but rather a flow of discourse and discovery occurs with the group's sharing. All members of the group are respected for their contribution to the group, which results in collaborative learning. A gaining of information, or even a change of one's perspective with regard to circumstances of a given environment, are factors to be considered when designing collaborative learning.

Individual Learning Styles: Dunn and Dunn

Over time, many educators have noted that different individuals within their classroom perform better at some tasks than others. And individuals who perform well in one discipline may perform badly in another and vice versa. Drawing from these observations, educators and theorists have concluded that individuals possess varying learning styles that correspond to the individuals' differences in perceptive ability, cognitive processing, information management, and sensory variability.

Keefe (1979) noted the learning-style movement emerged from the reform movements of the 1960s and 1970s as a key element toward increasing instructional responsiveness to individual students' needs. Keefe and Languis (1983, p. 56) "describe learning style as the consistent patterns of behavior and performance by which an individual approaches educational experiences." "Learning styles, therefore, are the composite of characteristic cognitive, affective, and physiological behaviors that serve as relatively stable indicators of how a learner learns, interacts with, and responds to the learning environment" (Schiering, 1999, P. 17).

A popular learning-style model in the United States is that of R. Dunn (1984) and Dunn and Dunn (1978; 1992; 1993). It rests on research conducted during the past three decades. The theoretical cornerstone of the Dunn and Dunn model is based on the brain lateralization theory. It's noted that within an individual a particular hemisphere of the brain *may be more dominant* than the other. Or, in another case, a dual brain dominance, where both sides of the brain function equally, is evidenced. Additionally, this model relates that most individuals can learn;

different instructional environments, resources, and approaches respond to different learning style strengths.

The Dunn and Dunn learning-style model begins with the environmental strand, which includes a preference for or lack of interest in sound, light, temperature, and room design. The emotional strand is next and addresses the elements of motivation, responsibility, persistence, and structure. Six elements characterize the third strand of sociological factors. These include what type of work collaboration one prefers, or for which one has a low tolerance. These include working by oneself, in pairs, with peers, on a team, with adult authority, or varied groupings.

The fourth strand is the psychological one with elements of perceptual preferences (auditory, visual, tactile, or kinesthetic modalities), intake, preferred time of day, and mobility. The final strand is that of physiological, and the elements in their model are analytical and global (field independent and field dependent), with the former exhibiting a preference for math and science and the latter for the arts. Also this strand refers to processors being reflective or impulsive. Researchers observed that the right brain processes information in intuitive and holistic ways. The left hemisphere, conversely, is more analytical and sequential in its manner.

The strands and the elements within them represent factors that, in different combinations, can influence the learner in the process of learning. This model is not an alternative to established theories of learning, but is rather seen by Dunn and Dunn as a complementary model based on neuropsychological and cognitive theories.

Overall, when a student is learning new and difficult material by reacting to certain elements within the strands, hemisphericity is evidenced with preferences for (a) no sound being present or some sound—even the whirring of a fan being necessary; (b) high-intensity lighting or soft illumination—such as a table lamp; (c) formal room design with a desk and chair or informal room design where one studies while sitting in a chair or lying on the carpeted floor; (d) working alone or in partnerships, in groups or teams; (e) no snacking or food intake or taking frequent breaks for food; and (f) sequencing material, or seeing the whole picture.

"The first one of each of aforementioned indicate what's referred to as an Analytic processor (Field Independent). This is where left brain dominance is demonstrated as the individual constructs information in a structured sequential manner while working on one project at a time to completion. The latter of those referenced in *a* through *e* signify a right brain dominance or Global (Field Dependent) processor who needs to see the whole picture, and works on many projects simultaneously without necessarily completing any of these by the assigned date or time" (Schiering, 2008, pp. 1–3).

Individual Learning Styles Applied to Teaching

Teachers who adhere to a learning-style philosophy create a classroom design that is both informal and formal. These respectively address preferences of global processors, who like soft illumination and an informal room design with sound present, and analytic processors, who like to have high-intensity lighting and a desk with a chair for learning tasks. The informal area may be a comfy corner that has carpeting, throw pillows, or the like, and accommodations such as individual headsets for listening to music softly played while concentrating on material.

Other classroom accommodations would include working alone or with others, in partnerships, in teams, with peers, responsiveness to authority figures, and the opportunity for healthy snacking, with the rule of "if you abuse this privilege—you lose it" being applied. Of course, the losing it would only be for a short period of time, as opposed to a full day or week. The child that is hungry is most definitely not able to concentrate on learning. Analytic learners would not respond to this particular "intake" provision, as they are not in need of snacking.

Practitioners' Use of Dunn and Dunn's Method of Teaching

The most important components for practitioners for this model are that each of the five strands and elements within them are addressed on an individual basis. Also, small-group learning situations are recommended. Learning style teachers provide opportunities for working in partnerships, as global processors do not like to work alone, while analytics do. Since perceptual preferences are not indicative of one being right- or left-brain dominant (global or analytic processors), teachers would be sure to have all modalities implemented for application of varied instructional techniques.

This means that some projects or assignments would require tactile/kinesthetic involvement, while others may be more auditory and visual.

Realizing that the left-brain processors are usually highly structured, motivated, responsible, and persistent, the teacher would want to create assignments where different processors may work together in small groups or on a team, and allow for some "alone" time for those field independent learners.

The basic premise within the classroom and at home regarding learning styles is that the elements represent preferences that should be acknowledged. A learning-style inventory, as well as teacher observation, may provide preference information. Children who are physically comfortable in their learning environment are more likely to learn and approach it in a positive fashion than those who are continually working without recognition of their preferences in some or all of the strands. Ultimately, differentiation of instruction is evidenced when student learners' favored ways of learning are addressed.

Self-Efficacy Learning: Bandura

One's sense of self-efficacy and how this influences learning is the focus of Bandura's (1977) theory. Primarily this addresses the various factors that impact a person's development in feeling that he or she is in a state of well-being. It specifically focuses on the principal ways of understanding efficacy as a part of development.

This is with respect to how it affects the quality of a person's psychological perspective. How a sense of efficacy operates in individualistic and collectivistic social systems is given attention. There are many factors that influence development of collective efficacy and the way a person struggles to regain control over conditions that affect their feelings about themselves.

Bandura (1997) maintains that individuals struggle to exercise control over events that affect their lives. The capability to produce a valued outcome and to prevent undesired ones therefore provides powerful incentives for development and exercise of personal control. A strong sense of efficacy in a socially valued pursuit will be conducive to human attainment and well-being. As such, a person's level of motivation, affective states, and actions are based more on what the person believes.

To understand what motivates a person, Bandura (1997; 2003) explains, requires that we need a framework that synthesizes the origins of beliefs of personal efficacy, their structure and function, the process through which they operate, and their diverse effects. These are simultaneously imposed and include:

- Cognitive processes: These influence a personal efficacy in a variety of forms. When a person sets goals, they are influenced by self-appraisal of capability. The stronger the person perceives self-efficacy, the higher goal challenges they set for themselves. Actions are initially organized in thoughts. What a person believes about his or her efficacy shape the types of scenario they construct and rehearse.
- Motivational processes: These refer to a person's foresight, motivating the actions one chooses. What a person believes influences the expected outcomes and motivation. Foresight is a personal guide and influences one's motivation for choosing or not choosing a particular action. A person's level of effort and need for success mobilize the person to use or not use their capability and resources.

  There are three different levels of cognitive motivation: causal attribution, outcome expectancies, and cognized goals. Motivation influences the goals people set for themselves, how much effort they expend, how long they persevere in the face of difficulties, and their resilience to failure.
- Affective processes: These involve how a person copes with difficult situations. Personal capability to cope with stress and depression affects one's level of motivation. Efficacy beliefs also affect how a person perceives and cognitively processes stress and controversy.

  If a person believes that potential threats are unmanageable, he or she will look at many aspects of his or her environment as fraught with danger. This distress can impair one's personal level of function. Conversely, if a person looks at situations as being nonintrusive and relatively calm, then the level of functioning is a state of acceptance and comfort.

- Selection processes: These are when a person believes his or her own efficacy can shape the course of his or her life related to the types of activities and environments, which cultivate certain potentialities and lifestyles. He or she will avoid activities that he or she believes exceed his or her coping ability and select activities that he or she believes he or she is capable to manage. Various factors influence a person's choice and affect the direction of a person's development.

Self-Efficacy Learning Applied to Teaching

An important action for the teacher is to develop a learning environment where all students have the possibility of developing their own self-efficacy and motivation for the activity. When learners are able to do activities that they believe they are capable of doing, higher levels of student self-motivation will result. Following this theory, teachers must be aware of the need for the learner to believe in himself or herself, value who he or she is, and feel secure in the learning environment.

Implementing a self-efficacy learning perspective may be achieved by teachers providing guidelines for being persons of good character. Defining and modeling respect in the classroom impacts learners' sense of self-worth. Motivation then is a central factor and essential to creating interest in learning. A stimulating learning environment can affect the learners' personal development and self-efficacy in a positive way, taking care of the learners' need for experiences that give them mastery and acknowledgment.

Practitioners' Use of Bandura's Method of Teaching

The teacher needs to create an environment with opportunities for mastery, giving the talented student academic enrichment as well as giving attention and support to those who struggle academically. One of the teacher's main tasks, therefore, is to create a learning environment that focuses on the learners' strengths and to devise solutions for intervention where weaknesses are present.

In schools there is pressure to report on tasks mastered and not mastered. However, if success is to be achieved for the learner, it is important for the teacher to start with activities that the learner will be able to master. The academically talented learners often get a lot of positive feedback, while learners who struggle often feel that they get negative feedback. This lack of positive feedback can influence the motivation of these students in current and future academic activities, and teachers must be conscious of rectifying this situation.

Empowerment Perspective: Dunst, Trivette, and Deal

Different theories of empowerment share a common theme, namely that the primary emphasis is on the strengthening of an individual's ability to control personal events within daily school situations. The empowerment perspective focuses on how human needs and concerns are viewed, how one addresses concerns and desires, and how one's operational outcomes are related to indicators of success (Dunst, Trivette, and Deal, 1994).

Five years later these authors relate that empowerment has been championed by a number of behavioral and social scientists and practitioners in diverse fields, such as education, early childhood intervention, family-centered intervention, and participatory research. The idea of empowerment serves as a major force challenging entrenched thinking about the capability of people and the role they can play in shaping their own destinies.

Empowering refers to both the behaviors and the beliefs that reflect the individual's sense of mastery and control over important aspects of his or her life. There are some key factors that are important in the empowering of a learner. These are enabling, enhance and promote, capability, and supporting and strengthening.

- *Enabling* is used to refer to opportunities that are afforded to individuals to use existing competence, as well as to learn new competencies necessary to mobilize resources to meet needs or achieve aspirations.
- *Enhance and promote* are used to facilitate pro-social and positive aspects of behavior that strengthen a sense of mastery.
- *Capability* refers to knowledge, skills, and competences that individuals use to mobilize resources to meet needs, achieve aspirations, and fulfill the individuals' functions.

- *Supporting and strengthening* refer to the outcomes of human service practice resulting from efforts to enable and empower individuals.

Empowerment Learning Applied to Teaching

The empowerment concept relates that teaching is incumbent upon an individual's ability to learn, dependent on how the person feels about himself or herself. If the individual feels enabled or sanctioned, he or she may approach the learning situation very differently than if he or she feels uncomfortable, ill at ease, or diminished.

Practitioners' Use of Dunst, Trivette, and Deal's Method of Teaching

Educators who follow this model strive to place students in situations where they will feel some sense of confidence in approaching the learning task. Teachers understand as well that students who have achieved some sense of mastery on one learning task will approach the next task with more confidence, and there will be a higher chance of success in learning this new task.

Viewed in extreme by critics, teachers who follow this model are seen as being soft on content, wanting for students to only "feel good about themselves." But building on various research, the educators who subscribe to the theory of empowerment look back on the evidence that demonstrates that pupils who have succeeded will succeed again, and that those who feel no sense of empowerment will approach each new lesson with trepidation and, therefore, may not succeed as frequently.

Biological Brain-Based Learning: Jensen, Damasio, and Brandt

Biological theorists focus on the anatomical and physiological changes that occur within the brain as learning occurs. These theorists are concerned with describing the ways in which memories are formed and understanding the variables that impact these processes. Brain-based theorists connect holistic health issues such as exercise, emotions, stress, nutrition, and positive attitudes to healthy brain functioning.

Subsequently, more effective learning occurs (Jensen, 2008; Damasio, 1994; Brandt, 1999). At its core, biological brain-based education is founded on the simple observation that the brain is shaped by experiences the individual has—modifying and shaping the experiences one has can shape and modify one's brain.

Brain theorists have also noted that the brain, like muscle tissue, grows and develops from usage and can be shaped and molded from the performance of specific exercises. Damasio (2008) mentioned that a lack of physical activity and mental activity results in reduced brain capacity. Subsequently, the active brain functions better than one that is not involved in creating physical activities and/or mental exercises, so that learning best occurs when one is involved or engaged in that process.

While various parts of the brain are associated with different functions, there also appears to be a difference in the way information is processed by the two hemispheres. Drawing on the original work conducted by Nobel laureate Roger Sperry, researchers observed that the right brain is more visual in nature, processing information in intuitive and holistic ways. The left hemisphere, conversely, is more verbal in nature, processing information in a more systematic and sequential manner.

While subsequent research has indicated that these processes aren't quite as polarized as originally thought, researchers and educators have noted that some individuals tend to favor one hemisphere over the other, relying more on the type of processing of information that is associated with the right or left side of the brain.

Biological Brain-Based Learning Applied to Teaching

Educators who follow the science emanating from brain research will structure their lessons to accommodate for the individual differences students bring into the classroom, designing activities that allow for sequential thought and/or holistic thought, as well as convergent and divergent thinking.

Brain research conducted on individuals who have lost functionality in some parts of the brain, due to injury and disease, have shown remarkable plasticity, with the brain compensating for loss of functionality by relying on similar functions to compensate. For example, the loss of brain function on the left side of the brain leads to difficulty with speech. The same area of the brain on the right side is devoted more to the language expressed through song and rhyme. This being the case the individual can still communicate through song and the right side of the brain can be taught to compensate for the loss of left-brain functionality. Teachers armed with this knowledge know that they can approach the teaching of language in different ways, allowing the usage of song to assist those individuals who might be more right-brain dominant. The predominant idea is to have active engagement in learning so the brain is stimulated.

The research on the impact of stress on learning also posits the teacher to be more attentive to the classroom environment and the impact of feelings on learning. Stress can and does impact learning and as science indicates, stress can vary from environmental to emotional issues in individuals.

This theory promotes structuring the classroom's environment to diminish stress and provide opportunity for exercise to allow the brain to function better. Brain-based education supports the inclusion of physical education within a school and also presupposes that a school must be concerned with providing good nutrition to its pupils. A whole pedagogy of techniques has been developed geared at awaking the brain and stimulating it to enhance performance.

Connecting Theoretical Perspectives

Each of the learning and teaching theorists' perspectives presented in this chapter have useful and viable components in and by themselves. However, none of them, as with most learning and teaching models, are comprehensive. Most present one or two constructs with regard to the learner and teacher interplay. However, a model for academic and social cognition incorporates something from each perspective while adding to them.

This is done by providing an interconnection of social and academic cognition, and reciprocity of thinking and feeling. Additionally, there are external components that influence common social and societal realities and belief and value systems. Realizing these provides the knowledge about *who* one is as a learner and teacher. This results in the formation of an all-inclusive theoretical construct that may be implemented with practical classroom applications.

Theoretical Framework of Teaching and Learning: A Model for Academic and Social Cognition

Collectively and independently, as theoretical practitioners of cognition, we have researched a wide expanse of learning and teaching models. Numerous researchers' perspectives, and various theoretical frameworks developed by other theorists, have been examined, and we've added our own observations to come to a *comprehensive model* combining academic and social cognition's impact on learners and teachers for information processing and dissemination techniques, as well as classroom implementation.

At the most basic level, we begin with the observation that thinking is a natural process. When observing the behavior of a toddler, even at a prelanguage level, one can observe the presence of thinking. Various cognitive processes interplay at differing levels of complexity; simple observation, experimentation, classification, or hypothesis formation leading to a realization of the child's place in his or her environment.

The child or adult displays these various levels of cognitive processes in a classified manner. "These are addressed as the *Reciprocal Thinking Phases*. They're termed: Beginning Awareness and Acknowledging, Critical and Creative Thinking, and Metacognitive Processes" (Schiering, 1999, pp. 32–33; 2003, 554–55). At any age, individuals move seamlessly between and among these various cognitive phases in a mutual manner (Bogner, 2008).

At the very beginning of the life spectrum there are behaviors that connote the cognitive process through nonverbal actions. Each of us interprets these through our own experience as new meaning is constructed. A basic example is seeing a baby smile at the sound of a voice. The cognitive function of acknowledging this reaction is clearly evident. This process continues until the baby develops speech that expresses thoughts, ideas, opinions, judgments, and feelings. This is done by forming meaning, as a result of what is happening in and around his/her home, neighborhood, family, community, and ever-increasing expanse of social/societal structures.

Feelings and emotions, as well, impact thinking. Thinking and feeling are joined and influence each other within and between one another in a reciprocal fashion. This concept is termed the *cognitive collective* (Schiering, 2005). As thinking and feelings influence an individual and/or groups of varied sociocultural standings, an awareness of *who* one is as a learner impacts *how* one learns.

This includes attitudes and dispositions, as well as behaviors toward learning and teaching. We explain that this awareness then impacts on the methods used when one learns and teaches, resulting in reliance on acknowledging, recognizing, and realizing what one thinks and feels.

Individuals' concepts regarding self-awareness within organized religious and social, academic, economic, and political settings and situations are enhanced through reflection. Such reflections create an individual, as well as group definitions of one's perceived place or sense of belonging within those varied environments. Sociocentricity may come into play. This is where the group defines the individual's membership in it by adherence to its rules or standards.

If one does not comply with all the rules of the group, then one is excluded from it. Subsequently, a sense of belonging doesn't exist. What is important to know is that as easily as one is socially part of something so is one separate from it. Nonetheless, individuals come to relate to various situations through the experiences they have within them.

What one thinks and feels forms belief and value systems. These begin in the nuclear family, regardless of its configuration with two parents, one parent, guardian(s), or the other circumstances of caregiving in this setting. These beliefs and values then continue to be formed outwardly and inwardly, as a world sociology influencing one's own and the impact of others' thoughts, ideas, opinions, judgments, and feelings with reflection on religion, economics, academics, and politics, affecting learning and teaching.

We believe that there is a sociology of the world and within this there are common social and societal realities that encompass and transcend one's culture. It is these common social and societal realities that serve as a basis for discussions and exchange of viewpoints. They are the effects we experience each day and are as ordinary as how one gets to work, the places one likes or dislikes visiting, and movies and/or multimedia formats preferred, as well as a multitude of other things.

The social cognition exchanges bring solidification or modifications of individuals' cognitive collective. In turn this brings one back, in cyclical fashion, to the concept of who one is as a learner being an ever-changing natural process. This happens as new experiences are encountered and meaning from them is constructed. As such, the authors believe that equal emphasis should be placed on *who* one is as a learner and teacher, as well as on *how* one utilizes the model for learning and teaching.

The overall theoretical framework of *Teaching and Learning: A Model for Academic and Social Cognition* relates that while learning is a natural process, it is certainly a complex phenomenon, which is interconnected. Learning and teaching are impacted by common social and societal realities experienced on a life-cumulative and daily basis, the belief and value systems one has, the individualistic and varied ways in which information is remembered and processed, the thoughts and feelings that emerge, and the social groupings and relationships in which the individual finds himself or herself.

Linking all of these factors together into one holistic model would be advantageous to the learner and teacher. A model for academic and social cognition does that and is the topic of chapter 3, with its elaboration and practical application in the K–16+ classroom addressed in the remaining chapters of this book.

Chapter Discussion and/or Journal Questions

1. On what does the experiential learning theory reside? How would you practice it?
2. What is meant by hierarchical learning? What is one way to implement this perspective in a lesson?
3. How would you explain the social component of learning?
4. What are differences between actual, potential, and proximal zones in Vygotsky's philosophy of learning?
5. What are the strands of the Dunn and Dunn learning-style model, and what are some ways these and their interior elements can be applied in a classroom?
6. How does the perceptual preference section of learning style equate to differentiating instruction?

7. What are the four components of empowerment learning, and how are they used in a classroom situation?
8. What is the focus of biological and brain-based learning?
9. What is an example of someone experiencing self-efficacy?
10. How does a model for academic and social cognition differ from other theories and perspectives presented in this chapter?
11. What are four components of a model for academic and social cognition?

CHAPTER THREE
AN OVERVIEW: A MODEL FOR ACADEMIC AND SOCIAL COGNITION

The Child That Dreams
(M. Schiering)

I am still the child
And I shall spend these years
In dreaming
Of what I have not
But wish for and could be
And you shall teach me
So that I may grow with
Truth and knowledge
To become the person within my being
Who will turn one day to teach another
Who is still the child that dreams.

Who are you as a learner and teacher? What comprises who you are in being these? How different do you suppose one teacher is from another one? What are common traits and what comprises differences in one's learning and teaching? What do you suppose influences the style of teaching, implemented methodologies, and personality characteristics that impact the learning environment?

The answer to these questions begins with the thought that each of us is the recipient of learning in academic and social settings—just as we are the creators of these. Who one is as a learner and teacher is incumbent upon this exchange premise—being the learner as one is the teacher. The overview of the model includes its philosophy, history, and concepts, as well as cultural and other influences on learning. A definition of a learning model is given attention in this chapter.

Key words: model, philosophy, umbrella term, reflection, SOW and REAP, phenomenological perspective, culture

The Model's Philosophy

You are invited to think of yourself standing somewhere, as a separate entity from all others. What surrounds you? On what are you standing? What objects are nearby and what ones are at a distance? As you reflect, recall those things that bear a resemblance to you now, whether in physical appearance, thinking, and/or feelings. Write down what you see in the journal you're keeping about the book's discussion questions. You are still you, but in some ways are aware that you're connected to others through places you've been, ones you want to visit, things you desire to experience, and a multitude of images that put you where you are presently.

Yesterday, you were in another place alone or with other people, listening and/or seeing things the same or differently than you did today. Growing up there were experiences that shaped you and those around you who helped to influence who you were then and who you are today. This truth for you and is true for those you teach or will teach. In some manner, there's an irrefutable connection. This learning and teaching model is based on that concept and its philosophy serves as the sustaining component of a holon—everything being connected to something.

This linkage may also be stated as nothing being removed from anything else. Koestler (1978), as cited by Wilber (2000, p. 40), relates, "One whole part is part of another whole." Each section of this model is connected to every other part of it with an intertwining like that of a finely woven tapestry. Each section is reliant on the other sections in that there's synchronicity among and between the foundation upon which it rests, core components, reciprocity of thinking and feelings, and the four external factors of the model.

In the classroom, there are multiple factors at play that impact learning. In keeping with the concept of a holon, these factors are interconnected. Teaching is most effective when the teacher attends to the multitude of factors, understanding their interconnectivity. Understanding, for example, that how a student feels about himself or herself, the presence of a positive classroom environment, the way in which a lesson is presented, the teacher's affect, and external events such as home life all impact learning.

At its core, our education philosophy is based on an understanding that there's an interrelation between thinking and feeling in the academic and social spectrums. This combination has not previously been presented as primarily and fundamentally linked, but rather has been seen as separate one from the other. This chapter joins thinking and feeling cross-culturally. The learning goals focus on the presentation of new terms for comprehension of learning and teaching.

There is an ongoing learning and teaching exchange with respect to how and what cognitive skills and feelings impact one's actions. We propose that the way in which this exchange of learning and teaching occurs for the betterment of all is by active engagement in the experience. This is such that one's remembering it is a natural occurrence.

We asked one another, as you might, "What's the tipping point between thought, feelings, and behavior?" We responded with an agreement that the place where thoughts become actions relied on knowing about one's thinking and feeling. With that being the case, we wondered about what encompasses our thoughts and feelings right now. We agreed with Million (2007–2008) when he said in a conversation that "the 'now-being' of a particular moment is when one witnesses an experience, or is 'in' the experience and therefore impacts thoughts and feelings in the present."

Schön (1983) refers to this concept of thinking being reliant on reflection "in" and "on" action, where the former is within the moment and the latter is referencing that time. "Subsequently, we extended their philosophies to include one's attention (focus), orientation (awareness in the present time), memory (recalling), and problem solving (addressing solutions to situations) in the actions one takes now. This partially forms who you are as a learner and teacher" (Schiering, 2000–2010, pp. 32, 27).

Our educational philosophy also addresses observations students and learners make in the now being of a person having substance because of an experiential past from which to draw. These would be for interpretation, decision-making, problem-solving, or general relating. Subsequently, our perspective is expanded to include a comprehensive awareness that there's a foundation of belief and value systems which influence actions through not just thinking and feeling, but knowing what one is thinking and feeling.

This all-encompassing philosophy refers to a time continuum of thoughts, ideas, opinions, judgments, and feelings passed along through generations of home, neighborhood, school, community, cultural, group, and individual interactions—with accommodations that meet the present "now" of one's being, regardless of geographic locations.

Included in our educational philosophy is an underscoring of a pervasive relevance to "positive" thinking and acting, and modeling of respect, caring, fairness, responsibility, being trustworthy, and being kind with good citizenship. Taking these concepts and exhibiting these through your behaviors serves much like a plant's root system, where life-giving water, sun, and soil nutrients are essential for the plant's growth. In the educational field, we believe that learning is akin to the plant, in that nurturing one's thinking and feeling allows for growth.

Sustaining life in the field of learning and teaching relies on modeling concerned interest, loyalty, open-mindedness, appreciation, and acceptance in teaching each individual by meeting the needs, interests, or styles of the learner. You are invited to do that as you take the learning and teaching concepts presented in this book into your life behaviors.

Further addressed and called attention to is the process of teaching—realizing that each learner requires life experiences upon which he/she may reflect. This is accomplished through memory acquisition and implementation, synthesizing, and analyzing information by knowing what cognitive and metacognitive skills are being utilized.

Additionally, there needs to be an understanding that thinking and emotional learned responses become natural through practice to form *who* one is as a learner and teacher. It is that naturalness which may take a lifetime to complete. But nonetheless it is passed on from generation to generation, as we reciprocally learn and teach the child that dreams of what he or she may become, and dwells within the self or another.

The Model's Historical Overview and Concepts

A model for academic and social cognition was developed by Schiering in 2003. However, the implementation and ever-modified practice of it began in 1965 in her fifth-grade, inner-city, culturally diverse classroom in mid-America. In the years that followed, she implemented the model in various international and national geographical locations, when teaching varied grade levels, which included college undergraduate and graduate courses, as well as during her conference presentations, and in educational journal publications.

In 2008, as she worked with Bogner and Buli-Holmberg, the final model was developed and presented to various international groups of educators. These presentations and the audience's responsive sharing resulted in the following synthesized concepts:

1. each learner and teacher knowing who he or she is when learning and teaching,
2. each learner and teacher realizing they're individuals and acknowledging their learning preferences,
3. both the learner and teacher understanding the phenomena of learning so that they may be effectively managed, and
4. using the model to promote a holistic view of learning and teaching for realizing a classroom community that encompasses an overall sense of security and well-being.

As individuals, both the learner and teacher in the roles of students and/or educators experience phenomena through interaction with the environment, responding cognitively or emotionally. In order to be an effective teacher, one must realize who one is as a learner and teacher, thereby gaining a working comprehension of individual uniqueness and strengths, as well as being aware of what one is thinking and feeling. This is done in conjunction with realizing students' thoughts and emotional responses, resulting from their shared and/or internalized experiences.

Knowing more about these with respect to you is commonplace. However, knowing about those of your learners is less often experienced. It requires you becoming aware of your students as individuals, persons grouped together in a classroom, and how each one best learns. Now, that's not an easy task, but with some background information, which is presented in the following chapters of part I, you have the opportunity to become aware of what makes the "you" of you, and what makes "your students" your students.

It is critical that both the teacher and the students understand how learning happens. Teachers are learners too, constantly expanding their knowledge of content, learning about themselves, and refining their craft, ultimately as educators. The goal then is for both the student and the teacher to come to the point of realizing how they learn and who they are as learners, and having the means to manage their own learning situations.

Culture and Other Influences on the Model

Let's think about your culture with respect to teaching and learning. It may be "'considered a medium for growing things' (Eisner, 1997, p. 353). For each of those in the school setting, there is a mutual exchange with an intertwining of the 'roles' each is expected to play. In a fashion, we are growing students as we ourselves grow, so that *who* we are as learners and teachers are in a state of culturally-influenced learning, and teaching interaction" (Schiering, 2003, p. 554).

What are some characteristics you have that are a result of a cultural group? Are these the same as those you teach or have observed in preteaching classrooms, or remember from your earlier years in school? Were you in multicultural classrooms? If so, how did differences come to be similarities, or did they? Was there classroom harmony, friendships that brought everyone together? Were some excluded while others were included in social ways?

Those are tough questions and probably as difficult to address today as in your yesterdays. But in order to comprehend the differences in students, it's important to know what brings us together and what might separate us, which is reliant on what's called the "Phenomenological Perspective—the study of perceptual experience in a purely subjective format" (Trigwell and Prosser, 1997, pp. 241–52; Schiering, 1999, p. 28; Schiering, 2003, pp. 555, 556, 558).

This perspective is a descriptive or classificatory account of any life event that is apparent to the senses. Subjectivism, we realize, provides a very broad range of thinking and feeling. As a learner and teacher, it is the art form of bringing learners together to appreciate different cultural influences and shape these into a cohesive group. Just being aware of that is important.

Students come together in a classroom with cultural influences; what might some of these be? There are style of dress and preferred foods, activities, and even ways of communicating with one another, as well as learning. "In the anthropological sense, a culture is a shared way of life" (Eisner, 1997, pp. 349–53), and encompasses the art, beliefs, behavior, and ideas of a particular society.

In the collective sense this provides recognizing individual and societal commonalities and/or differences that include cultures, as well as the thoughts and feelings that formed them. Most of our reactions to cultural influences in the classroom will depend more on how teaching is conducted than what is being taught.

One task of the teacher is to imagine and then configure the situations/experiences through which the student learner's thinking can be operationalized. This is where thoughts, ideas, opinions, judgments, or feelings can ensue and a memory is created, because the experience has meaning. Of course, these are personal or idiosyncratic, where differentiation is exhibited through interpretation, one's point of reference, and perception. Concurrently, as the learner and teacher conceptualize the need for varying instructional modes to foster learning and one's response to the experience, there needs to be comprehension concerning thinking and learning, as well as the language of thinking and social literacy, or conversations that occur, as Schiering (2003) states:

> The experiences shared in academic settings, as well as those outside it are influenced by books that are read, and television programs viewed. Whether inputs are reports on current events, situational comedies, drama or the like, Internet research, video games, and the myriad of overt and subliminal discourse that is encountered on a daily basis, each should be taken into account when addressing who one is as a learner and teacher.
>
> Social and societal contexts, form and have formed, shape and have shaped the physical, cognitive and emotional learning environment we have come to create as parents, siblings, relatives, friends, teachers and even strangers. (p. 554)

Definition of a Learning Model

Since this chapter addresses our learning model, we think it's worth mentioning the definition of a model. "The noun model implies an active, personal construction of one's own theory, as well as its inevitable change in content and function with experience" (Bretherton, 1985, p. 33). That's a relatively simple way of stating that models of learning and teaching address things such as cognition and metacognition, and strategies used to teach. To be effective, a model must be accessible to learners and teachers with ownership, as opposed to borrowing some components while disposing of others.

A pervading attitude that this belongs to me, because I adhere to its philosophy, techniques, and instrumentation while internalizing and personalizing it, is recognized when using a model (Borkowski, Estrada, Milstead, and Hale, 1989, p. 64). "To own a model, in this sense, implies that a teacher/student must practice its major components, receive guidance in modifying related instructional techniques, adapt the model's characteristics to the unique circumstances of the classroom, and update the model based on personal experiences" (Borkowski, 1992, p. 253). As Idol, Jones, and Mayer (1991) stated, "Students using models and guides allow for exposure to critical thinking competencies within the curriculum content and do not require the creation of a separate timetable, but allow for a natural transfer of thought" (p. 52).

You might look at a learning and teaching model as being similar to constructing a model airplane. First you go to the store and select the exact model you want. Since there's a picture on the cover of the box, you find this relatively easy. Then, your model preference in hand, you open the box at home. Here you begin to put it together, realizing that someone put all the pieces you need to construct this in the package for you, along with some instructions. Working diligently, you put each piece together with a bit of glue, until you have the finished airplane, ready to fly. It's yours and you made it. You take ownership of it and use it.

Then, a friend comes over and you play with the model airplane together. You take turns and enjoy the experience. Each of you takes ownership of the model in this using of it during the time you're sharing. A learning and teaching model is like that, as when you use it, it belongs to you. Maybe you'll make your own one day and maybe not. Nonetheless, it's yours while you use it.

Taking the definitions and operations of a learning model, a model for academic and social cognition, is like that model airplane and we've presented it in this and the following chapters of part I. It takes into account the "now being" concept. It provides learners and teachers with the opportunity to examine who they are as individuals in educational settings as well as social/societal ones. This is because the model deals with thoughtful practices and experiential learning and teaching, along with reflection on the mutual exchange of these, which forms who one is in these realities.

The model partially rests on the culture, which was addressed earlier, that is designed to develop thinking and the related learning that goes with it. Our model is addressed in the next chapter with specific reference to the foundation upon which it rests.

Chapter Discussion and/or Journal Questions

1. What is the philosophy of this model?
2. How did the model come to be created?
3. What are the four "concepts" of a model for academic and social cognition?
4. To what do "culture and other influences" refer?
5. What's the definition of a learning model?

CHAPTER FOUR

THE MODEL'S FOUNDATION: SOW AND REAP AND THE UMBRELLA OF REFLECTION

As discussed previously, when you were reading about culture, the text related that "in a fashion we are growing students as we ourselves grow." As educators, we are sowing learning seeds. We hope these will reap knowledge, as thinking, feeling individuals and as persons who are informed, active members of our classroom, neighborhood, community, society, and world. How we model what's to be learned connects with many outside-the-classroom influences. Through reflection on these influences, a sociology of the world (SOW) is realized.

Four external factors that impact this reflection include religion, economics, academics, and politics (REAP), which are internalized to recognize *who* we and our students are, as learners and teachers. A model for academic and social cognition attempts to bring together the various interconnected phenomena that impact learning and as such shape effective teaching.

An illustration of the model is provided (figure 4.1) along with the definitions of the acronyms SOW and REAP. Schools, seen as the neutral meeting ground for students of varied cultures, are examined in two different schools. This is with respect to a world sociology and in respect to religion, economics, academics, and politics. A summative analysis is also provided. Making a personal connection to SOW and REAP is given, as the chapter culminates with questions for reflection, the model's umbrella of reflection, and an introduction to the model's interior components.

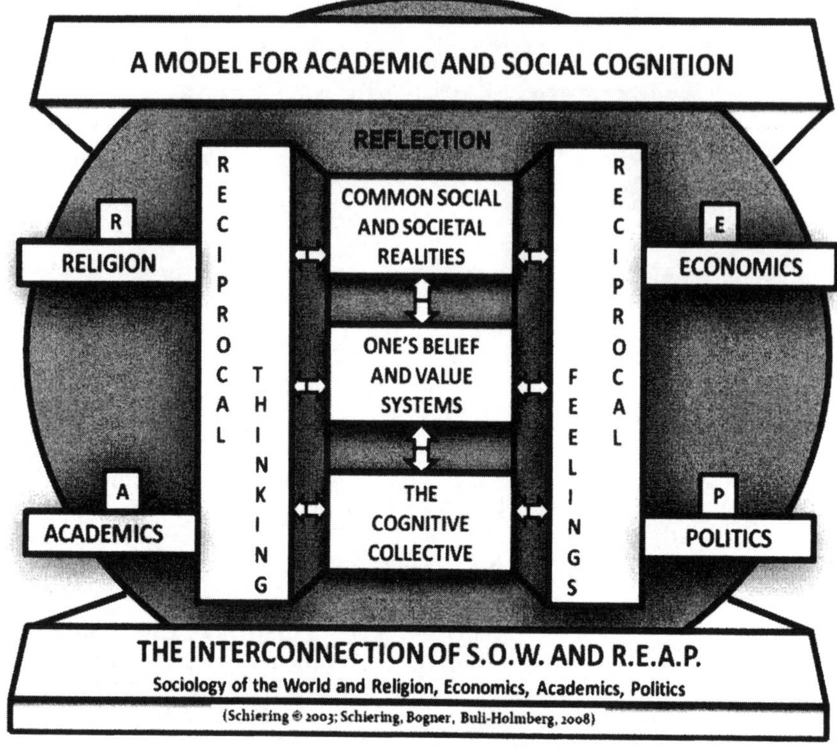

Figure 4.1. The Interconnection of SOW and REAP

Key words: sociology of the world, external factors, religion, economics, academics, politics, comparisons, umbrella of reflection

The Acronym of SOW: Sociology of the World

Sociology is defined as the science of human society and of social relations that exist within and between organizations. This includes changes within those settings, which specifically addresses the needs and development of such groups. In that simplistic definition, this concept is reliant upon linked experiences—those read about, modeled, observed, or listened to, that are universal and conventional within and between varied groups of people . . . in a neighborhood . . . in schools . . . in classrooms . . . everywhere.

Taking this explanation into account we examined the idea of there being a sociology of the world (SOW) in that there are areas, within all cultures, of familiarity. This is a result of shared customs/traditions, routines, and social structures that have come to be accepted ways of conduct, whether in the way one speaks or acts. "A Sociology-of-the-World is formed through the interconnection of the things that contribute to unifying people regardless of their age, gender, ethnicity, socioeconomic or educational level, race, religion, cultural mores, or language" (Schiering, 2003, pp. 556, 560).

What are five customs, routines, or social structures that you think shape the "you" of you? Here are some question clues to assist in finding these. What's your usual routine for getting up and going about your day? What are the holidays you celebrate? Is the clothing you wear similar that of to those with whom you work or play? With whom do you share traditions or customs? Does sharing these traditions and customs cause you to feel connected to them or these persons? What are the social structures in which you participate? Are these work ones, organizations, volunteering, or all, or some of these? The answers to these seven questions provide you with, hopefully, a comprehension of the things that bind us together and/or separate us in a sociological sense.

Considering the sociology of the world concept, we invite you to recognize that external factors regarding your religious beliefs, economic situation, academics, and political views and laws will impact each social structure. This is the social structure of you and, yes, your students. Also, the external factors of others will impact you and your students, and ultimately be determiners in how you teach, and sometimes, what you teach. This is because these form the customs/traditions and routines with which each of us is most comfortable and exhibit by what we say and do on a regular basis.

The Acronym of REAP: Religion, Economics, Academics, and Politics

Within the context of the classroom, in respect to SOW it is helpful to identify specific factors, external to the teaching and learning instruction, that may shape or influence what happens to both the teacher and the students. There are many, but we have chosen to focus on the primary ones that are identified by the acronym REAP. These are the four, with definitions of each, for our comprehensive learning and teaching model.

Religion refers to the belief or nonbelief in a deity, adhering to this belief, and worship of a supreme being or beings' controlling power. It is based on a faith practice that adheres to worship and traditions imposed by either humankind or a deity/deities concept that attempts to explain the unexplainable.

Economics refers to the science that deals with material or emotional-based welfare, in that material welfare influences perceptions of life experiences.

Academics refers to the scholarly activities of a school or learning setting that impact the student learner's belief systems, self-actualization, and achievement levels.

Politics refers to the influence of governing agencies and the exercising of power in the government or public affairs of a state, municipality, home, or school.

These four factors of religion, economics, academics, and politics move inwardly and outwardly to influence behaviors and attitudes in the commonality of groupings, regardless of their geographical location. REAP is an understanding of a disposition of these situations that addresses what come to be recognized as habitual behaviors within cultures and noncultural congregates.

How would you identify and explain the influences of REAP in your daily routines?

Connecting SOW and REAP to Learning and Teaching

In addressing the external factors, let's look at the connection of these four (religion, economics, academics, politics) in learning and teaching, as each one separately and together impacts a world sociology. Also, they do affect learning and how teachers teach. For example, individuals' or whole groups' religious/worship/faith practices, beliefs, or lack thereof, have an effect on an individual's affective behaviors and dispositions.

This is realized through the attitudes and values proposed, generated, and practiced by that grouping. Religious practices of others in our communities and on a world spectrum impact our lives as differences and similarities cause discord or harmony. Or they may reside somewhere between these two perspectives, where toleration provides collaboration or cooperation, irrespective of exhibited dispositions.

These attitudes and values are demonstrated in specific and general demeanors displayed in learning environments with traditions surrounding observance or nonobservance of such things as ideologies: what's considered right or wrong, or rituals and ceremonies recognized by that religious group. With respect to learning and teaching, religion may shape curriculum and the culture and social mores of the school. In private faith-based schools, religion is considered an appropriate subject to be taught and prayer is encouraged. In public school, religion exerts a push and pull on curriculum.

There is pressure on one hand to remove all religious references and a push on the other hand to include religious references in the curriculum. For example, the Bible as literature and prayer at school events connect to religion. Some curriculum items such as evolution become focal points of discussion, serving as both social and political touchstones that can divide or bring together a community, as demonstrated practices, beliefs, and values are held to as truths.

Religion may be viewed as a connection to the underlying economics of an individual family. This could be through its impact on the overall demeanor/dispositions concerning the affordability, as well as permissibility, of materials being available to assist and/or stimulate and encourage education in the home. Are there books available to read sitting on the bookshelves at home?

Some other questions regarding economics might include whether the family owns a computer or provides access to the vast stores of information available on the web. Does the family have the resources to travel, visit museums, the library, other countries, or places of historical significance? On the most basic level, can the family provide nutrition and shelter, essential to the child's ability to concentrate and focus on learning in school?

Economics, correspondingly, of the community at large, also impacts teaching and learning in an education-based setting. Some school districts have many more resources available for technology, safe and inviting school facilities, and up-to-date textbooks. The realities of failing school bond issues and narrow declining tax bases force many school districts to increase class size. This might also limit or remove supplementary educational experiences such as art, music, or foreign language.

Academics, including subject matter and pedagogy, greatly influence learning. Can students relate to the subject matter? Is the content taught in ways that allow for meeting students' needs, interests, or varying learning styles? Is there an opportunity for students of varying ability levels to pursue their own interests and relate to subject matter at differentiated stages of intricacy?

If we believe that the commitment to external assessment and published test scores precludes any innovative teaching techniques, we may eschew or avoid them at the onset, rather than finding ways to be creative concerning how we teach what must be taught. If we believe that the students, because of their socioeconomic background, will not be able to learn as well as students from more affluent backgrounds, we may often teach with less enthusiasm, challenging them less and expecting less of them.

Or the converse of this may be viewed and realized with respect to social justice being part of beliefs or values. This causes one to discover ways to circumvent the financial issue by seeking outside funding through grants or charitable organizations, or to make necessary contributions to enhance the economically depleted learning environment. With that in mind, the political situation comes into perspective.

Politics is closely linked to religion, academics, and economics, as the politics within a school can influence what is taught. It also impacts how teachers view themselves and teach with comprehension of what is considered acceptable in educational settings. The idea of support for a more open classroom or the district being heavily committed to teaching to the test comes into play.

So too does one's ability for political correctness. This is with respect to what may or may not be expressed, emphasis or de-emphasis on alternative means of assessment, creativity and imagination being honored, or rote memorization being favored. All these and more are understood in the political arena.

Does the school encourage and support innovative teaching techniques? What government-assisted programs are available and the criteria for eligibility impact what may be part of the political agenda. Politics can also influence academics by determining what content is taught and what textbooks are selected, depending on the governance structure adhered to by the overriding laws, constitution, or parliament of that agency. How do you think the political atmosphere impacts your school and/or teaching?

Each of the external factors of this model is reciprocal in nature and part of one another, as they're joined. This is with regard to the context from which we choose to reflect upon and evaluate these SOW and REAP acronyms. And their inherent meanings are to be considered, as this provides personal beliefs about how and what one learns and teaches. The following pages compare two classrooms with respect to SOW and religion, economics, academics, and, lastly, politics. After each comparison there's an overview of the material presented and then a culminating summary.

Classroom A: SOW and Religion

Ms. Jones, a fifth-grade teacher at the Ninth Street School, had twelve girls and fourteen boys in her class. While they were bused to school from different areas, they had been in each other's company since kindergarten. They were of varied European, Asian, and African ethnicities. "Quite a group," she'd once commented when talking about loving teaching them and learning from them as well.

The students' religious beliefs, values, and having good family relationships were very important to everyone, and so was doing well in school and being good in sports and Scouts. These factors partially shaped their sociology. Students came from one- or two-parent households. Some were with half sisters and half brothers, due to their parent's divorce and remarriage. And some lived with grandparent(s), which wasn't so strange, as Ms. Jones had once lived with her grandmother.

Everyone had their own situation and everyone knew about the others' home lives. In their classroom there was a community of caring about one another. The social setting was quite harmonious. This was partially because they'd come to respect and accept their religious differences and/or similarities during the five years of their being together.

Religious practices included adherence to many students being from Christian homes. There were several Buddhists, two Quakers, a few Hindus, and several Muslim children in the class. Their positive belief and value systems were based on their nuclear families' religious backgrounds, with their traditions shared during the year through discussion.

Classroom B: SOW and Religion

A conversation with Heidi, a fifth grader in the Thompson School who'd moved from Oslo in Norway, was really interesting. First she'd shared about her coming to the area because her mom remarried and her new dad's family lived close by. Things were quite different in the "new place," she'd once said. For one thing, there were eighteen girls in her class and only ten boys. In her former school there was a more even ratio.

Regarding beliefs and values, which were primarily a result of their family's religious teachings, neither Heidi nor her classmates were separate in their thinking. She'd made friends with girls and boys from different ethnic backgrounds. Yet, while they observed and practiced different religions, there was a commonality of purpose to be kind. And, even though they had very different roots, everyone got along well. By midyear Heidi discovered that everyone didn't go to church. Where she'd come from almost everyone was Lutheran and this religion was part of the school's curriculum.

In the community in which she now lived there was a Buddhist temple and a synagogue, as well as many churches near one another in the center of her town. Throughout the year she'd come to realize that religious practices played a major role in their lives regarding what was valued. This was, overall, an accepted way of life for everyone and brought about a sociological meld. It wouldn't be uncommon for a student to be absent due to celebration of a specific religious holiday that other classmates didn't observe. The students shared a sense of togetherness with respect to believing in a "higher power."

Overview of Classroom A and B: SOW and Religion

Both of these classrooms demonstrate a composite sociology of the world in that there are different ethnicities and religions practiced. The classrooms bring the students together with a sharing of life experiences. These promote the common need for learning and gaining information that will serve to unify the respective students in their futures. This is with regard to accepted societal norms and their overall religion-based beliefs and values.

Classroom A: SOW and Economics

Economically, this was a "mixed bag" classroom. It was common knowledge that not everyone lived in the same type of house. The "projects" around school were where half of the class lived. Others had houses of varying size—some with yards and some without them. Some children were bused to school, and when there, shared in celebrations of upcoming holidays and one another's birthdays.

They didn't visit in each other's homes, as feeding an "extra" person was not in the budget. But they did stay after school for various programs and socialized there. Then, during the year, there was a Multicultural Day where they shared different ethnic foods brought from home. This was a looked-forward-to day, as everyone partook in the partying, with each student sharing their cultural heritage.

Many of the children's parents were out of work, which affected home economics a good deal. But their children's education was considered a priority, so school attendance was good. One interesting common social area for the students in this class involved affording a pet. Several children had a dog and most of the classmates had one sort of animal or another, ranging from fish and reptiles to cats and birds. Only one child did not have a pet and kept pestering her mom to get one.

As for the school itself, each of the thirty-five classrooms, had at least one computer, and there was a computer program class where all students went once a week. Only two of the students had computers in their homes. There were school morning, lunch, and after-dismissal programs, Scouts and art classes being two of the latter. This was commonplace since the mid-1990s. Economically, the school was relatively sound, and relied on some federal funding. Nonetheless, it was noted that local community and general aid-to-school programs had been utilized for over twenty years.

Classroom B: SOW and Economics

Heidi lived in a really big house and so did most of her classmates. They had huge yards and almost everyone had a dog or cat for a pet. And the community even had training schools for dog obedience. Economically, they'd be considered affluent. Overall, Heidi thought that her neighborhood was pretty neat, and so was her class, where everyone took part in national holiday celebrations.

Most everyone walked to school and met along the way. Things like celebrating holidays, spending time together during vacations by visiting each other's homes, and even having a sleepover now and then on a weekend were pretty common. And when there, "getting to eat different types of foods was cool," Heidi had thought. Once she'd brought a special Norwegian dish her mom loved to cook and everyone thought it was terrific.

When Heidi went to a sleepover, she found out that everyone, like her, had a computer at their home and a pet, and most had more than one cell phone. They played the same video games, and liked similar music. But Tom's dad was an executive and recently lost his job and he told his friends that they were "strapped" for cash. Heidi couldn't relate well to that, but empathized with her classmate.

Most of the children in Heidi's class got a weekly allowance from their parents. The school did not rely on federal funding, but it was available. The PTA sponsored events for any "extra" money needed to buy things for a class or the school. There was a strong sense of community and shared interest areas. Most moms didn't work and it was common practice for them to visit their child's classroom and share in projects that were sponsored by the library, or be involved in classroom-related programs during the year.

Overview of SOW and Economics

The B classroom experienced an elevated economic level as compared to the A one, where the home front found many parents on unemployment. Unifying socialization factors included national holiday celebrations, various types of pets in the home, awareness and use of computers, and children having get-togethers, as well as good nutrition through familial endeavors or school programs.

Both classrooms evidenced the sociology of the world with attention to initiatives/programs that were considered part of the times. Socialization in and, for classroom B, outside the classroom, were present for addressing a conglomeration of beliefs and values that affected societal norms. Monetarily, although funds came from different sources, the students' and schools' economic needs were met.

Classroom A: SOW and Academics

When it came to academics, there was a wide range of ability levels in the students' classroom. There were four English as a second language (ESL) teachers, because many students were bilingual, and there were four resource rooms for special-needs students. Two years ago a gifted and talented program had been added. At this point there were enough children in it to warrant its continuance. The school followed the national and state standards by providing instruction that met these requirements. While the national test scores varied in this classroom, the school met the mark for maintaining good grades.

Teachers were given latitude regarding academic modes of instruction and biweekly meetings found the teachers sharing ideas and methods that met the needs of a varied student population. One teacher's idea addressed creative writing with many photographs on the hallway bulletin board. Children wrote as if they were either someone or something in the picture, and/or expressing thoughts and feelings about it. This resulted in everyone getting involved in writing or having conversations about the writings. A sociology of the world was experienced through a sense of school unity both academically and socially with a central focal point being the meeting of students' needs.

Classroom B: SOW and Academics

When it came to academics, everyone was pretty much on the same page. Nonetheless, there were two ESL teachers who came into the classroom daily, because of a few students being bilingual. There were two resource rooms for special-needs students in the school. Also, there were two gifted programs, in the arts and sciences. Heidi and eight of her classmates attended these.

Heidi's classroom/school had programs in place that involved the students experiencing state and national tests. Means of instruction varied in her classroom and in the school. Each semester the teachers met to share their teaching methods, and sometimes students visited classes to share projects and/or special discipline-related programs.

Recently, the entire school got together and created a wall display of things they'd learned. One statement was "I learned to ice-skate. Jess: age 4." This was considered a fun project, while being academic in that it had all the children reflecting on things they'd learned. The school was academically sound with a cross section of grades being substantially above average.

Overview of SOW and Academics

Both classrooms experienced the academics required by national and state programs. The students varied in ability, with accommodations being provided for the children to meet their instructional needs. The methods varied and meetings were held to share ideas concerning helping children learn. At one point during the year both classrooms were part of a schoolwide project that involved a hallway display focusing on students reflecting and having their thoughts and feelings shared. The school projects served as unifiers for the school population by joining it together in a sociology of the world.

Classroom A and Politics

National politics found the class had had a unified view of who should be president in the last election. They'd studied about the three branches of government and brought to class the viewpoints of family and other organizations where they'd heard adults talking. Sometimes this was at the local Ys they attended, or at the after-school programs, and even at home. These influences continued throughout the year and impacted classroom sharing.

Ms. Jones knew the politics of the communities had affected the children, because many parents were experiencing unemployment and relied on government money to make it possible for them to survive. This affected the children most profoundly, and yet there was an overall understanding of "making do" with what one had.

Classroom politics, for the children, involved elections for who would have specific responsibilities there. This included a president, vice president, and student council representatives. And these roles changed as each new semester of the year began. Shared governance was important to everyone in the class. Initially begrudgingly, but over time acceptingly, the students had come to understand the idea of compromising when it came to voting on issues that affected them.

Classroom B and Politics

With respect to national politics, there weren't many differences in the classroom. Viewpoints were shared about the previous year's presidential election preferences. This had been addressed with mock debates before the November election. And afterward, opinions about who'd won and how this was achieved were a focal point of discussion for several weeks. This seemed to carry over as new national incentives were brought forth. One addressed increased property taxes, with the children learning about how new political policies might affect their home life both socially and economically.

For Heidi, the biggest issue was having a president instead of a king as the country's leader. Needing to learn about the three branches of government was interesting to her as she compared her previous country and municipality's governance system to her new one. The class was politically arranged in a similar fashion to the state government.

Representatives for the school's student council were voted on each October. While there wasn't a classroom president or vice president per se, once a week there was a time set aside for discussing the dynamics of shared governance. Politically, each classroom and the school at large was considered to be a democracy.

Overview of SOW and Politics

The political situations in the two classrooms (A and B) did not evidence vigorous differences in the sharing of governance. The former year's national elections were part of both classrooms' discussions. These had continued throughout the year as political situations affected their sociology. Voting took place on a variety of responsibilities, with student council being an added area for classroom collaboration. The biggest issue was learning how to compromise when it came to these elections.

The A-school students had parents who were unemployed. The politics, on national and community levels, had subsequently affected their home life regarding what could and couldn't be afforded. Beliefs and values were influenced when it came to having money to buy things in order for their families to survive.

In Heidi's class elections were held for student council and within-room responsibilities. The three branches of government were new to Heidi, but she'd come to understand how this political arrangement worked, as did her classmates. The students' parents talked at home about how the newly imposed national programs addressed an increase in property taxes for the community. This issue was brought into school and students discussed how this might impact the family both socially and economically. They questioned whether this might change their sociology. They soon realized that answers would not be readily forthcoming.

SOW and REAP in Two Different Classrooms: Summary

As you could probably tell from reading these scenarios, classrooms A and B were in different geographic areas. They experienced different economic levels, and are affected by the political scene with new national government-imposed programs. However, religious and social traditions of home, family, and community cause these classrooms to be a congenial neutral meeting ground. Collectively, concerning SOW and REAP, these classrooms and the schools in which they reside represent a miniature sociology of the world. Two reflection questions: Were the schools you attended like the ones presented on the previous pages? What were your schools like with regard to academic and social cognition?

Making a Personal Connection to SOW and REAP

On what do learners and teachers reflect? That is a most expansive topic for discussion in, of, and by itself. And we think it's too broad to address. And yet those daily reflections that you may not even think about form your personality. Together, these create a big picture we call a sociology of the world. Positivity of thoughts and opinions, as well as feelings and ideas, may be favorable and provide a sense of well-being in a society. Negative ones do the opposite. So on what exactly do you reflect when connecting SOW and REAP?

In our daily encounters we most likely reflect on what's happening now. Oftentimes, these reflections are not complex, but rather routine. Things like being satisfied or dissatisfied with where you live, the school you're in or to which you may be assigned, who's driving today, whether you like the car you're driving, what you can afford to buy car-wise, what will be for dinner, whether you make it or someone else, if it's someone else what your relationship is with that person, how much you love teaching, what this school is really like, and what the students are thinking.

When we answer these reflection questions they shape the "us" of you and me. They may not even be something of which you are conscious, just happening, triggered by a comment from another, or simplistically a thought that comes into your mind. We are joined together and separated from one another, simultaneously, by the responses to these questions—these and a thousand more that you are sometimes aware of and frequently unaware of even asking. *Reflection* serves as the umbrella term for this model.

An invitation: We present a reflection/practitioner invitation to bring the thoughts of your days to the forefront of your mind—you, the teacher in training and/or the one who has a classroom.

Questions for Reflection

1. How would you describe your schools when you were growing up?
2. What were the social and academic situations in your school?
3. Who were the persons with which you had friendships?
4. What sort of programs did your schools have for all children?
5. Were you part of these programs, or which ones did you join?
6. What were the differences and/or similarities regarding religious practices?
7. Did you celebrate religion-based holidays with school concerts, and how was this received within the school/community?
8. How were national holidays addressed?
9. Did you go on vacation?
10. If you vacationed, where did you go, and would you visit these places again? If not, where would you like to visit for a vacation period? Why?
11. Were places you'd been addressed in your classrooms?

12. What things where acknowledged and given attention in your schools, and what were not?
13. What was the community like around the school you attend/are attending?
14. What are the religious, academic, economic, and political situations you experience, and how do you handle these issues?
15. Are you one who joins organizations? If so, what are these, and if not, why not?

How do you suppose that the answers to these questions have shaped *who* you are as a learner and teacher? When you're ready, share the answers with other teacher candidates, teachers, or someone with whom you'd like to hold a conversation. Or you may want to place the answers in the journal you're keeping for this book.

The Model's Umbrella of Reflection

In this chapter the process of reflection responds to SOW and REAP in that these bind together the various components of the model. Reflection is meant to refer to individuals and whole societies thinking about former and future events in their lives. In a manner of speaking, each of us is a byproduct of our individual and shared past experiences. This is because our present is affected by emotional and cognitive reactions to personally experienced familial, school, and community, as well as national and world, events.

Reflection is a looking back in time and a looking forward in which we realize life experiences that have made us *who* we are in the present and influence personality characteristics for actions to be taken in the future. In that context, "We are our experiential past and people can only address, perceive particulars, configure generalities, respond through emotions and interpret what they find to be important in their life experience through the viewing—reflection on previous experiences. One's points-of-reference are based upon his/her reflection" (Schiering, 2003, pp. 558–59).

A concrete example of one's reflection in practice may be looking for a job in a particular field of interest for training. The experiences evidenced in the past will impact the present and future. The learning and teaching done today is reliant on the learning and teaching done previously. Each experience, in general, relies on and is built upon what was recognized to be instructional, and/or life-forming influences along one's experiential life path.

As this model is being presented, you are hopefully realizing that for each of us as teacher candidates, classroom educators, parents, or concerned individuals the mastery of learning and teaching occurs over time. And, as with all cognitive processes, it relies at its core on effective and ongoing reflection.

Learning and teaching are improved when we engage in ongoing refection—our own about the thoughts and feelings we have about learning and teaching. Also, our reflection on the effectiveness of (1) a given strategy, (2) adaptation, (3) motivational technique, or (4) evaluation process, as to whether it worked, why it worked, or how it could be improved, serves as the overall umbrella for what's experienced in the classroom.

Our reflection on our students, with respect to what they bring into classrooms; their feelings, thoughts, attitudes, and belief and value systems; and the way in which these impact learning, influences and shapes that environment. "As teachers, we are engaged in a noble undertaking, wrestling with the vastly varying dreams, hopes, and beliefs of individuals and society, helping to fashion anew each day a different but connected reality for improving the task of learning and teaching" (Bogner, 2008, p. 3).

The Interior Components of a Model for Academic and Social Cognition

In the next few chapters you are presented with the core of the model, which refers to the two interior components of common social and societal realities and belief and value systems and the model's paradigm of the cognitive collective: reciprocal thinking and reciprocal feelings phases. It is the thinking we do and the feelings/emotions we have that result in the ways we learn and teach. Sometimes these interior components are so closely intertwined it's difficult to separate one from the other. They become part of an intuitive consciousness.

Additionally, what one thinks and feels results in the combining of individual beliefs and values attributed to whole societies for a social and societal commonality being realized. The thoughts, ideas, opinions, judgments, and feelings one has result in not just how learning and teaching occur, but *who* one is as a learner and teacher. These three interior components of a model for academic and social cognition are addressed in the following four chapters.

Chapter Discussion and/or Journal Questions

1. What is meant by the acronym SOW, and what are examples of it in the social context of a classroom setting?
2. What is meant by the acronym REAP, and how do these impact a classroom's environment?
3. Why and how do you suppose one's reflection, the umbrella term for the model, influences learning and teaching?
4. What are the interior parts of this model?
5. How do you suppose the "culture of learning" is influenced by SOW and REAP?
6. Why is a model for academic and social cognition considered to be comprehensive?

CHAPTER FIVE

TWO INTERIOR COMPONENTS OF THE MODEL: COMMON SOCIAL AND SOCIETAL REALITIES AND BELIEF AND VALUE SYSTEMS

There are areas of commonality within all cultures. Schools serve as one of the places for experiencing this, as they're a neutral meeting ground for diverse populations. Educational institutions bring together, in a designated location and time, the similarities of those in such settings. The similarities and differences of persons, within formal and informal places of learning, allow for harmony or the converse among those persons. This happens as they share practiced beliefs and values. In the companionship indicative of the social and societal settings, one comes to partially define oneself as a person, learner, and teacher.

This chapter first introduces the concept of common social and societal realities and belief and value systems, which are two of the interior components of the model. In narrative fashion each is addressed individually. Beliefs and values in schools with changes since 1965 are presented in nine examples (Schiering, 2010). These include the practice, change, and learning issue of each belief and value presented. Next, the nuclear family's common social realities are chronologically provided and followed by a wider view of this chapter's interior components.

Dewey's six areas of multicultural commonality, the model with respect to common social and societal realities and belief and value systems, are provided, with connections to the holon philosophy, and SOW and REAP. One classroom example of common social and societal realities about an ecosystem concludes the chapter.

Key words: common social and societal realities, beliefs and values, social, society, holon, nuclear family, birth, death, success, failure, tradition, and love

Common Social and Societal Realities

You may wonder, "What are common and social realities?" They may be explained as being the broad, familiar, or ordinary things we share as persons living together as a group in that dealing with one another affects our welfare. Subsequently, these realties address interconnected, interdependent individuals and cultures. The conduct, standards, and activities of the setting form the definition for the word *society*. Each person is not unto himself or herself, but rather lives in an assemblage governed by mutual needs. In a society of learners we share many common social and societal realities.

Our individual and oftentimes shared viewpoints influence dispositions, character, temperaments, spirit, desires, hopes, beliefs, and values, as well as our behaviors. Some of these realities stay the same and some do not. Common social and societal realities may be seen as defining us through personal perceptions and those shared by those around us, or, on a wider scale, the world.

Most times in a person's daily routines, the things we have in common are not given much thought. We just go about doing what's expected and unless something interrupted these familiar actions, we'd say, when asked about what's happening, "STDD—same thing, different day." That's a normal response and part of one's social reality. Yet it's these commonalities—general daily occurrences—that bind us together into a society where we discover *who* we are as individuals and members of units, as well as learners and teachers. Please reflect on this topic of common social and societal realities for a moment by creating a list of them, as you relate to your routines that join you with others.

Done yet?

Not necessarily in the order in which they were shared, here's what we came up with in just a few minutes: what's for dinner, who we go to work/school with, friends, where we live, restaurants liked and disliked, clothes, income, savings, credit cards, types of jobs, birthdays, anniversaries, age, gender, ethnicity, grade level, gardens, responsibilities, where we're going when vacation time comes, preferences regarding pets and/or sports teams, sense of spirituality, games (video, iPod, computer, board, card, chance, Wii), television shows, types and use of cell phones, text messaging, beverages (soda, alcohol, tea, coffee, milk, water), movies, wishes, dreams, college assignments, getting good grades, fears about the unknown and a variety of things, general health, going to the gym or exercising, pizza, parents and parenting, relationships, relatives, family members. That's quite a list—we think you'll agree!

Common Social Realities

These are the areas that form one's sense of environment—social norms. They comprise the understanding of how things may vary by place and culture, where common experiences shape a general comprehension by bringing those in that space together. Attending to these or not can shape learning and/or teaching. Common social realities are the things we like, as much as those for which we have distaste, whether experienced individually or together. And these may vary by community or age, gender, and the external factors mentioned in the previous chapter. Overall, they're the things we regularly find to be part of our lives.

Belief and Value Systems

Belief systems are concepts that incorporate feelings on whether something is true or untrue, good, bad, or even exists. Values are ideas that focus on whether something is important or the magnitude of its worth. Values include beliefs regarding right and wrong, or the level of importance something has, resulting from one's experience. The word *systems* refers to the grouping of one's beliefs and values.

What are some beliefs and values you have? Make a list of them in your journal or on a nearby piece of paper. If you've the time, take a few minutes, call a friend or share with those around you what you've written. Start a discussion and find areas of commonality and difference. Put a star next to those that intrigue you the most—this may be all of them.

Belief and value systems are at the core of this model. They represent the mental convictions and attitudes that are held by individuals or whole groups of them and influence behaviors. These behaviors are learned and form beliefs and what's valued—it's a cyclical process. Beliefs are originally established within the nuclear family in whatever structure or pattern it may entail. And they are attributed significance as appreciated, respected, treasured, prized, and/or cherished ideas. Beliefs and values are referenced as a system in that, when combined, they define an individual. They're observable through the actions the individual takes and the discourse that conveys the substance of their meaning for that person—what that person says and does.

Belief and value systems extend from the immediate family outward to extended family, neighborhood, community, schools, state, and the world, expanding as one ages and is exposed to an ever-widening set of others' belief and value systems. When this exposure to differing viewpoints takes place, one's own beliefs and values may change. This is a common situation and a "natural" occurrence. Concerning a school-system's set of beliefs and values, these oftentimes become rules—unspoken or written—and subsequently are incorporated into what's allowed and what is not permitted—the hidden curriculum.

The main point about beliefs and values is that while some are unchanged, others are in a state of flux—continually being modified during short or extended periods of time. As a very simple example, a young child may hold to the belief that green is his/her favorite color only to see in later years that this belief changes, with deep purple being preferred over all other colors.

Some beliefs become strengthened over time as reflections upon experiences solidify already held assumptions. For example, religious belief in the power of prayer, or a political belief in the sanctity of a free-market economy, will become a concretizing influence subsequent to our reflections.

A value system, however, is a different matter. For example, holding fast to the concept that all female adults are kind and giving may change as future experience demonstrates this to be otherwise.

What one comes to value is changeable in accordance with what one is thinking and feeling. Nonetheless, there are values that may be held by whole groups of people, such as the importance of good nutrition, providing for others, or the acts of being caring, respectful, and kind. Also, some values are being a good citizen, being responsible, being fair, doing well in school, getting along with others, being acceptable at sports, being in organizations, volunteering, and those behaviors which are socially common in the places we live.

Beliefs and Values in the Schools: Changes

To illustrate the point about beliefs and values being in a state of change/flux, some modifications are presented in what was accepted and became unacceptable over short and extended periods of Schiering's (2010) teaching career. Examples given first address educational or school practices in the mid-1960s. These schools were first in the center of this country and then in the southern portion, where some schools were not yet ethnically integrated. Although the federal government had laws requiring this, the community socially rejected it. The schools in the last examples were in the northeast.

Being new to education in the role of teacher, there was a lot to be learned about what was permissible and what was not allowed. Nine educational beliefs and values are given specific attention along with practices, changes that occurred, and the learning issues that resulted from these changes and practices.

Many of the changes were slow in coming, but were primarily due to beliefs and values that resulted in school program modifications to accommodate the public viewpoints regarding individual equality and common social and societal issues coming to the foreground. When you read these you may find that it's difficult to believe that these ideas were actually held as truths for people across this country. Nonetheless, the enforcement of "proper practice" proved them right then and inappropriate now.

1. It was improper for women to wear slacks or pantsuits, as this was considered men's clothing. Women should wear dresses or skirts, with the length being slightly above the mid-calf level.

   Practice: Women teachers were to wear dresses and/or skirts. Their length was to be two inches below the knee. It would be considered insubordinate to dress otherwise, and considered a possibility for loss of one's teaching position if not rectified.

   Change: Pantsuits became popular attire for women. Later, miniskirts and minidresses were accepted, and now jeans and more casual wear are permitted for female teachers.

   Learning issues: Conforming to this practice in the mid-1960s meant retaining the teaching position. Dress codes were in place. Communities influence what's accepted as being a "normal" appearance. This is part of permitted behavior and signs of the times. As beliefs and values change, so do these codes, and common social and societal realities with respect to the cognitive collective.

2. Students would learn best from being spanked or paddled if they disrupted a class. Corporal punishment was the most influential way to teach children proper behavior. Fear of being paddled would prevent what were considered to be their unruly actions.

   Practice: If girls' or boys' misbehavior interrupted classroom instruction, or disrespect was shown toward adults, paddling would be instituted. Refusing to paddle children would get teachers referred to the school's principal for reprimand.

   Change: Corporal punishment was nationally banned by the early 1970s.

   Learning issues: Spanking and/or paddling a child in a classroom is a form of child abuse. Social justice in schools needs to be addressed. Forcing one to administer this form of punishment is morally wrong. "Hurting" a child in this manner sends a message, through modeling, about what's acceptable authority figure behavior. A child may be scarred for life if punished in this way, and subsequently this does not create a sense of classroom belonging or community, or facilitate learning. Experience being a formidable teacher, paddling or spanking sets an example of accepted adult behavior that may result in this being copied as the individual becomes an adult—thus continuing the practice.

3. Various ethnic groups were thought as being inferior to other ones.

   Practice: Whole communities adhered to the idea of schools being separately built and utilized for students of varied ethnicities. This was the case even after federal government imperatives, and rested on the concept that some ethnic groups were intellectually inferior to others.

Change: Schools are a multicultural/ethnic meeting ground for learning and teaching.

Learning issues: Separation by ethnicity is a detriment to society and impacts future generations in a negative fashion. Thinking for the overall betterment of society through social justice, and a positively based unity of purpose, helps growth and development of children, communities, and whole nations.

4. Women seeking higher education is not necessary, as they are to be at home having babies and raising their children. Men are the accepted breadwinners.

   Practice: Females finishing high school were fewer in number than their male counterparts. It was accepted that women's role was "in the home."

   Change: More females than ever before attend college and seek advanced degrees. Women entered the workforce in a multitude of varied fields, including corporate America. Equal pay was instituted for job responsibilities.

   Learning issues: Gender discrimination is not acceptable. Increased social acceptance of the rights of women has developed over time. Educational opportunities for women should be equal to those of men. A woman's place may be in the home as well as outside it. Equal pay for job performance is a human right.

5. The number of students in a class doesn't matter, as everyone is entitled to schooling and if each pays attention he/she should learn.

   Practice: Unlimited class size.

   Change: Teacher associations voted to limit class size, as research evidenced that fewer children in a classroom was one important and viable means for optimum learning to occur. In most states, class size was limited to twenty-seven students.

   Learning issues: An unlimited number of students in a class thwarts teacher effectiveness and student success. Experience in the classroom proved that the opportunity for individualized and differentiated instruction with fewer students was a key component for a diverse population's optimum. Also, students' sense of ownership and classroom management issues were more formidable with class size limitations.

6. Music, physical education, and art classes are not necessary until high school. Students being bilingual are not appreciated or necessary until students learn a foreign language, as an elective in upper grades.

   Practice: Classes in music, art, and physical education existed in districts that could afford these programs. However, they were not provided everywhere. The language in the United States is English and foreign language is considered an "elective" class. It would not be instituted in elementary school as a part of the school's curriculum. Children should be taught English at home.

   Change: Music, art, and physical education classes at early and later grade levels in public schools became commonplace. Foreign language was introduced during the elementary and middle-school grades in some states. Students being bilingual became appreciated as our population experienced expanded diversity. And English as a second language (ESL) instruction was instituted in the early years of schooling, as well as later, when it was realized that there were many foreign-language speakers in classrooms and home instruction was customarily very limited.

   Learning issues: Adding to the arts provided potential for creating a more well-rounded and educated population. This was especially true when introduced and practiced during the elementary-level years and extending through grade twelve. Good physical and mental health is important at all age/grade levels, and these programs facilitate that being possible. Learning a foreign language was easier when introduced at the first- or third-grade levels, as opposed to waiting until the high school years. ESL classes in schools facilitated non-English speakers learning the English language.

7. Programs for children with special needs, whether due to learning disabilities or giftedness, are not necessary parts of the school curriculum. These children should go to special schools that can accommodate them. These learning-disabled or advanced children weren't normal and shouldn't mix with able ones.

   Practice: Most schools did not have classes for children with special needs, whether due to learning disabilities or giftedness. Special schools or tutors for learning-disabled children existed if their families could afford them. Some children with exceptional academic abilities were advanced in grade levels.

   Change: Mainstreaming children in regular classrooms became the practice in the 1980s. "Gifted" programs were also provided, as teachers of special education children were brought into the classroom. Or students were pulled out to receive special instruction. A decade or less later the inclusion classroom was realized.

   Schools of higher education now require in-practice teachers to take courses regarding how to teach special education students in all disciplines. And special education is a certification area program provided by most colleges for teacher candidates teaching all levels.

   Learning issues: We live in communities that have people of varied abilities. To separate whole schools by learning disabilities or giftedness thwarts getting along with others, due to lack of exposure and/or experience. This causes difficulties in creating relationships that acknowledge those with learning differences later in students' lives.

8. Technology, such as having computers in every classroom, is for districts that can afford it. It's not a necessity or viable accommodation for all schools.

   Practice: Classrooms did not have computers. Teachers need not use these for instruction or as a means for students gaining information and/or conducting research.

   Change: Classrooms have computers and are hooked up to the Internet. Blocks for inappropriate websites are in place.

Research and search engines are readily available. Families having PCs at home is relatively common.

Learning issues: Technology advanced to a point where it has become a necessity to be part of an advanced information age. Nationally and internationally, news media has moved from paper print to going green with computers. This form of technology enhances students' ability to conduct research and be informed about current events on an international level.

9. Behavior issues with regard to teaching children about being persons of good character should be taught in the home.

   Practice: Schools removed civics classes from the curriculum. School violence increased nationally.

   Change: School violence prevention programs became mandatory for schoolteacher's certification at all grade levels. School-wide codes of conduct were instituted. Character development instruction has been made part of the school's curriculum.

   Learning issues: It is the responsibility of home, school, and communities to join together to educate children in ways of appropriate social conduct. Teaching respect for others starts with self-respect. Defining and modeling these is important for beliefs and values of substance regarding appropriate moral conduct.

After examining these nine beliefs and values with the practice, changes, and learning issues presented, what are some educational situations you've seen change since you were a student and/or teacher? Do you think this was for the betterment of our common social and societal realities? Why or why not?

Common Social and Societal Realities/Belief and Value Systems: Nuclear Family—The Starting Point

"Where do we get our common social and societal norms? Where's the starting point?" you may ask. Well, the first instance of knowing about *who* one generally is, in respect to social and societal realities, begins in the nuclear family. It is here where likes and dislikes are formed and what's important, as opposed to unimportant, takes on meaning. The home is where common social and societal realities link up with belief and value systems.

Nuclear family common social realities are chronologically provided here:

1. An infant comes to distinguish the similarities in his/her immediate environment through the sensory experiences of touch, smell, taste, and hearing.
2. A few weeks later, sight is added to these as visual acuity develops. In this initial stage of awareness, comparison and contrasts are made to determine the personal significance of individuals and objects within the nuclear family setting. This refers to those that feed the infant, hold, comfort, and interact on a regular basis, as well as provide sustenance of a physical and/or emotional nature.
3. The crawling toddler explores by first putting things into his or her mouth to determine taste, size, and feasibility of handling. It is here that beginning awareness, comparison and contrast, and classifying emanate, as some things are too large, too uncomfortable, just right, comforting, unimpressive, or pleasing.
4. Caretakers' tone of voice help to determine what is acceptable and what should not be explored. This is a time of extensive watching by the nurturer(s) and advanced sensory experimentation by the young child, as well as reactionary observations when varied experiences take place.
5. Exploring continues as language is developed through imitating those encouraging development. Persons, places, things, and objects are given names. Discernment is evident.
6. Later, feelings are titled. In each of these previous five areas, which are reciprocal as well as developmental, the infant, explorer, and beginning language learner makes observations of

what is anticipated with respect to behavior and values. Children come to value things resulting from the acknowledgment, recognition, and appreciation by the recognized nurturer(s) who resides in and shares the nuclear family dwelling. The number of persons in the core family configuration provides a multitude of influences.

Each of these persons help establish the initial approach, feelings, and mind-set, as well as the viewpoint of the child, and begins the comprehension of what is valued and later becomes either accepted or challenged. Things like being toilet trained, getting dressed and feeding oneself without assistance, playing with toys, listening to different types of music, foods, clothing—the basic needs, and experiencing an expanded social setting—become *common social and societal realities*, as decisions are made about likes and dislikes.

7. During these growing-up years in the nuclear family, learning is occurring by recognizing what is appropriate and inappropriate behavior. What is important and what isn't becomes evident through voice tone and praise or reprimands from those of significance to the child. Decision-making is happening regularly, although perhaps unknowingly.

   Acclaim, support, and reinforcement for instilling self-efficacy and a sense of personal empowerment impact the social construct to form attitudes and behavior that are in alignment with the way life is lived. Whether the child takes on the values and beliefs of those in the core family depends on the way the information is processed and reacted to by the individual, as much as the amount, variety, and consistency of experiences encountered.

8. The invocation of making decisions may be added to in the formal education stage, depending on the institution's mission. This may carry over to the home with thoughts on what will be worn to a particular place, what place to visit is preferred, communicating likes and dislikes most exactly with reasons why, solving generic problems, and differentiating between normal, strange, and different people or surroundings.

It is the home base where those things termed as common social and societal realities come to be part of personality. Considering that learning occurs in social settings first through observations and then leading to established norms within the nuclear family, one may determine the composition and development of what is to be valued. This also applies to what's devalued, regarded or disregarded, rejected or okayed, and accepted, for establishment of what is believed to be true.

9. As one ages, the number of experiences that occur are increasing exponentially by rapidly becoming greater in number. The individual is now more influenced by his or her ability to reflect, compare, and contrast what has been modeled with what he or she feels in a sensory and reactionary/emotional manner when these new circumstances are presented.

   What have come to be known *as* common social and societal realities may be modified or remain unchanged during this time period. However, in all likelihood, this will be commensurate with what has been established within the core family that is part of the extended social groups one experiences. Codes of conduct impact on manners as they encompass common social and societal accepted behaviors, dispositions, values, and beliefs. Each of these in their own right configures a substantial portion of *who* one is as the learner and teacher.

In each aforementioned instance, there is what has been presented as the nuclear family's common realities. These foster belief and value systems and what the child personally feels when varied stimuli and situations are encountered. There's an independence and interdependence coexisting, impacted by genetics as well as experiences. All the while the child is reciprocally developing, through new circumstances, his/her memory, cognition, and metacognition, resulting in understanding what the parameters are for a given time and place.

Each of these causes the formation of personal preferences: This feels good, this does not. This is safe, while this is not. I am secure here or I am insecure in this place. This pleases me, I am comfortable. I can do this. I'm not sure I can do this. I can't do this. I like/love this. Everyone does these things. Someone or no one I know does this. I'm good at this, but it's not recognized in the way I want it to be. Each scenario provides a formation or shaping of beliefs and values unique to the individual, but influenced by the group to which one belongs.

Common Social and Societal Realities/Beliefs and Values: A Wider View

In order for any given culture and/or social/societal mores of a group to function, there need to be set in place common social realities. At some point these affect the neighborhood, school settings, community with businesses and service industries, city, state, municipality, country, and world. By their very nature, beliefs and values that influence common social and societal realities are considered to be generalized, rudimentary, interconnected, and prevalent ways of acting and conducting oneself.

And these beliefs and values are considered to be fundamentally factual, or true to life. They are part of what's happening now, what happened in the past, and the proposed future. Subsequently, common social and societal realities encompass belief systems and values that are practiced wherever one resides during any portion of the day, or greater expanse of time.

Each setting is unique to its own rules, practices, and regulations for conduct and discourse, and assists in one's knowing, as well as others realizing, *who* one is as a learner and teacher. An example might be the use of humor. Where some places it is okay to be sarcastic, in others this would be considered very offensive—the singling out of one person to be made fun of at the expense of that individual for the sake of the grouping.

Common social and societal realities comprise individuals and groups, cultural or otherwise, dispositions, temperaments, spirit, makeup, values, beliefs, and character originating in the nuclear family in the empirical sense. Within this core "observations are made and behaviors are modeled and it is the observation and copying of these that initially form the distinctiveness and functional value of individuals" (Ormond, 1999, n.p.), which is stated by Bandura (1977; 2003) as being part of a "social learning theory."

Six Areas of Multicultural Common Social and Societal Realities

Dewey (1937) referred to six areas of multicultural commonality where individuals demonstrate similar attitudes, definitions, and reactions to birth, death, success, failure, tradition, and love. All cultures/societies have these six common areas that influence the social interior behaviors of persons living there. These are interconnected and influence everyone's beliefs and values.

For example, it's understood that birth refers to new life, while the ending of life encompasses a passing on to another dimension. This closure may be seen as entrance into a new life form, or at least its finality to the existing physical configurations attributed to human beings, which is referred to as death.

Success is viewed as a result or achievement in areas of significance to an individual or individuals within a group. Most commonly, this is referred to as wealth or monetary acumen. However, one's success may incorporate the societal norms addressing things of value such as the number of possessions one has of a particular form, or emotional/physical well-being.

Success, in a broader context, may mean one's achieving fame, social standing, personal achievement, self-worth, or association within and between affiliations that attest to what is important. "Important where?" you might ask. It would be within a particular group, as well as in relationships that have value in a social/societal spectrum. Failure, on the other hand, relies on the nonachievement of the established criteria. Tradition may be linked to success and failure in that tradition is a long-established custom or practice that has the effect of an unwritten law.

Success and failure within and linked to the tradition of a culture would depend on the significances of value to that civilization or society. Tradition also refers to the practices of particular cultures. There are the traditions of holiday celebrations, vacation areas, and daily routines. There are the traditions that establish a pattern and are acknowledged by varied groups as being important while binding the person of that assemblage together for a common purpose. In this sense, tradition serves as a unifying factor when members participate in the established norms of that group.

Finally, love is explained as an emotion with numerous variations, in that there's love of a child, which is usually different from that of or for a parent, or another person, or an object. The feelings that are attributed to any of these are incumbent upon an emotional or sensory/phenomenological reaction of and to individuals or groups.

There is a love of animate and inanimate objects, such as love of a particular sport or love of a plant, animal, or picture. *Love* is the universal term used to describe affection or terms of endearment. Strong feelings regarding love impact any of the common social and societal realities through the degree to which these are envisioned and acted upon.

Common Social and Societal Realities/Beliefs and Values: Holon Philosophy

As stated in chapter 3, the concept of a holon is that nothing is removed from anything else. As individuals develop, they become part of many social groupings and have common social and societal realities, as well as beliefs and values. Each of these helps to define the individual and contribute to his or her identity. Well, that, along with an ongoing revision of beliefs and values, as well as acceptance or rejection of the things that shape that group.

Do you recall that the membership in varied groups has been explained by Koestler (1978) in a book by Wilber (2000, pp. 40, 52), *A Theory of Everything*, when he pointed out, "One whole part is part of another whole." And building on that, "A nested group of holons forms a Holarchy." We explain that these holarchies are what we have in schools and in our classrooms, as well as in social, work, committee, and various other groupings outside of the academic arena.

There are many cultures living in close proximity to one another in any given country, and each of these is part of the whole, but separate from it during, before, and possibly after the present time. That is a natural occurrence—to be part of something and apart from it at the same time, connected to it over an expanse of time including the past and present, but separate from it at any given moment (Million, 2007). This addresses the concept of change or modifications with respect to holons in that nothing remains exactly the same from day to day, year to year, or generation to generation. So, too, our common social and societal realities change as much as do our beliefs and values.

As related in the *Tao Te Ching*, "Everything is in a process of change, and is constantly evolving." If one puts one's foot into the river and removes it and then places one's foot into the river again—it is now a different river (Lau Tzu, 2500 BC), because the original flow of the river changed, due to the interruption of the foot being originally placed in it. Nonetheless, the authors call attention to each animate and inanimate object being a holon. Who we are as learners and teachers is realizing we're holons and part of holarchies. "This overall linkage of a holon also may be seen reflectively. In this instance, the past may be related and attached to the present in the form of an ongoing continuum. Just as one is connected to the past so too does that past impact and influence the present and future; each is a part of the other—connected to the other—a holon" (Schiering, 2009b, p. 68; 2010a, p. 6).

In conversations with James Million (2007–2008), he gives a more detailed explanation of a holon when he relates, "A more finite example of a Holon would be the thumbnail itself being a whole entity with specific configurations, but it is also part of the thumb, which is part of the hand, which has its own definitions, and is part of the arm. Nothing, therefore, stands alone, but is part of something else. The trees are part of a forest and so forth."

And, examining this thumbnail explanation, it is of significant value to also be aware that while the thumbnail is part of a whole thumb, it is not the same as every other thumbnail. Similarly, an individual may be part of a social setting or organization and considered a member of it because of the definition of that group and its requirements for membership, such as a school, and still not be conforming to the entire requirements for membership and be part of it and apart from it, simultaneously.

The concept of the group membership is defined by the group. This forms a social structure and impacts on common social and societal realities. While one is a member of a college's graduate program, one may not necessarily be the same age as each member of the group, nor have the same interests of those in the program, but will still be a member of that assembly.

Finally, regarding the "parts of a whole" conceptualization, it could be related that students and teachers learn and teach themselves, simultaneously, with their reactionary awareness and organization—a trading of perceptional knowledge. Subsequently, the more one knows about *who* one is being, as a learner, the more informed someone is, the better one's learning situation. The holon of a classroom environment is the connection of the learner, teacher, and traditions of that place. The holon of daily living is realized through the traditions of a sociology of the world and the external factors that are part of its common social and societal realities, as well as belief and value systems.

When it comes to teaching, we as educators need to realize the interconnection of students' beliefs and values, their common social and societal realities, thinking and feelings. Each of these, due to the closeness of the classroom, influence attitudes, behaviors, demeanors, and ideas concerning what will be accepted and/or rejected and taken in for gaining knowledge, or just information processing. The holon concept affects each part of our lives.

Common Social and Societal Realities/Beliefs and Values: SOW and REAP

In everyday experiences within and between cultures in schools, social and societal norms are established as the cornerstones—basic elements for common social and societal realities. Subsequently, the world sociology concept resides in and is reliant upon the shared circumstances and situations that are universal and conventional within and between cultures.

As you now know, a person has a belief and value system that is formed in the family and continually reformed as the individual ages and encounters new and varied social groupings' experiences. As a social being, common social and societal realities influence and impact the learner. REAP represents some of these external factors that impact the learner's belief and value system and his or her thoughts, ideas, opinions, judgments, and feelings.

As Dewey, Vygotsky, and Bronfenbrenner have maintained, there is a close relationship between people, culture, and an individual's development. Bogner and Schiering (2008) relate, "Individuals do not operate outside of the social context in which they find themselves. One's own belief and value systems that form the basis for making decisions through reflection and lead to learning are shaped by common social and societal realities. External factors impinge upon and simultaneously support and challenge these beliefs. These same external factors may elicit strong feelings about self and others that subsequently influence thinking and the effectiveness of learning."

Common Social and Societal Realities: A Classroom Example

It has been explained that through individual and shared common social and societal realities' experiences, belief and value systems are formed. These can transcend the vast differences individuals bring into the classroom and provide teachers the opportunity to fashion accessible lessons and build community. These common social realities assist us in solving what is surely the conundrum of education, assisting students of vastly different backgrounds and abilities in mastering goals. This requires looking for commonalities out of individuality.

The following lesson finds the teacher addressing common social realities in a school setting where the school becomes an expanded area for learning in a social context. The teacher, Bogner, relates a time when asked to guest teach the topic of ecosystems in a fifth-grade classroom.

Preparation for the lesson: The teacher had, of course, an array of handouts and overheads of various ecosystems. These included land ones with mountains, a coniferous forest, and areas around the community. Water ones displayed rivers, oceans, a tidal pool, and smaller water areas, such as rivers, lakes, and ponds.

School type: The school served a mostly lower socioeconomic area of some diversity that was not necessarily physically near these types of ecosystems.

Establishing connections: The teacher began by trying to establish areas of common experience before moving on to the introduction of various concepts about ecosystems. "How many of you have been to the mountains?" the teacher asked. Two hands went up. "How about the ocean?" Four more responded. The teacher said, "Okay," and asked, "How about a pine forest?"

Recognizing the connection: Two hands went up, which showed there was not a formidable connection to the topic, as yet. Clearly the members of this fifth-grade class had not traveled much. The teacher introduced the concept of a land ecosystem by addressing one communally experienced by these students. This was the playground, a grassy area outside the school.

Questions: "What's an example of an herbivore—something that eats plants to survive?" "Grasshopper," one girl responded. "Good," the teacher replied just after other examples had been provided. "Now what eats the grasshopper? Remember it has to be a carnivore—something that eats other animals for survival." "A bird," one girl offered.

Many more responses comprised the answers. "These are parts of a land ecosystem," the teacher explained. "Ecosystems are a community of plants and animals living together in an environment. They rely on one another for their survival. Other types of ecosystems may be water and air ecosystems."

Common social and societal realities: The lesson continued as the fifth graders identified the word *predator* with the spider feeding on herbivores and animals that ate these animals. In short order, the students had recognized an entire ecosystem they experienced, which was that of the playground outside the school the students attended. They'd built the entire ecosystem using a commonly held social and societal reality—the school yard at recess, one they evidenced each day.

The introduction of the spider as an herbivore in an ecosystem led to more sharing of common and social realities with the expression of thoughts and feelings about spiders. One student said, "*My* mom hates spiders and I don't like spiders either." Another student shared that he thought all insects were cool. The students' past experiences of sharing a similar geography, the playground and the nooks and crannies of this area, as well as the ones at home and places they'd visited on vacations all served as a basis to teach the general concept of an ecosystem.

The teacher made the connection to other ecosystems by explaining that people who lived far away, in other states and countries, also might have similar feelings about spiders in their ecosystems. A wider group of individuals having similar thoughts, ideas, opinions, judgments, and feelings all revolved around common societal realities.

It had taken the teacher a few minutes to find the normal ground to which the students could relate. And, by finding this shared experience, the connection of the lesson on ecosystems had been established—thus making the lesson meaningful to the students through a common social and societal reality.

Chapter Discussion and/or Journal Questions

1. What are the interior components of this academic and social cognition model?
2. To what do "common social and societal realities" refer, and what are some you have?
3. To what do "belief and value systems" refer, and what are four of yours?
4. What are three beliefs and values and their corresponding practices, changes, and learning issues addressed in this chapter?
5. In the empirical realm, what is the composition of common social and societal realities?
6. From where does the initial connection between common social and societal realities and belief and value systems begin, and how does this connection chronologically progress?
7. What is one of the first examples of knowing *who* one is as a learner and teacher?
8. What are the six areas, according to Dewey (1937), of common social and societal realities and belief and value systems?
9. What is meant by the term *holon* and what's an example you can give of this?
10. On what does the world sociology concept reside?
11. Using the explanation provided in this chapter, what is one example you can relate as being a common social and societal reality?

CHAPTER SIX

THE THIRD INTERIOR COMPONENT OF THE MODEL: AN OVERVIEW OF THE COGNITIVE COLLECTIVE

Joining Thinking and Feeling
(M. Schiering)

I think . . . therefore I am.
I feel . . . therefore I am.
Where did I learn that?
Perhaps it's not as important as realizing
What we think and feel.
By knowing that . . .
You come to realize who I am
And
I come to realize who you are.
All said and done
We are a combination of what we think and feel.

Reciprocal thinking and feelings are the thoughts, ideas, opinions, judgments, and emotions you and everyone have. They result in a continual structuring and restructuring of our reality—beliefs and values upon which we take action. This is accomplished through personal and shared reflection, represented by the model's umbrella term of reflection by encompassing past and present experiences. All of the model's elements of common social and societal realities, belief and value systems, and the model's foundation of SOW and REAP are impacted by one's thinking and feelings.

This chapter is an overview for you of the cognitive collective (Schiering, 2005). A definition of this is provided and followed by the progression of thinking and feelings. The relevance of these to effective pedagogy is addressed with how feelings impact thinking and vice versa. Emotions are presented with a follow-up listing of some thoughts and feelings one might have during the course of a day. A college student's experience at a British English festival is a story that relates the reciprocity of thinking and feelings. Key points about the cognitive collective culminate the chapter.

Key words: cognitive collective, thinking, feeling, reciprocal processes

Defining the Cognitive Collective

Human beings think as well as feel. This happens within the classroom, as well as outside it. Throughout a person's day, the individual moves between varying cognitive processes and emotions. As teachers, we must address this natural progression and interplay by recognizing first that it occurs, and second that in order to be effective teachers, we must know how this happens and attend to it.

The cognitive collective is comprised of two parts, so it forms a paradigm called reciprocal thinking and feelings. Each is referred to as being reciprocal because there is a natural movement between thinking and feelings. Each impacts the other, and individuals move simultaneously through, among, and around these.

Sometimes they can be envisioned as the interweaving of one's thoughts, ideas, opinions, judgments, and feelings. And sometimes they can be envisioned as simply being present without a connection being evident. Furthermore, in some instances, it's important to note that thinking and feelings are so infinitely connected that it's difficult to separate one from the other.

The combining and joining of thoughts and feelings occur on a regular basis, with students of the classroom having different reactions to what is being presented. Different feelings at different times and varying cognitive processes or thinking phases occur at various times, or at the same time. The teacher also may evidence thinking and feelings as he or she traverses through these aforementioned phases. It is, however, one of the teacher's roles to manage this complex symphony of individual processing to move students toward effective learning.

As stated, generally, the cognitive collective is the "interplay" of thinking and feeling—reciprocal thinking phases and reciprocal feelings. The former has been put into a graphic organizer format for specifically identifying different cognitive skills in three phases, which show movement among and between one's beginning awareness and metacognition.

The reciprocal feelings have not been put into a chart format, but are presented as a list of feelings that one may evidence when being aware of the cognitive skills one is using. Again, the paradigm of the cognitive collective refers to the thoughts, ideas, opinions, judgments, and feelings a person has and the various cognitive skills and emotional processes that produce them.

The Progression of Thinking and Feeling

Thinking and feeling are the most natural of human processes. It is apparent that even in the infancy stage, individuals are almost immediately conscious and responsive in making cognitive connections and feeling responses relating to, for example, differentiation of voices. Those having been heard, mutedly, in the womb, now have become classifications between the mother and father, and later, males and females. This categorizing becomes apparent as a result of beginning awareness and results in identification in an infant's reactive mannerisms.

The same can be said for classifications based on the senses of smell and touch, which have previously been presented as "feeling" or sensory responses to stimuli. Additionally, the reaction to favored persons is evidenced as prioritizing results in the baby being more eager to be held by one individual than another. Although verbalization is not yet exhibited by the infant, certainly reciprocity of cognition and metacognition are in play, resulting from observable responses to any given experience.

In later years, in the academic setting, between a learner and teacher there's a continual, if you would, ongoing exchange of what one is thinking and feeling. What brings about optimistic thoughts and emotions is in direct proportion to individuals' positive self-esteem. Sometimes this happens naturally, due to the demeanor of the teacher and learners, and there are many circumstances that may produce this empowering sense. However, regardless of where one resides, is schooled, or works, there are a few concepts that connote individuals or whole groups feeling comfortable and thinking about self-actuating because of this feeling of ease.

The concepts referenced are those involving motivation, a sense of security, self-respect, success, and acceptance. These are coded in the common social and societal realities we experience on a daily basis. This being the case, then, what causes thoughts and feelings to evoke motivation, a sense of security, self-respect, success, and acceptance, which result in exhibited behaviors and belief systems? The answer is inherent in the idea of life experiences being cyclical, on the positive spectrum, and individuals' evidencing personal empowerment.

By applying the cognitive skills within the reciprocal thinking and feeling phases, as presented in chapters 7 and 8, to practical learning experiences, a sense of security emerges and takes hold in the psyche. This is first accomplished when individuals are able to identify what cognitive and metacognitive skills are being addressed—by oneself or others. The overall sense of security is forthcoming, with students feeling successful, as a result of accomplishing tasks set forth that address and ensure their being successful by knowing what is being thought.

Subsequently, feeling secure and/or having a sense of well-being about the learning environment becomes the mainstay and allows one to have and exhibit self-respect and self-acceptance as a learner and teacher. These concepts then are exhibited in attitudes that convey what one is thinking through one's behaviors and belief and value systems. We state, "This is difficult to refute. Why?" Because if one is feeling comfortable with one's learning and/or teaching environment and experience, whether this be teaching oneself or not, the sense of well-being becomes part of who one is as a teacher and learner.

The Relevance of the Cognitive Collective to Effective Pedagogy

How Feelings Impact Thinking and Vice Versa

Examples of the relevance of the cognitive collective are apparent every day. Within the classroom, teachers are confronted with students who are dealing with feelings as well as cognitive processes. These interactions shape the dynamics of the classroom and the likelihood that students will achieve the desired learning outcome.

Casual observation may attempt to delimit the episodes of strong feeling to early grades where students are more immature, or to middle grades or high school where students are struggling with definition of self. Nonetheless, the truth is that what one is thinking and/or feeling is present in all educational settings with students of all ages. Perhaps to best understand the influence feelings have on thinking and vice versa we need to look at some of the thoughts and feelings students regularly experience in a classroom.

What follows is an example of an American college student's presentation at a British English festival with respect to the situation and later effect and affect of the cognitive collective concerning the scenario.

Situation: A female undergraduate college student's presentation of a paper on Shakespeare at an English festival detailed the use of animal imagery in Shakespeare. It was a scaled-down version of a paper she'd written the semester before, during her studies at Oxford. She had tremendous confidence in the paper and had conducted a considerable amount of research in its preparation. Following the presentation a professor from another school raised his hand and began his critique by listing numerous items that should have been included, in his opinion, and examples from other plays, as well as various references.

The student was unprepared for his critical response. Almost immediately, with quick reflection on the comments, she felt strong emotions of embarrassment, hurt, and then anger fueled by her sense of injustice. These strong emotions and feelings prevented her from responding in a more cognitive manner.

Had she been able to be more thoughtful, she could have explained that the traditional British interpretation of Shakespeare was different than the American one, or that the paper was not meant to be exhaustive, but rather an illustration of animal imagery in Shakespeare's writings. She opted for remaining silent as her feelings of social injustice in a public forum encompassed her cognitive awareness.

Examining the combination of thoughts, ideas, opinions, judgments, and feelings from the perspective of an uninvolved observer of the events in the presented story, the following analysis serves as an example of the effect and affect of the cognitive collective.

1. If the professor had realized, recognized, or meant his comments as instructive, his actions prohibited this response on the part of the student, due to the strong emotions that hampered an interactive exchange.
2. A further observation of the example reveals another striking fact about the role that thinking influences emotions and feelings in instructional settings.

These two components can disclose, to the keen observer, attributes about the learner—attributes that can influence subsequent learning. In the student's case, as an undergraduate, her strong emotions revealed the discerning presence of a sense of social justice. This guided her reflection and uncommunicated cognitive response to the professor's critique.

The observation and analysis the college student made was that her paper was limited in length, not meant to be or even allowed to be exhaustive, and was being critiqued in a synthesized and noncollaborative manner. And, she thought, the evaluation was from a graduate perspective rather than from an undergraduate one.

Additionally, upon further evaluation and examination of the situation, one could easily ascertain that there was a high level of emotional expectation for her in doing the presentation, as well as it being an honor to be accepted to present. That the audience would be of a caliber where there would be reciprocal respect for the studies conducted, and that she'd been afforded the opportunity to share in a collegial sense, was of substance to this young author.

The student's sense of injustice regarding the professor's comments resulted in her emotions impacting what she was thinking, in respect to thoughts, ideas, opinions, and judgments, and feeling. While cognitively and metacognitively she was capable of a formidable response, the social context of the situation evidenced her limited reaction. She recalled other presentations and her mind reeled between a sense of being shamed in front of the audience, her extensive work being marginalized, and her feelings regarding her presentation being flawed, versus the work she'd conducted being of import and significance.

She wondered if others in the audience felt similarly and, if this was so, why? She was a student, not a professor. Her work was of an exploratory nature, meant to have others recognize the work she'd conducted, while revealing the work she'd conducted, which had previously not been assessed, examined, or spoken about in the context of this gathering.

With simultaneously self-imposed emotional and cognitive social and academic realities of this experience impacting her response, she opted for an explanation of her work, rather than reminding the professor of the "place" and "status" of those presenting. She reacted with inner emotions impacting her to a high degree, but revealed an academic response, as she explained her work being strongly research-based, and preliminary in nature.

With all this in mind, the context of justice for her will continue to influence her subsequent learning situations. "Forewarned is forearmed," as the saying goes. This is the second main observation to be made about feelings and emotions. These core responses can be windows into deeper invitations of learning. As such, they are appropriate contexts to be considered in designing a learning environment, where one's thoughts are superseded by emotions and vice versa. Therefore, the manner in which she reacted was inwardly emotional and outwardly cognitive.

How many times are learners so overwhelmed by the critiques of another that there is a total nonresponse, except to later be wary? In the college student's case, intimidation by the professor evidenced by his socially unjust "critique" may cause the presenter and those persons surrounding the situation to be acutely aware of what was modeled by the student and the teacher, for future reference.

The emotions found in judgments and fostered by this and other life experiences cause one to react as the teacher, either in a similar manner as the professor, or by taking a higher road and responding with emotional respect for differentiation of learning. At the very least it is clear that one's feelings, emotions, thoughts, ideas, and even opinions have serious impact on the cognitive and metacognitively adapted skills, which are utilized within an academic setting and form a portion of the cognitive collective.

Students' Experiences: Thoughts, Feelings, and Emotions

We know that each of us, learners and teachers, experience many thoughts and feelings each day at any moment. And these change or might not even be associated to the learning that's being anticipated.

However, in order to talk with you about the learning and teaching of a lesson, we need to address children's thinking and feelings. What situation did they bring to school today—do you know that? What life experiences have shaped them into the student in the classroom?

Some information may be observed by looking at the student's record from previous grades. Some might come from talking with his/her former teachers, or those who are caregivers during parent/teacher nights at school. And some knowing of our students may come from talking with them. There's also our own sense of intuition that informs us of how our students interact with others and learn. The thoughts and feelings that shaped them may be like those things that helped shape your personality and/or won't be similar at all. Here are some of the things that students experience when a lesson is being presented.

Thoughts and/or feelings:

- about self, and the ability to perform well in a given situation;
- about others, and how they will do in comparison to you;
- about the justness of the teacher's actions;
- about the appropriateness and relevance of the curriculum, as well as activities and events that occur within the classroom;
- about what's for lunch or dinner;
- about who's going to be at the after-school program;
- about how you'll do on the upcoming test;
- about who will be home when you get there;
- about how you feel uncomfortable with the material being presented;
- about the sense of elation you have when doing well;
- about whether you walked the dog before going to school;
- about so many things. . . .

That's just a partial list of what students may be thinking or feeling, and the same list could apply to you, as the teacher. It's probably not possible to actually know or even realize what anyone or everyone is thinking and feeling during the school hours. However, being aware that, as the teacher, you need to be somewhat cognizant of what's going on in your classroom, is vital.

The Cognitive Collective's Key Points

- The cognitive collective is the interplay of thinking and feeling. It occurs during prelanguage and progresses to language acquisition.
- It involves the reciprocal thinking phases and reciprocal feelings.
- Reciprocal thinking and feelings are the thoughts, ideas, opinions, judgments, and emotions you and everyone have, which result in a continual structuring and restructuring of our reality—beliefs and values upon which we take action.
- The reason for using the term *reciprocal* is that there's movement between and among what one is thinking and feeling. Each impacts the other and individuals move simultaneously through and around these.
- What one is thinking and or feeling is so closely woven together it's oftentimes difficult to distinguish one from the other.
- Thinking impacts one's feelings and vice versa.
- These interactions shape the dynamics of the classroom and the likelihood that students will achieve the desired learning outcome.
- What one thinks and feels results, oftentimes, in what one says and does.
- All of the model's elements of common social and societal realities, and belief and value systems, as well as the model's foundation of SOW and REAP, are impacted by one's thinking and feelings, which is the cognitive collective.

- The presence of these thoughts and feelings is a representation of the reality that human beings feel as well as think. This reality happens within the classroom as well as outside of it.

Chapter Discussion and/or Journal Questions

1. What is the cognitive collective?
2. To what is the cognitive collective connected in the model?
3. What are examples of thinking terms?
4. What are examples of feeling words?
5. What is the progression of thinking and feeling?
6. What is, in your opinion, the relevance of the cognitive collective to effective pedagogy?

CHAPTER SEVEN

THE COGNITIVE COLLECTIVE'S RECIPROCAL THINKING PHASES

The reciprocity of thinking refers to the ongoing exchange of comprehension that forms memory within and between phases of thinking. What you are thinking may not be what I am thinking, but awareness of what is transpiring, cognitively, empowers the learner and teacher while providing self-efficacy. Knowing what one is thinking helps to clarify learning, with the learner and teacher acknowledging the infinite identification of the cognitive and metacognitive processes being experienced at any time. *I think therefore I am.*

This first portion of the cognitive collective's reciprocal thinking phases, cognition and metacognition, is provided in a general overview. Then, a historical perspective is given, which is followed by an explanation of each phase's cognitive skills. These are examined in a summary.

A graphic representation, figure 7.1, illustrates the phases being reciprocal, and is followed by a section pertaining to the definitions of cognitive skills within each phase. How we, as adults, move seamlessly between the three phases is discussed by asking, "What are you thinking?" regarding a woodland walk scenario. The chapter's final topic is about prelanguage thinking, with an example of this and some final thoughts on the reciprocity of thinking.

Key words: reciprocal, cognitive collective, cognitive skills, beginning awareness, critical and creative thinking, metacognitive processes

Reciprocal Thinking: First Portion of the Cognitive Collective

The ways in which one thinks is critical to an understanding of how learning occurs and how teaching can best be structured. Within the cognitive collective, individuals have thoughts, ideas, opinions, judgments, and feelings, moving between those in a reciprocal fashion. Well, you are probably aware of that at this juncture and might be wondering, what's the connection to the interior components of the model?

The belief and value systems and common social and societal realities we come to experience are impacted by what we think. The sharing of this in the conversations we have, and the observations we made yesterday and configure today, as well as project for tomorrow, also influence these components of the model.

Each individual's thinking may be characterized by a number of specific cognitive skills that can be identified by the learner and teacher. This being the case, the learner can hone and develop these skills, identifying when he or she is using each and becoming more proficient in their usage. "Tasks for the teacher, therefore, would seem to be attending directly to helping students 'know what they are thinking', helping each student to identify when he or she is using a particular skill and assisting them in developing mastery over it" (Bogner and Schiering, 2008).

Reciprocal Thinking Phases: History

The concept of reciprocal thinking phases was originally created by M. Schiering, as a paradigm titled *The Phases of Thinking: Evolving from Cognition to Metacognition* (Schiering, 1999; 2002). This was a major component in her doctoral dissertation, as one goal was to develop students' cognitive and metacognitive skills for student empowerment. It was published with the aforementioned title and appeared in over twenty articles and national and international presentations until early 2007. In 2008, she reconfigured the graphic design. Working collaboratively, Schiering and Bogner moved away from the concept of thinking "evolving" to its being "reciprocal."

The reasoning for the use of the word *reciprocal* in the title is that it demonstrates that the processes of cognition and metacognition are occurring simultaneously, as opposed to being developmental, with thinking moving from one phase to the next, sequentially. Also, the use of the word *reciprocal* emphasizes that thinking is ongoing and conducted within and between the thinking phases.

Reciprocity of Thinking

The reciprocal thinking phases are a compilation of cognitive skills involving thoughts, ideas, opinions, and judgments that ultimately result in discourse and/or self-actualization. These are generally explained and defined in an overview fashion on the following pages. However, detailed definitions of these cognitive and metacognitive thinking skills are addressed in appendix A, along with examples of each in an explanatory sentence.

The names of the three thinking phases are: basic awareness and acknowledging, critical and creative thinking, and the metacognitive processes. They are explained by Schiering (1999) as follows.

Phase 1: Basic Awareness and Acknowledging

This first phase involves skill development in recognizing, realizing, classifying, and comparing, and contrasting, as well as information gathering and acquisition. It emphasizes a beginning knowledge of learners' and teachers' competencies by implementing a targeted number of thinking skills. These skills relate to fact-finding and ordering techniques that include initial awareness and cause the learner to start making connections to personal experiences and those presented orally or in written formats.

Learners are able to respond to various stimuli in conversations as well as configure answers to literal comprehension (fact-based) questions with accuracy. This phase takes into consideration an individual's earliest forms of awareness through differentiation of voices and sound, as well as observations (comparing and contrasting), the feel of animate and inanimate objects, and later, verbalizations that address these skills.

Phase 2: Critical and Creative Thinking

This phase involves the transcendence and inclusion through movement from beginning awareness with transference from cognition to metacognition. Learners process skills through visualizing and verbalizing the connections they have made resulting from prior experiences and awareness with prioritizing, communicating, inferring, active listening, inventing, predicting, generalizing, sequencing, initial deciding, and initial problem-solving.

It can be determined that the combination of critical and creative thinking relies on past discernments to construct new meaning. The learner may hypothesize, imagine, or visualize making connections from his or her own experiences or reading material for applied comprehension. Subsequently, determining outcomes from actions taken provides a comprehensive set of thoughts for problem-solving, which is addressed as a metacognitive process.

Phase 3: Metacognitive Processes

This phase occurs when the thinking goes beyond the cognitive and the learner actually knows what he or she wants to realize—exhibiting a control over his or her intake of material. The juncture of cognitive processes in phases 1 and 2 are realized with actions influenced by evaluation and critiquing.

By being able to identify what one is thinking, self-efficacy ensues. Also, a sense of personal empowerment, enabling one to know what he or she is thinking for increased cognition and metacognition, is evidenced. There is synthesizing information and critiquing accompanied by self-actuation through evaluation and synoptic exercises (general and summative overviews) occurring. Additionally, there is a realization of action or actions that need to be taken to facilitate the acquisition of knowledge.

Metacognition is domain dependent as it is instantiated (firmly grounded) in a context or learning task (Tobias and Everson, 1995). This refers to learning that addresses a specific subject area and refers to students working in a format that is structured and sequential. Abedi and O'Neil (1996) defined metacognition as consisting of strategies for planning, monitoring, or self-checking cognitive/affective strategies, and self-awareness.

The metacognitive processes in phase 3 require self-assessment and self-adjustment through evaluating, organizing, critiquing, collaborating, tolerating, advanced deciding, risk-taking, analyzing, synthesizing, advanced problem-solving, recalling, reflecting, and self-actualizing.

The result of learners and teachers identifying and implementing the higher-order thinking skills in this phase is inherent in their ability to address implied comprehension questions, where the answer is only evident through conjecture or clues that lead one to think a specific answer is viable. An example would be a sentence about seeing birds' footprints on the sand. It's implied that previously a bird had walked on the sand. Implied comprehension is based on context or illustrative material being presented in auditory, visual, tactile, or kinesthetic formats.

Reciprocal Thinking Phases Overview

As we have mentioned and you may recall, regardless of one's cultural mores, geographic location, age, ethnicity, race, level of education, or gender, there are common social and societal realities. These are influenced by the cognitive skill terms in the reciprocal thinking phases and affect belief and value systems. Specific cognitive processes can be identified for each of the three thinking phases. Being able to identify the cognitive process in use is helpful to both the student and the teacher, helping each to become proficient in the use of that skill. Figure 7.1 details these various cognitive processes.

The general definitions of cognitive and metacognitive skills are provided for you in the following three sections by phases. By referring to appendix A, you'll find full and detailed definitions of these thinking skills with examples of each one in statement/sentence format. This is done to provide you with explicit clarity regarding comprehension and application of these thinking skills.

General Definitions of Cognitive Skills: Phase I

There are five cognitive skills that can be identified in phase 1. These are recognizing, realizing, classifying, comparing, and contrasting. Recognizing helps a person be aware of or identify things. Realizing focuses on the skills that help a person make real by comprehending. Classifying refers to arranging things into groups according to established criteria. Comparing demonstrates the similarity of things while contrasting denotes their differences.

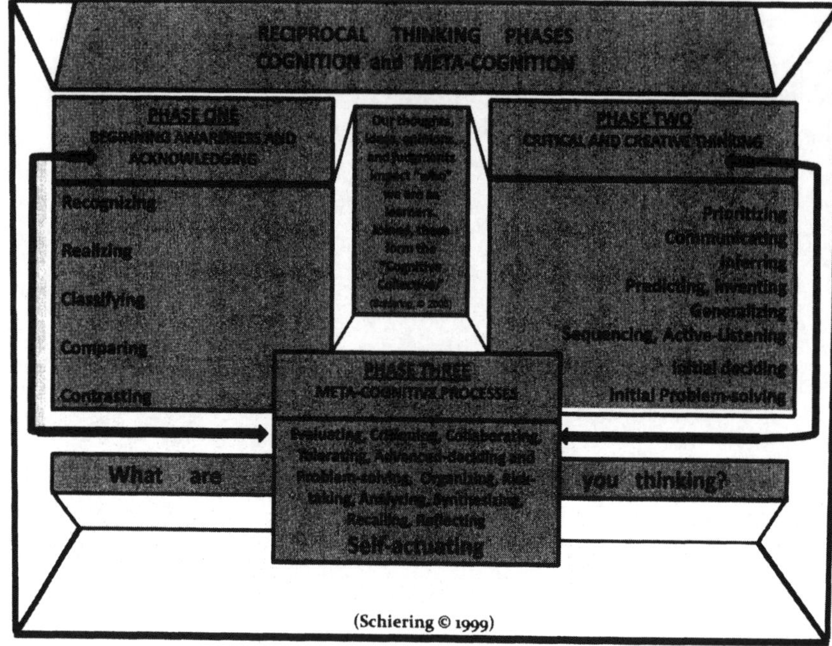

Figure 7.1. Reciprocal Thinking Phases

General Definitions of Cognitive Skills: Phase 2

In this phase, there are ten skills at a higher level of cognitive ability. These are prioritizing, communicating, inferring, active listening, inventing, predicting, generalizing, sequencing, initial deciding, and initial problem-solving. Prioritizing refers to ordering by importance. Communicating refers to the exchange of information in varied formats. Inferring relates to supposing, as a result of contextual clues. Active listening relates to being attentive when someone is speaking.

Inventing pertains to creating something new. Predicting means forming an idea of what's upcoming. Generalizing enables one to take an expansive view of something. Sequencing is an ordering of things. Initial deciding refers to a beginning choice or judgment. Initial problem-solving addresses a beginning solution to a situation.

General Definitions of Cognitive Skills: Phase 3

In this phase, the metacognitive processes take place, and there are thirteen cognitive skills. The beginning skill is evaluating. It has to do with assessing something. Organizing deals with a systemization process. Critiquing involves an evaluative means of examining things. Collaborating involves working together in a cooperative fashion. Tolerating concerns the patterns of recognizing and respecting for acceptance.

Advanced deciding and problem-solving involve the level of difficulty of a choice or resolution being realized. Risk-taking means to take a chance. Analyzing concerns the act of cautious examination of something. Synthesizing is the act of bringing things together by compacting components. Reflecting involves realizing something after thought, or contemplation. Self-actuating has to do with one's self going forward and taking action.

After reading these definitions and looking at the ones in appendix A with examples . . . what are you thinking?

In the ordinary span of a day, individuals move easily between the three phases of thinking, by using the cognitive skills in each one, reciprocally. As an adult, one does not even realize this unless one's attention is called to reflect on what was said, thought, or done. By looking back at the reciprocal thinking phases, in figure 7.1 at the bottom of the chart is the statement, "What are you thinking?" To realize this in a concrete manner, the following scenario, originally written by Dewey, and later adapted by Bogner (1990), states, in parentheses, cognitive functions, regarding whether the sentence expresses thoughts, ideas, opinions, or judgments.

Scenario

Suppose you are walking in a wooded area where there is no regular path. You are observing the different types of trees and forestation by making note of size, height, and shape of the flora and fauna (thoughts, ideas, and opinions). Your already-formed habit of hiking may take care of knowing in which direction you'll travel (judgment). You have a sense of security, as long as everything goes smoothly (thoughts). However, you find yourself saying, "I'm not familiar with this area." Experience tells you to expect the unexpected (idea, judgment).

Suddenly you find a wide ditch in your way (thought). You think you will jump it (idea), but to make sure, you survey it with your eyes, and you find that it is pretty wide and that the bank on the other side looks slippery (thought). You then wonder if the ditch may not be narrower elsewhere (idea), and you look all around to see how matters stand. You do not find any good place to make this crossing possible (opinion). So, you are thrown back upon forming a new plan (thoughts, ideas, and opinions). You take out your cell phone and call a friend and explain the situation, as you present the problem you're having (idea, opinion, and judgment).

Next, your friend suggests looking around to see if there's something that can help you get across the ditch. You thank him for the suggestion (idea) and end the call. Looking about, you discover a log that might be useful (idea). You ask yourself whether you could haul that to the ditch and get it across the ditch to make a bridge (idea and opinion). You judge that the idea is worth trying (thoughts, ideas, and opinions), and so you get the log, manage to put it in place, and walk across the log bridge and continue the venture (opinion). This confirms your thoughts, ideas, opinions, and judgments, which may later influence you in taking another wooded-area walk.

In this example, the individual moves back and forth between the various reciprocal thinking phases. This becomes evident when addressing basic awareness and acknowledging, critical and creative thinking, and the metacognitive process in conjunction with one another in the following manner:

1. *Recognizing* the walk in the woods
2. *Realizing* there is no regular path in the forested area where the walk occurs
3. *Comparing* and *contrasting* the size, height, and shape of the flora and fauna
4. *Recalling* that this already formed habit of hiking may assist in knowing in which direction to travel
5. *Recognizing* and *generalizing* that as long as all goes smoothly a sense of security prevails

6. *Realizing*, *synthesizing*, and *reflecting* on the lack of familiarity with the area
7. *Evaluating* that there's a problem continuing the walk, due to a large ditch that needs to be traversed, and ways it might be traversed
8. *Generalizing* by *recognizing* this isn't the usual walk and surveying the area to *realize* the ditch is wide with a bank on the other side, looking slippery
9. *Sequencing* and *synthesizing* means to solve the problem
10. *Recognizing* and *realizing* assistance might be needed in finding a means to continue the walk
11. *Classifying* the options and *recognizing* there may be more than one way to get across the ditch while *reflecting* on expecting the unexpected
12. *Predicting* that jumping across the chasm might be possible while *comparing* and *contrasting* alternatives, noting if the ditch is narrower elsewhere so crossing over it would be possible
13. *Tolerating* the interruption in this woodland walk and then *communicating*, *active listening*, and *collaborating* with a friend, by calling on the cell phone, to explain the situation and get ideas for *initially deciding* and *problem-solving*
14. *Inventing* and *prioritizing* a way to do this when *recognizing* alternative means for circumventing the problem
15. *Inferring* it will be possible to get past this obstacle and continue the woodland walk
16. *Recognizing* a new plan when *realizing* a nearby log might be dragged across the ditch and serve as a bridge
17. *Risk-taking* and *advanced deciding* and *problem-solving* by trying this "log-pulling" idea while *organizing* and *classifying* the steps needed to be taken

18. *Analyzing* the woodland walk by *generalizing* the events that occurred even as they were happening
19. *Self-actualizing* when managing to put the log in place and continue the woodland walk

The cognitive skills in each phase were addressed, almost seamlessly, with movement within and between them, when reviewing the thinking about the scenario.

Woodland Walk Scenario Overview: Self-Knowledge for Enhancing Effective Cognitive Ability

Each of the three reciprocal thinking phases contains definable cognitive skills. These can be identified and honed over time by answering the exemplified question about what you are thinking. Evidenced in the scenario about walking in a woodland area, this is observable. Asking this simple question about what you are thinking illustrates the importance of one's being aware of one's cognitive function for later enhancement. This is accomplished through knowing which cognitive skill the person is using at any given moment.

Developing greater facility in each of these cognitive skills allows the individual to be thinking in a most effective manner. The final cognitive skills result in reflection through self-accounting and self-actuating. These skills provide for empowerment and self-learning and self-efficacy with attention given to gleaning information from the presented material's content, as well as implementation and application of skills for decision-making and problem-solving.

Two essential observations flow from this idea of developing greater capability. First, the learner will learn better if he/she can identify the cognitive skills being used while practicing this skill. Second, the teacher can structure and teach lessons that do this by using the chart or having peer or student-to-teacher discussions that address these skills.

What about Prelanguage Reciprocal Thinking?

As teachers, we're aware that thinking occurs prior to language acquisition. This has been mentioned in the overview of the cognitive collective. You may recall reading this in the section titled "The Progression of Thinking and Feeling." We stated that it is apparent that even in the infancy stage individuals are almost immediately conscious and responsive, making cognitive connections and feeling responses relating to, for example, differentiation of voices.

As the learner and teacher, you want to know that thinking occurs all the time even when language is not present for expressing specific thoughts. Why? This is because the awareness of the mind working enhances your comprehension of the whole individual through your realization of our being thinking beings from the moment of birth forward.

Using the cognitive skills in the reciprocal thinking phases, a scenario is provided in the following section to illustrate possible prelanguage thinking of a baby between nine and twelve months of age.

An Example of Prelanguage Reciprocal Thinking

The situation: A grandmother has been asked to babysit her grandson, who lives in a different state than she. It's the first occasion for this experience. He's ten months old at the time of her extended stay in the area. She wants to make a most favorable impression. Because she's going to be staying overnight, she knows she'll be feeding him dinner.

Checking with a pediatrician for permissible foods for him to eat, she brings a treat of whipped cream and pureed pineapple that is mixed with green food coloring for dessert. At the end of the meal his grandmother presents the dessert with an elevated voice telling him, "This is a new thing and you'll love it!" The baby opens his mouth and enjoys the new food.

The baby's initial reciprocal thinking: He recognizes his grandmother as someone new to him and realizes she is feeding him when his parents are not present. He classifies the food items, which are usually presented to him each evening in the same order. At the end of the meal a new item is put forward that looks different from the other foods.

He's reluctant to try this, but his grandmother's elevated voice and things having gone well up to this point encourage him. He generalizes that the experience has gone favorably so far. Perhaps he has even tolerated this change in caregivers at meal time. He decides to accept what's offered, as he opens his mouth. This is his form of communicating, as is his facial expression, connoting delight once he has tasted the new food.

He may be recalling previous meals and comparing and contrasting these foods by color or initial tasting of them.

Quite importantly, he recognizes that nothing has tasted so good previously. He moves back to comparing and contrasting the new item to the ones that preceded it, and reflects on whether this will be repeated in the future. (At this juncture, each of the reciprocal thinking cognitive skills from phase 1 has been evidenced by the baby's reactions to the situation. Some of the cognitive skills from the other phases have also been evidenced. You're invited to use the scenario to try identifying these.)

Next ten visits—baby's reciprocity of thinking: These grandmother visits occur weekly and the baby, recalling and reflecting on the previous visits, with the presentation of the green dessert, responds most favorably to his "Grams" coming to care for him with self-actuating smiles and making a "Gih-am" sound. He also communicated this with delightful squealing. At mealtime he recognizes and realizes the pattern that has been set. He points to the green food item and demonstrates a priority for having this first.

He compares, contrasts, and classifies each food, using reflection on which ones are most preferred. He demonstrates his preference by reaching for the dessert. When the food is not presented that way, he evaluates the situation and invents actions to get what he wants, thus communicating once again. His advanced problem-solving is communicated by reaching for the green dessert that sits on the high chair tray.

This action was a definite risk-taking experience, as he didn't know how his Grams would react. Realizing that she removed the food from the tray, he recognized his communication technique didn't work. Getting the dessert would require collaboration. Recalling past meals, he sat quietly and ate the items presented and finally self-actuated by eating the green treat. (The act of self-actuating was continually evidenced when the baby had an action that evidenced moving forward to do something. This involved pointing, reaching, eating the food presented, and finally enjoying the dessert. Nearly all of the cognitive skills were utilized.)

In this scenario the cognitive skills were attributed and determined by the thinking of the grandmother. Her attention to the actions that were taken by her grandson seemed to provide the evidence of his thinking.

A prelanguage demonstration of cognitive skills will vary in any given situation, but the fact that there is prelanguage cognition is important to realize.

Some Final Thoughts on the Reciprocal Thinking Phases

The reciprocity of thinking occurs within and between phases at all levels of cognitive and emotional development. And this reciprocity is not age-specific. It is not developmentally imposed. Some may exhibit the critical and creative thinking skills at a very young age. This also applies to metacognition being evidenced. Conversely, a person of forty years may not have the ability to think reciprocally in these phases. However, by teaching students and ourselves about these phases and the cognitive skills within each one, as well as practicing using and identifying them, the opportunity to develop thinking skills is enhanced and exemplified.

Chapter Discussion and/or Journal Questions

1. What does it mean to have reciprocity of thinking?
2. What are the three headings on the reciprocal thinking phases graphic organizer?
3. What are some of the components of the history of reciprocal thinking?
4. How would you explain phase 1 of reciprocal thinking?
5. How would you explain phase 2 of reciprocal thinking?
6. How would you explain the third phase of reciprocal thinking?
7. How does the Identification of Reciprocal Thinking Terms Chart assist in building cognitive and metacognitive skills?
8. How do you suppose knowing what you're thinking brings about students' and/or your own sense of self-efficacy and empowerment?

9. Is there such a thing as prelanguage reciprocal thinking, and if so, how would you explain this?
10. What is at least one way that using the Reciprocal Thinking Identification Chart might assist students' realizing what thinking is occurring?

CHAPTER EIGHT

THE COGNITIVE COLLECTIVE'S RECIPROCAL FEELINGS

Feelings/emotions exist. They are not right or wrong—they just are. They happen sometimes with foreknowledge and other times without it. A multitude of feelings may be realized and/or exhibited, during any situation. We know this from personal experience. One's reactions to one's own or another's feelings are what create additional emotions. Feelings are reciprocal in their nature within and between varied circumstances. They may also be cyclical (Schiering 2000a; 2009a; 2010a).

The important thing is to be aware of what one is feeling and express this through communication involving verbal discourse, or even nonverbalizations. Learning and teaching rely on this interchange of expressing what one is feeling as much as on conveying what one is thinking.

Focus on the feeling phases, for the second part of the cognitive collective, is first addressed in this chapter. Perceptual feeling experiences are given attention. These are followed by an example of a prelanguage feeling narrative. Each phase is explained with how feelings impact learning, teaching, and test taking. How feelings impact effective pedagogy and learning are listed. Two experiments are provided for realizing the interconnection of thinking and feelings. These include the results of each experiment and then pertinent information regarding that. A few feeling reflection questions are presented.

Next are sections on how feelings serve as motivation and their impact on learning. Two feeling events with the involved person's and classmates' feelings are provided. Event scenario summaries and questions follow that and basically, these scenarios are for your reflection, discussion, and analysis. A final experiment provides a concrete way to identify and determine whether it's one's thinking or feelings that have been expressed by realizing the differences between them.

Key words: feelings/emotions, experiments, reciprocity, interconnection, prelanguage, and postlanguage

Explaining Reciprocal Feelings

Who one is as a learner and teacher is incumbent upon the interrelationship of the model's interior and exterior components. These are evidenced in one's knowing what one is reciprocally thinking and feeling. Knowing is a byproduct of reflections about common social and societal realities, and belief and value systems—what one lives each day. Feelings we have assist us in realizing who one is as a learner. This is based upon individuals', as well as whole-groups', past experiences, which ultimately impact on the dispositions, demeanors, and attitudes brought to school, the workplace, home, and everywhere. *I feel, therefore I am.*

Reciprocal Feelings: The Second Portion of the Cognitive Collective

We are thinking and feeling human beings—in a sense we're humans in the act of being. The operative words are *in the act of*, because feelings relate to our rationality or lack of it when experiencing varied situations about which we're thinking. Theorists have described how feelings about self can and do impact learning. How one perceives a given situation is influenced by emotions/feelings from past experiences and those in the present.

To be effective learners and teachers, individuals may well consider being able to identify how feelings impact learning. Teachers need to address the structure of their learning environments so that feelings/emotions positively assist learning. Doing that is at the highest level of intricacy, due to several factors.

These include the style of delivery of curriculum, the overall classroom environment, and learners' and teachers' demeanor and dispositions, as well as levels of interaction, discourse, and opportunities for a sense of well-being. Most importantly, identifying the feeling that one experiences in a learning and teaching situation is important for overall student success in the classroom.

You know about feelings. They are divided into two categories, which are physical and emotional. The physical ones are when there's a sensory response to some stimulus. Examples might be you feeling hot or cold, having a ringing in your ears, tasting something that's spicy and your tongue burning, seeing a balloon fly, or smelling the fire in a fireplace. These physical or sensory responses involve one's senses.

Emotional feelings are in a category somewhat exclusive to a nonsensory response to stimuli. And yet it may be that such sensory stimuli cause you to have an emotional response. An example would be that you felt elated when the wind rushed over your face on the amusement park ride.

Nonetheless, something causes you to feel happy or sad, elated, nervous, excited, and so forth. The response may be due to external or internal factors. With the latter, it may be a memory that triggers an emotional reaction. And this memory perhaps will cause a sensory feeling.

It's important to know for clarification that part of our common social and societal realities connects these two words *feelings* and *emotions*. They're interchangeable, and we use the word *feelings* throughout this chapter to convey emotions as well, when we express ourselves on the topic of feeling this way or that way.

To some situations you react in a vibrant manner, and this is in direct proportion to the value you attach to the situation. This means that your reaction to, let's say, a roller coaster ride will be different than another person's, or it could be similar. Overall, feelings and/or emotions exist. As stated in the introduction, they are neither right nor wrong—they just are.

What are you feeling right now?

Reciprocal Feelings: Perceptual Experiences

At the core of the concept of feelings and emotions is the idea that they are perceptual experiences that are presented and displayed through individuals' subjective analysis of a situation. This encompasses one relating a particular event by conveying it in a sensory or emotional manner—an affecting reaction to life experiences. These may be the same or different from those within our nuclear family, classrooms, friends, or strangers.

Our feelings may be in compliance or discordance with others whether in the geographic surrounding community, in cultural and general groupings, or society-based. And it's important, we think, to relate that in prelanguage circumstances, delineating feelings and emotions are somewhat limited in that these are interpreted by the observer(s) of the behaviors.

Nonetheless, there are prelanguage feelings and emotions, just as there are these once one is able to verbalize. As we shared in the preceding chapter, this is the same for prelanguage thinking. The main idea is that feelings are present and the observer's reactions to them are what determine the needs, wants, and desires of the prelanguage person.

What are some prelanguage feelings you think you may have observed?

An Example of Prelanguage Feeling

The situation: In the previous chapter's reciprocal thinking prelanguage scenario, the baby was shown to demonstrate thinking by the interpretation of his actions by his grandmother. This was when she came to babysit over a period of time and then fed him a tasty dessert. Looking at the same scenario, one might attribute the following feelings the baby had.

The baby's reciprocity of feelings: When the grandmother came to babysit the first time, the response from the ten-month-old was one of complacency and possibly acceptance. He neither cried nor showed emotions displaying rejection, but rather a sense of inquisitiveness about being cared for and/or nurtured. As the meal items he was used to were presented to him, the feelings were those of having a sense of security, with him being congenial.

Then, when the dessert arrived, a new feeling was expressed with his response to the green whipped cream and crushed pineapple showing pleasure and even excitement. This was followed in subsequent visits of his grandmother with him acting happy, cheerful, and ecstatic when she walked through the door. This was certainly the case when she fed him his dinner meal.

He was feeling eager to see her and his desire for having the dessert before the oatmeal, carrots, and mixed meats was demonstrated with pointing and making sounds that showed this. One might say that during the feeding time he was absorbed, which confirmed his interest, curiosity, and being engrossed while his grandmother was babysitting him.

Questions: How do you suppose the baby's feelings might change if the green tasty dessert were not to be presented at the end of the meal, after the baby was used to having this when Grams babysat? Hmmm.

In addition to verbal communication techniques for those who have language, there is nonverbal conveyance of feelings and emotions. This is much the same as with prelanguage children, with facial expressions, body stance, or gesturing conveying feelings. Nonverbal feeling emanations may depict excitement with a wide opening of the eyes and mouth, hands in the air, and/or jumping up and down. Sadness might be demonstrated with a slumped-over body stance, lowered head, and eyes focused downward, with the mouth in the same position. Moderate or unemotional feelings may be exhibited with an inattentiveness, or lack of the aforementioned exuberance-type expressions.

Phases of Feelings

To link the phases of feeling to those of thinking is nearly an impossible task. This is because so many different feelings may be evidenced at any given time for any cognitive skill. However, in a fashion, the following phases are presented to show a progression and interconnection of feelings with thinking with respect to one being in the act of feeling.

Phase I

An individual's earliest forms of awareness through differentiation of voices and sound, and the feel of animate and inanimate objects, as well as recognizing, realizing, classifying, and categorizing these sensory responses, are demonstrated by feeling as if one is discovering something and being orderly, contemplative, supposing, questioning, comparative, efficient, effective, self-examining, and creative.

Identifying and implementing the feeling terms in this phase results in learners and teachers experiencing a selective range of emotions focused on explicit comprehension. This is with an understanding of what they're experiencing having certain sentiments. Comprehension may be literal, applied, or implied.

Phase 2

The progression and reciprocity of feelings occurs in this phase as learners come to convey connections they have made resulting from prior experiences and acknowledging. In this phase, individuals most likely experience being discriminating, determined, communicative, hesitant, mystified, flexible, sequential, inventive, unrestrained, intrigued, resourceful, decisive, critical, creative, positive, predictive, inspired, uncertain, contemplative, and exhilarated.

While some of these words appear to be opposites of one another, they're presented to demonstrate how a feeling might be construed that way by different individuals in response to their corresponding cognitive skills. The result of learners and teachers identifying and implementing the feeling terms in this phase is their ability to be productive and innovative. Also, addressing and making connections to one's own experience, or reading material for answering applied comprehension-type questions, is important. This is significant when connections are made to past experiences for constructing judicious decisions.

Phase 3

The transference and transformation from beginning awareness and initial deciding occurs when learners process the skills that allow them to visualize and verbalize connections resulting from prior experiences. There is awareness of oneself and surrounding persons, as well as greater world environments. Self-adjustment and checking are apparent, with one being evaluative, empathetic, conciliatory, understanding, collaborative, tolerant, sympathetic, adventuresome, analytical, holistic, critiquing, constructive, disquieted, participatory, discerning reflective, and self-actuating.

The result of learners and teachers identifying and implementing the terms in this phase is their ability to make inferences, which are based on context or illustrative material being presented in oral, visual, tactile, or kinesthetic formats. Identifying and implementing the feeling terms in this phase results in learners and teachers experiencing philosophizing and hypothesizing. Multiple meanings are constructed, resulting from reflection.

A wide range of emotions are evidenced as innovative ideas are considered with respect to addressing problem-solving and/or decision-making, which involves acceptance of self and others. Each of the feeling phases are interconnected and exchangeable within and between themselves, as well as within and between the thinking phases, simultaneously. Also, there are a wide variety of feelings that can be attributed to any phase. There's such an expanse of emotions that it is difficult to impose exactness to any reaction for each individual.

Feelings Impact Learning, Teaching, and Test Taking

To be effective learners and teachers, individuals may well consider being able to identify how feelings impact thinking and vice versa when it relates to learning and test taking. For the last of these, we know there are many variables regarding why students do well on tests, perform poorly, or are someplace in the middle. The feelings of individual students impact their learning, and the subsequent proof of this through assessment. Regardless of whether a teacher is using a straight multiple-choice test, a true/false one, or some alternative means such as a project, there are considerations that require the teacher's attention, so best performance is a result of best classroom instruction.

Things to consider regarding effective pedagogy with feelings include:

1. Teachers need to address the structure of their learning environments so that feelings and emotions positively assist learning.
2. Assisting learning is at the highest level of involvedness, due to:
   - the style of delivery of curriculum,
   - the overall classroom environment,
   - learners' and teachers' demeanor and dispositions, and
   - levels of interaction, discourse, and opportunities for a sense of well-being.

3. Identifying the feelings that one experiences when learning and teaching is important for overall success in academic and social settings.
4. Most importantly, it's vital to be aware of your feelings and equally important to be aware of the feelings of others.
5. The feelings one has in the classroom or anywhere serve as the strongest motivator, whether this results in one taking action or remaining idle.
6. Feelings and thinking are so closely related and intertwined that it's often difficult to know which one is which, as one affects and touches the other—am I thinking this or feeling this?

The Interconnection of Feelings and Thinking (Schiering, 2010a)

Experiment 1

a. Fold your hands together and mentally label the right hand "feelings" and the left hand "thinking."
b. At the same time, refer to your hands, which are now together, as "learning."
c. Raise the second finger on your right/feelings hand.
d. Now raise the second finger on your left/thinking hand.
e. Answer the questions of whether when you did this any of your other fingers moved, did you touch the back of your hand, and was it difficult or easy to raise these fingers?

Experiment 1: Results

1. The other fingers didn't move when each second finger was raised.
2. The fingers touched the back of each hand when lowered.

3. It was relatively easy to move the second finger upward on both hands.

Experiment 1: Information

1. Sometimes thinking and feeling do not influence one another.
2. Still, thinking and feeling are involved in learning (represented by your interlocked hands). The interconnection of these in learning is commonplace and natural.
3. You are the teacher: the circumstances of teaching are related to learning through what one thinks and feels. This is true for you and students alike.

Experiment 2

a. Follow steps a and b above, but this time

b. raise the third finger on your right hand (remember, that's the feeling one),

c. raise the third finger on your left hand (remember, that's the thinking one), and

d. answer the following questions: When you did this, were your third fingers, separately, more difficult to move than the second fingers? Did the other fingers move even slightly when you raised the third fingers/thinking and feeling ones? Did you touch the back of your hand, and was it easy or difficult to move the third fingers on both hands?

Experiment 2: Results

1. It was not as easy to raise the third fingers as it was the second fingers.
2. The other fingers moved slightly when the third fingers/thinking and feeling ones were raised. These touched the back of the hand when lowered.
3. It was difficult to move the third fingers/thinking and feeling.

Experiment 2: Information

1. Some feelings and thinking are very closely related. Noting a difference between them is difficult.
2. Thinking and feeling are involved in learning (represented by your folded/interlocked hands). The interconnection of these to learning is commonplace and natural. On some occasions, thinking and feeling impact one another, even if this isn't the intent, and, separately, realizing, recognizing, and differentiating them is not possible.
3. You are the teacher: the circumstances of teaching are related to learning through what one thinks and feels. This is true for you and students alike.

Feeling reflection questions: What was your feeling and/or emotional reaction to reading this section of the book and doing the experiments? What was your reason for reading about feelings? Was it due to it being assigned; something you were interested in for learning about your own feelings, or those of your student learners, to gain insight on best practice by knowing *who* one is as a learner and teacher; or some other reason? As you were reading, what were your physical surroundings like? Were these ones of comfort and ease? Why or why not? Each of your reactions to these questions provides an awareness of your physical sensations, as well as emotional ones, which puts you in touch with yourself.

Feelings Serve as Motivation

Probably, the feelings one has in the classroom or anywhere serve as the strongest motivation to act or not take action. We suppose it goes without saying that this sentence is one which will shape and reshape your classroom when it's given attention. Feelings are around us everywhere.

We experience feelings in school, at home, when out visiting or shopping, when seeing a movie which evokes even more feelings, or when alongside a friend. Feelings are part of us as much as thinking is, and they serve to create desire or make us somewhat interested, or not interested in anything. If one has feelings of attachment to what's being said, seen, taught, or generally experienced, then one will be involved and engaged in it.

Let's say you're at school. Where do the feelings you have when there come from? From what place do the feelings you have, when there, originate? Feelings/emotions come from any place you go or recall having been. And they address a wide expanse of situations. Again, these feelings and emotions serve as the strongest motivation any teacher could imagine!

- Children, adolescents, and adults need to feel comfortable with learning.
- This requires a sense of security, safety, and overall emotional well-being in the classroom/ academic setting.
- Trust in those who occupy the classroom needs to exist. Each individual feels in a sensory manner as well as an emotional one.
- A common social reality is that feelings and emotions are considered interchangeable when explaining how one feels.
- The feelings that accompany optimum learning are mutual trust, caring, concern, and fairness being exhibited from educator to student and vice versa.

Ways That Feelings Impact Learning

1. Students need a sense of security regarding their feelings being safe to share.
2. If students feel good about themselves in relationship to learning, then they're most likely to learn.
3. Group discussions form a pedagogical perspective and feelings may get in the way of intended learning.
4. We learn all the time based on the feelings we have.
5. What others say and do when realizing the dynamics of one's environmental circumstance may inhibit intended teacher instruction. Then again, the converse may occur.

6. Liking one's surrounding, the teacher, and the lessons that are presented oftentimes results in a student's attention and attitude regarding wanting to learn.

7. If a student doesn't like the teacher he/she mightn't try to learn.

8. If a student doesn't feel the teacher cares about him/her, and/or is not excited about the material to be presented, then he/she may not perform well, saying, "these are just a bunch of hoops to jump through."

9. There needs to be a personal connection to learning experiences for students and teachers alike.

Realizing Feelings

To illustrate feeling responses and their complexity, the following two event scenarios are presented to illustrate just a few different feelings that may be experienced by different individuals in a given circumstance. Then, the involved person's and classmates' feelings are addressed in a summative narrative for each event.

Feeling words presented in the matrix were taken from a four-page list, which was the work of Marshall Rosenberg, published in 2004 by the New York Council for Nonviolent Communication, and are on the Internet at www.nycnvc.org.

The Event

Brad was standing near the teacher's desk when Karen bumped into him. She apologized for doing this, and he accepted her apology.

Involved Person's and Classmates' Feelings

Karen was upset that she had bumped into Brad, as he was near the teacher's desk and she'd simply been too close. She also felt silly about this accident and began to laugh nervously. Yet Karen was concerned that she'd hurt Brad, and this disquieted her emotionally. Overall, there was her sense of embarrassment over her being awkward. She felt the class being impacted by the event through them teasing her with a statement like, "Wow, your face is really red."

Brad felt concerned that he'd been bumped into and emotionally there was a sense of silliness, which caused him to giggle. It was rather funny that she'd not seen him and had bumped into him, but he was tolerant of her action. The impacts of these mixed feelings, as reactions to the situation, are relatively stable. There wasn't a "big deal" made over what had happened, as Brad wasn't physically hurt. The final result was that both Brad and Karen laughed at the encounter and emotions were light, as opposed to being resentful. This impacted their classmates observing the event, who felt similarly.

The Event

Ms. Smith distributed the results of the tests. She noted that one student had received the highest score that she'd ever achieved. Ms. Smith commented that she had believed in this student and knew she could do the work well. She'd been proven correct by the student's performance.

Involved Person's and Classmates' Feelings

Ms. Smith felt happy about the student doing well on the test and talked about how she'd believed in her ability to do well. The teacher was curious as to whether this was a turning point for the student and felt euphoric that this might well be the case. This caused an overall sense of joy. Although she was concerned about future endeavors of this student, who in the past had not done well in any subject-area evaluation, today she felt heartened.

The student felt happy, even euphoric, about her test results, and this caused her to talk about the test with classmates, with the teacher, and at home. She said that the teacher had believed in her, and she didn't want to disappoint Ms. Smith, or herself, by doing poorly on the test. So she'd studied more this time than in the past. The student was happy about her accomplishment and that Ms. Smith had reacted favorably to her doing well. She reveled in the moment of doing so nicely. Reflecting on what had been done to prepare for this test, she felt determined to have this feeling again when test taking, in order to repeat this success.

The classroom situation resulted in an overall sense of security for the student and the teacher. Classmates were happy for the student and congratulated her on this accomplishment. Overall, everyone had a communal feeling of well-being.

Event Scenarios Summary and Questions

By looking at the two different scenarios and the summative narratives, it's easily ascertainable that there were some feelings and emotions each held in common. Overall the characters and classroom's classmates were congenial, with caring and interest being demonstrated. This is ideal! However, what if in the first situation Brad had felt annoyed that he'd been bumped into and decided to retaliate by bumping into Karen? What if he'd called her clumsy? How do you think the feelings of Brad and Karen might have been different in that case?

What if in the second situation the teacher had just handed back the test and not commented about believing in the student? Would she try hard on the next test? Would the student's classmates think that the teacher's not reacting favorably and acknowledging the student would mean Ms. Smith would react similarly when they did well? And what if the student had done poorly on the test as was the case in the past? How do you think the feelings of the student, her teacher, and her classmates might have been different in that case?

You're invited to write your responses in your journal or discuss your thoughts, ideas, opinions, and judgments with someone.

Distinguishing Feelings from Thinking

As it has been related in each of the experiments, thinking and feeling are so closely related it's difficult to distinguish one from the other. Subsequently, students and teachers alike often express something as a feeling that is really a thought, idea, opinion, or judgment. Ultimately this results in confusion regarding what is felt or thought. And so there's a simple way for each of us to realize this difference by creating sentences that truly convey a feeling and knowing that.

This leads you to experiment three (Schiering, 2010a), where you substitute the words "I feel" for "I am." If the sentence makes sense in both formats, then you've expressed a feeling. Follow the directions below, and then look at the samples to ascertain whether you recognize expressing a feeling.

Experiment 3

a. Read the following statements.
b. Using the "I feel" for "I am" substitution, determine if each statement expresses a feeling.
c. Place an F in the space after the sentence if you think it's a feeling or a T if you think it's a thought.
d. Explain your reason for placing a "T" or "F" after the sentence.

Experiment 3 Activity

Do these sentences express feelings? Why or why not?

1. I feel it is important to check the work. ___
2. I feel that you don't like me. ___
3. I feel we should thank the teacher for the pizza party. ___

Each of these above examples is either a thought, an idea, an opinion, or a judgment, and *not a feeling* or emotion. This is because you can't substitute "I feel" for "I am" and have the sentence make sense.

Examples of Correct Feeling Statements

1. I feel secure when we go on a class trip. I am secure when we go on a class trip.
2. I feel upset that I arrived late. I am upset that I arrived late.
3. I feel happy that I got the answers correct for this third experiment. I am happy that I got the answers correct for this third experiment.

Each of these above examples is a feeling. This is because you can substitute "I feel" for "I am" and realize the sentence makes sense.

Final Thoughts about Feelings: Learning and Teaching

There are a multitude of feelings in a classroom that occur on a regular basis. You, as the teacher, concerned individual, or person who's about to embark on this career path, want and need to be cognizant of how feelings influence the classroom atmosphere. This is very important, because as Maya Angelou (2007) wrote, "People will forget what you said, people will forget what you did, but people will never forget how you made them feel." The feelings students have about themselves; about you, the teacher; and about the dynamics of the school all contribute to their sense of security and well-being.

Chapter Discussion and/or Journal Questions

1. What are feelings?
2. What are emotions, and how do these differ from feelings?
3. What is one major component of each feeling phase?
4. What are four ways a student's feelings may impact a classroom learning situation? (Provide a scenario or situation.)
5. How might one determine the feelings of a prelanguage child?
6. How does one differentiate feelings from thinking? (Write three examples in sentence format.)

PART TWO
PRACTICAL APPLICATIONS OF THE MODEL'S PARADIGM

If I am not for myself who will be for me?
If I am for myself alone what am I?
And if not now when?
(Hillel)

Being for Myself
(M. Schiering)

If I am for myself and others see this
Then
There may be an inclination to find out what I know
And others will join with me
In
Teaching and Learning.
But, if I am only for myself
Then others may well choose to be separate from me
And
Generally not interested in realizing
There's much to be shared.
I think that as teachers and learners
We are not alone or only for oneself.
We're in a field that connotes togetherness,
As
Each of us teaches and learns, simultaneously.
We are joined in a profession

That has an indefinite time continuum.
One experience builds upon another.
We are known to be those who
Care, show concern, and are responsible
By
Creating learning experiences that form
One's having positive self-images and esteem.
How?
By actively engaging learners in
Learning and teaching experiences.
If only concerned with what works for me
Being what should work for you
Then we're "separate from" instead of "together with."
So, I am for myself but not only for myself.
Where? Everywhere!
When? Now! Every day!

The introduction to the first portion of this book posed the questions about who we are as educators and who are our students as learners. With attention to the interior and exterior components of the model, those questions have been answered. We are thinking, feeling human beings influenced by a world sociology, belief and value systems, and common social and societal realities through our reflection on life experiences.

The second part of this text addresses how to implement the model in everyday school-related teaching and learning situations. One area that served to ignite our interest in writing this section was how subject-matter testing influenced student success. At one point all tests were pretty much the same. We could anticipate multiple-choice questions, some essays, and fill-in-the-blanks or true-or-false questions.

Basically, tests are important because they're used as a means of comparing students' achievement, as they determine, in many cases, who has done well and who has not. They may bring about one's retention, passing, or skipping a grade. Presently, there are alternative means of assessment, such as doing projects, role-playing, oral reporting, and creative interactive ways of evaluating one's comprehension of subject matter. Did you experience these?

You may wonder why alternative means of evaluation came to happen. We think it came about because children weren't learning the same material the same way at the same time. This was evidenced by test scores, both in the classroom and on standardized tests which were given nationally.

In many schools, both nationally and internationally, many learners and teachers have come to believe it is important that, as Dr. Rita Dunn (1997) once said in a course she was teaching at St. John's University, "if children don't learn the way we teach, then we must teach them the way they learn." Because of this reality, we have come to know that what one teaches is as vital as how one teaches.

You are invited to think for a moment of a notebook in your mind. It's a four-subject one, so there are sections for several different topics. In this notebook, these are (1) room design, (2) lesson-planning, (3) differentiated and interactive instruction: applying the model in the classroom, and (4) the model utilized as a character development factor.

Each one of these notebook sections has been selected for part 2 of this book. This is because separately and collectively they prepare you for managing a classroom in conjunction with the model. This is accomplished through practical applications of a model for academic and social cognition, for students' overall success in school.

CHAPTER NINE

PRACTICAL MODEL APPLICATION: CLASSROOM DESIGN AND INSTRUCTION

Aside from the means of the physical design of the classroom, there are also the components that relate to students having feelings of community. That may be accomplished with this space made to accommodate each learner and all learners, simultaneously. Hence, in the school or academic setting, classroom management relies partially on the physical configuration of the room and also on the environment being conducive to social interaction. These factors then connect to students' sense of classroom ownership.

Then there are the types of instruction that occur in that setting, as well as the teacher's style of delivery, which comprise another dynamic of the students' sense of belonging in that space. All these factors continually play a major part in creating a community of learners interested in learning by realizing the linkages between the sociology of the world concept and the model's interior, as well as external factors.

This chapter begins with examining a "notebook of the mind" and progresses to a history of the classroom setting across America with respect to how these settings were designed and the impact this had on instructional strategies. This leads into each classroom being "unique unto itself" regarding the community of learners. Room design and ownership in traditional and nontraditional physical and instructional styles are examined. The combined traditional and nontraditional classroom is also given attention, with respect to the physical and instructional components. Figure 9.1 provides an illustration of this type of setting.

Classroom management, with varied instructional techniques including key concepts and direct and indirect instruction with lists of strategies and functions follow. Convergent and divergent types of questions are addressed, with examples of each type. Teachers receiving answers to questions, with suggestions on how to appropriately respond to students' correct and incorrect answers to questions, is also addressed.

This section includes the effect on student learners that teachers answering questions might impose. Also, their sense of security, classroom belonging, and ownership are referenced for social cognition. The closing portions of this chapter address two types of reasoning. These are inductive and deductive reasoning for instruction. Definitions of these reasoning types, steps for implementation, and scenario-style examples are provided.

Key words: classroom design, community of learners, management, stringent, flexible, comfort zone, direct and indirect instruction, receiving, belonging, ownership, sense of security, convergent and divergent questions, inductive and deductive reasoning

Notebook of the Mind

In the introduction to this section of the book, a "notebook of the mind" was mentioned. Let's say this envisioned object had four tabs. The first of these is room design. The other three are the remaining chapters of this book, with practical applications of the model to lesson-planning, differentiated instruction, and character development.

Reflect for a moment on what you would have in this first tab section. You may see in your mind an illustration of a classroom or a photograph of one. In either case, it's anticipated that there will be students' desks; black, green, white, and/or Smart boards; display areas for students' work; computers; learning centers; wall space having posters; some type of lighting; art supplies; project-work areas; and possibly more. You may also envision where the teacher's desk is located.

What do you suppose caused you to think of this particular classroom? Is it similar to the one you experience now as a teacher candidate or teacher? Is it one where you've made observations over the years, or a composite of different classrooms' designs? Perhaps it's one you'd like to have in the future based on one you recall from your past?

The classroom you imagined, in all likelihood, will be similar to the one you design when teaching, if it's possible to do so in compliance with school safety codes and/or district guidelines. That classroom design is not just about furniture in different places, but a room configured to provide areas for students to work in ways that meet their needs. Ultimately, the room design impacts on whether students have a sense of belonging in the classroom setting.

Do you remember a few chapters ago when the school was referred to as the neutral meeting ground for children of diverse abilities and cultures? Other areas of diversity were mentioned. But what's important now is to realize that the school's classrooms must be places whose atmosphere establishes a sense of security, ownership, and comfort in order for learning to be optimized.

Children can and do learn in places where they say to themselves, "I feel comfortable here; I am comfortable here." This is accomplished by having a classroom design that accommodates learners' preferences for where they sit and areas in the room for their use. Classroom design is as important as the ideas presented in the first section of this book about knowing *who* you are as a teacher and *who* your students are as learners. That's because who one is as a learner is connected to one's sense of ease and contentment in the learning environment.

History of the Classroom Setting

Less than fifty years ago, the classroom had certain physical specifications which limited and/or prevented teachers and/or students from designing the room. Those physical limitations impacted instruction in that they were stringent, due partially to the lack of flexibility of the room's furniture. The physical environment set the mood for strategies employed.

Desks and bench-type seats were secured to the floor, which did not provide for movement of them into different configurations for, let's say, small-group work. A section of the room was built to accommodate coats and outerwear with closets. Most often books were stored in either desk drawers or the desk top, which lifted upward.

This was commonplace at the elementary level. And, at all levels, the classroom's bulletin boards and blackboards were also immovable, and this may still be the case. The concept of latitude for physical features was extremely restricted and instructional techniques seemed to follow suit. The idea of a television, computers, Internet access, phones, and whiteboards with use of markers, Smart boards, and learning centers were not even on the environment horizon.

Because the classroom setting has changed dramatically over the past two decades regarding academic and behavioral considerations, the idea of classroom design has emerged as being of tremendous importance. The physical arrangement of desks and chairs in a classroom communicates, through its design, the behaviors and instructional accommodations for the population that occupies it. Although things have changed dramatically regarding room design opportunities, the way one was taught has impacted teaching for decades, because oftentimes teachers teach the way they were taught.

Nowadays, when considering classroom design, educators can be concerned that those in the room have a sense of security. They may feel cozy and have ownership. This is possible, in large part, to being able to reconfigure the room's furniture to meet student needs. No longer is everything set in a specific space. Subsequently, instruction has been impacted, with differentiation of instruction methods—flexibility of furniture equates with flexibility of instruction. Today's classrooms oftentimes provide learning environments that are welcoming throughout the school year.

Community of Learners

Each classroom is unique unto itself. It's a space within a place of academia. And it's more than that, because of the desires you have for students' learning and fulfilling your own sense of purpose. In order for these things to happen—students learning and you realizing your goal(s) have been met—look at the classroom as a *shared environment*.

While we've addressed the elasticity of the room's configuration being important, let's now look at the concepts of unity and students' sense of belonging there. Creating a community of learners is being aware that in many respects your classroom is a minisociety of social and academic interaction that hopefully is harmonious.

Having this relies on several factors. There's the atmosphere of the room with respect to design/furniture arrangement, instructional methods, style of delivery, the questions asked, receiving of answers, types of reasoning, and the overall attitudes and dispositions that develop as a result of the interaction of these components.

Here's a starting place: ask yourself, "Are the student learners' auditory, visual, tactile, and kinesthetic modality preferences being met? Does the room convey a sense of comfort? How many places are for student learners' utilization and how many are for the teacher?" The answers to these questions are incumbent on the physical accommodations of that setting.

While some students prefer a formal setting for instruction, others prefer less structure regarding the configuration of the classroom. Regardless, in order to have classroom satisfaction for students, each one needs to recognize the classroom as a place in which he/she feels congenial. This assists in establishing a sense of ownership—"This is where I belong, this space is mine/ours."

Classroom Design and Ownership

Classroom ownership, for students and their teachers, results from having a sense of belonging when there. We've suggested this occurs when a classroom design fosters and promotes the idea of elasticity through knowing that the physical environment is reconfigurable, shared, and invitational to learning. One way in which ownership may be accomplished is by having the students give input regarding how the room is arranged.

Do you think that having students do a drawing of the room design they'd like and voting on the most preferred of these would serve this purpose? Perhaps it would, and then the top four could be used, consecutively, by quarters of the year, thus demonstrating the use of these four agreed-upon favored designs as a result of student input.

Since students learn differently from one another, as related in chapter 7, the classroom needs to make allowances for varied types of learners. This would include sections of the room where modalities are addressed, or differentiation of instruction provided in accordance with students' individualized preferences and processing styles (Dunn and Dunn, 1978; 1992; 1993; R. Dunn, 1984; 1997). Techniques regarding students' pace, level, interests, and/or styles of learning are also important for classroom ownership. This type of instruction is given attention in the next chapter.

The physical arrangement of desks and chairs in a classroom communicates, through its blueprint, the behaviors and instructional accommodations for the population that occupies it. In this case, one might think of traditional and conventional classrooms, as opposed to nontraditional and unconventional environments. Components of each follow with respect to room configurations and the learning/teaching, with instructional design strategies that accompany each one.

Components of Traditional Classroom Design: Physical Setting

This classroom has, at its core, a design that is structured and set in place throughout the school year. The students' desks and hard chairs are organized, with one being behind the other. The students face the teacher's desk, which is customarily in the front of the room and well within the line of vision of all his/her students. Except for the first student in a row, everyone else is looking at the back of another's head. How do you suppose that might influence instruction? To where is the students' attention drawn?

Components of Traditional Classroom Design: Instruction

The students' attention is focused on the teacher, because looking at the back of someone's head is certainly less appealing. Regularly, the teacher stands in the front of the room and primarily uses a lecturing presentation style of delivery. This is referred to as direct instruction, where students most often are the passive recipients of information. The classroom instruction is teacher-centered and subsequently teacher-controlled. Such instruction is familiar to middle school and high school students, due to departmentalization of subject matter.

Nonetheless, traditional instruction is frequently experienced at the elementary levels. Although things have changed dramatically regarding room design opportunities, which impacts on instructional strategies, the way one *was* taught has impacted teaching for decades, because oftentimes teachers teach the way they were taught.

Multimedia equipment is scheduled with the teacher overseeing its usage, whether in the room or part of an upper-grade schedule. An overall idea of presenting the same material to the same students, at the same time, and in the same fashion, is customary. Assessments are frequently pen-and-paper multiple choice, true/false, or completion (fill-in-the-blank) evaluations. This traditional type of classroom instructional design does not encourage social literacy, interpersonal communication, or sharing.

Classroom rules and/or practices that connote what's not to be done, such as not leaving one's seat, prevail. Generally, this type of classroom has advantages for particular types of instruction that require structure, explicit routine, and formal organization of assemblage, or individualization of assignments. There's a strictness that imposes a solidified routine both in the physical configuration of the classroom and the teaching methods.

The Nontraditional Classroom Design: Physical Setting

Because the students' desks are arranged in a U shape or semicircle, circles, or clusters, students are primarily looking at one another. Possibly, there's a section of the room where a carpeted "comfy corner" has been provided. Flip-style seats, or beanbags, a rocking chair or two, and/or cushioned television-style seating are present.

While it may not be possible or permissible to have this type of accommodations for students in sixth through twelfth grade, desks may still be rearranged in the aforementioned U or other accommodations to facilitate shared learning and discussions. Sometimes a couch may be present, if the school allows, for those who need less rigidity (informal design) as a consideration for optimum learning.

Also, seating may be arranged in partnerships and/or groups of four to six, and possibly eight. Student learning centers and/or activity areas are provided for small-group work. Students' books are placed in cubbies or in book bags attached to the desk's back and are easily accessible for student acquisition in grades K–5. Lockers for middle school and high school students are usually accessible between classes, so they'll need to have subject-related materials with them.

The teacher's desk may not be in the line of vision of each student, but nearby the classroom population. The room's varied boards may be movable, with attention directed to several boards in the room simultaneously for interlocking of disciplines, or students realizing the interconnection of subject matter. Learning centers are also viable options for all grade levels.

Computers and multimedia equipment are essential and placed for easy learner access. Movable chart boards are helpful, and then there are chalkboards/whiteboards and/or bulletin boards for displaying students' work. The overall configuration of the room connotes it being student-centered and the room design encourages social literacy, small-group and whole-class discussions, and interpersonal communication or sharing being important.

The Nontraditional Classroom Design: Instruction

The teacher delivers lessons using varied and/or multiple styles of delivery in different parts of the room. These may include anecdotes, storytelling, small-group collaborative exercises, hands-on activities involving the entire class, partnerships, some individualization, and/or learning centers where the teacher serves as lesson facilitator.

Chart boards are optimally used with students coming forward and recording their thoughts regarding subject matter being discussed or provided. This provides tactile and kinesthetic involvement. While customarily there is direct instruction (teacher-centered) for the start of lessons, the students realize that indirect instruction (student-to-student) is a substantial component for them being engaged in peer learning.

Lessons are planned to vary in accordance with student needs, with differentiated instruction and "adaptations" (see appendix A) being the mainstay. Alternative means of assessment and seating for those evaluations are varied, due to inclusion classrooms because of diverse learners and/or children with special needs.

Classroom rules are present and positive in nature, stating what is acceptable as opposed to what's not to be done. An example would be to encourage sharing of ideas. Most importantly, the physical design of nontraditional instruction in the classroom is focused on the learners. The teacher conducts lessons *with* the class as opposed to presentations being conducted *at* the students. Students most easily have a sense of ownership in the nontraditional room, due in part to the flexibility and variety of instructional methods.

Combined Traditional and Nontraditional Classroom Design: Physical Setting and Instruction

Most important, for the "combination" traditional and nontraditional classroom, is the concept of this shared environment precluding ideas of a classroom belonging to any one person in particular. The room is owned by each member. Instruction varies with regard to different techniques and strategies being provided.

The combination of these two aforementioned types of classroom design provides for formal (direct instruction) and informal/student-to-student/project-based collaborative lessons (indirect instruction), or even individualization to occur on a regular basis within the same classroom setting. Desks may be moved to allow for students working alone, in a partnership, or in a peer group, and/or teacher-directed work.

They may also be arranged to provide for small-group or whole-class instruction where student learners interact with one another on a team or may be exclusive in their studies. Room configurations promote and encourage behaviors most conducive to the goals of a lesson through the room's design being changeable at any given time. Oral reading, silent reading, and small-group sharing methods are all familiar to this type of classroom (R. Dunn, 2008). Basically, the combined room design encourages each of these. The idea of reciprocity concerning one being the teacher and learner simultaneously, and/or one teaching oneself, is viewed as favorable.

There is a sense of comfort for right-brain dominant/field-dependent learners. This is evident, with an area of the room being provided where there's a carpet, cushions, soft lighting, individual cassettes with headsets for listening to music, and conversations—a comfy corner. For middle school and high school students it's possible to have chair cushions available and/or a classroom couch.

Conversely, left-brain dominant/field-independent students have the formal desk and chair with bright illumination and quiet. Areas for working alone are provided. A discussion center area is made possible for small-group work, along with computers and a learning center or two. An overall understanding prevails concerning the students' brain dominance when it comes to classroom design. The combined classroom would have bookcases and learning centers. An illustration of a combined classroom is seen in figure 9.1.

It should be noted that arranging the combined classroom is definitely easier at the elementary-school levels, and that the figure illustrates that. However, as related earlier, it is possible to make arrangements for flexibility of furniture and sociological considerations for all grade levels.

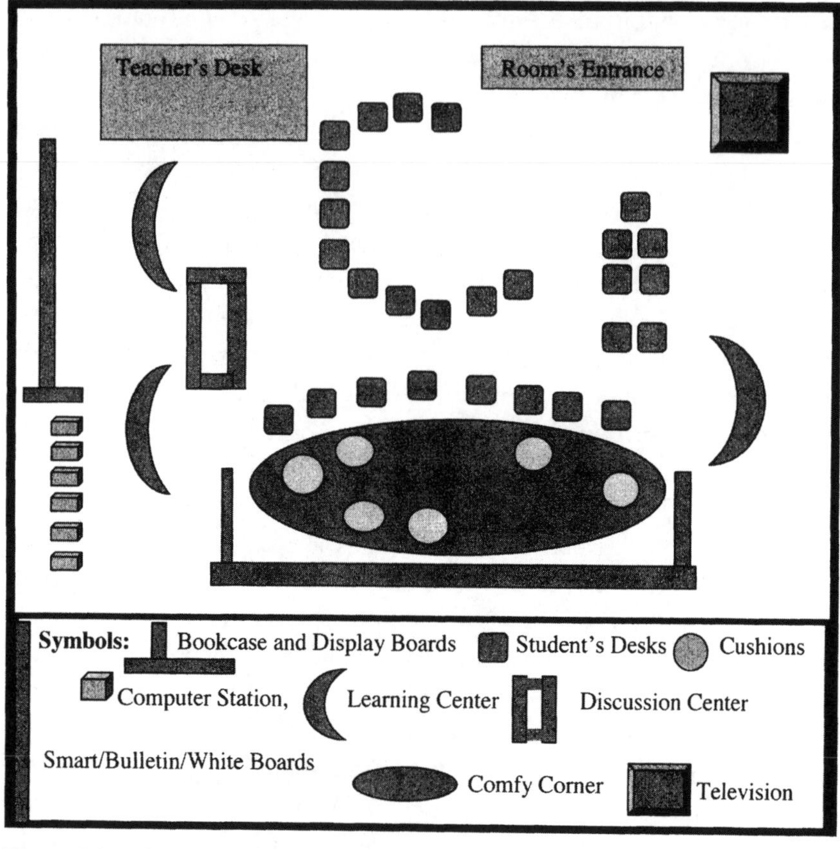

Figure 9.1. Classroom Configuration

Sometimes this requires a bit of imagination and creativity. One suggestion is to ask your students for their ideas.

Overall, the combined classroom provides a learning climate intended to be interactive, and/or modified for specific student environmental preferences. For those who prefer a formal seating type of design, there's a section of the room for that. And if these students preferred not to use the comfy corner or couch, they'd have their desks and/or chairs on the outer periphery of it.

As Murray and Keeves stated in 1994 (Schiering, 1999, p. 8), "Developing students' abilities to advance academically often requires that they be motivated to achieve, establish goals, and are persistent, responsible, and adaptive to 'varied learning environments.'" This can be accomplished with the combined room configuration implemented during the school year and application of mixed types of instruction within that setting (Schiering and Dunn, 2001).

Classroom Management

What do you think of when addressing the concepts of managing a classroom? The following pages provide definitions and conceptualizations concerning this topic and are from the course syllabi of Schiering (2000–2010; 2008). We concur that "customarily," classroom management has been the organization of instructional delivery being teacher-centered and his or her teaching styles and procedures. However, with the explanation of varied styles of classroom design, management connotes yet another dynamic.

When the setting allows for elasticity, then the instruction may logically follow in a like manner. You're asked here to examine and question which type of classroom design you prefer and why you suppose that's the circumstance. Now take into consideration the students in the room with respect to who each is as a learner. Are your answers the same?

We present some ideas concerning classroom management, beginning with the concept of the teacher not having absolute control over the classroom's inhabitants. This is because of the suppleness of the classroom's design, and student input as to how the furniture is arranged in the room. Generally, you reconfigure the room depending on the type of instruction you present, addressing the needs of your students.

If the students find the material interesting and relevant, they can learn in a way that makes sense to them. The students' focus will be on the learning. The concept of what constitutes a disruption or time spent on other tasks changes when we view learning as being multivariable. This is dependent on students' learning styles, instructional techniques, the teacher's style of delivery, and the classroom atmosphere. We've found that discordance is diminished when students are engaged in the learning exercise, unless there are many emotional problems (see "Adaptations" in appendix A).

Primarily, teachers are present to share what is known with those that choose to learn, and everyone can learn something. Therefore, a teacher's first responsibility is to create an environment that is safe for the minds and bodies of the students. This is accomplished through the teacher's comprehension of making the classroom malleable for diverse learners. We present some key concepts to include with the physical arrangement of the room, accommodating attitudes toward learning with these social literacy ideas:

Key concepts include:

1. Teachers and learners share the classroom environment.
2. Teaching and learning are reciprocal arrangements between all those present.
3. The person (teacher) with true power and control is the one who empowers another to be the most he/she can be.
4. The one thing everyone wants is acceptance—be accepting.

Classroom Management and Instructional Techniques

The design of a classroom is impacted by the types of instruction occurring there and vice versa. The classroom's harmony and the teacher and students' sense of security, as well as everyone's comfort level, is partially dependent on the configuration of the room. It also relies on this dependency in conjunction with instructional practices, techniques, and/or strategies. These are as important as how the lessons are delivered.

There are two types of instruction addressed here, and these are labeled direct and indirect instruction. The former implies an "undeviating," sometimes considered a "straight," means of disseminating information. The latter is incumbent upon a relaxed or casual style of presenting material where students are teaching themselves or one another. The teacher serves as a lesson facilitator. The content of the lesson as well as types of questions asked to foster learning are important. Two types of questions, convergent and divergent, are evidenced. And how you respond to students' answers is also vital.

Finally, concerning classroom management and instructional techniques, there's the student's reasoning ability to be considered. Is the reasoning inductive or deductive, or a combination of both? All of these are parts of instructional techniques to be considered for optimum learning by a diverse student population.

Whichever instructional type is used, you, as the teacher, want to proceed with a style of delivery that's designed to meet the needs of your learners by understanding which you believe will work best for whom. This means taking into consideration the students' common social and societal realities, belief and value systems, and thinking and feelings about the subject matter to be addressed. Additionally, you want to be excited about the lessons you present. Your enthusiasm may carry over to the students being interested in learning. Student motivation is a key factor in teaching.

Remember, the way you conduct yourself by being supportive and being positive in your demeanor and disposition is what will, in all likelihood, command the students' attention. This is because they feel comfortable in this "shared learning environment." The instructional techniques, types of questions you ask, response to students' answers, and awareness of students' reasoning strategies most definitely impact student learners' comprehension for mutual ownership and management of the classroom.

Direct Instruction

Direct instruction is teacher-centered learning strategies in which the teacher is the major information provider. The teacher's role is to pass facts, rules, or action sequences on to learners in the most direct way possible. This usually follows a traditional teaching format, with lecturing. However, the direct instruction format also includes the dissemination of information with explanations, examples, and opportunities for practice and feedback. There are large amounts of teacher verbalization, teacher-learner interaction involving questions and answers, and review and practice with correction of learner errors being provided.

Full-class instruction, organization of learning around questions posed by the teacher, provision of detailed and redundant practice/drill work, and presentation of material so that learners master one new fact, rule, or sequence before the next is formally presented prevail. Additionally, the arrangement of desks in the classroom is most often structured in rows—a formal room design with the teacher at the "front" of the classroom and learners facing the teacher.

Direct Instruction: Strategies

- Clearly presented goals and main points
- Focus on one thought at a time
- Content presented sequentially with explicit, step-by-step directions
- Use of an outline when material is complex
- Specific and concrete model or skills presentation
- Check for understanding by making sure the students understand one idea/concept/informational piece before progressing to the next one, question comprehension, provide a summary of main points, and reteach the areas where difficulty was observable

Direct Instruction: Functions

- Daily review and checking homework
- Presenting and structuring new content and providing an overview
- Guided student practice with prompts/probing questions provided during initial learning
- All students having a chance to respond and receive feedback
- Teacher observation for student learner understanding/comprehension
- Reteaching, using small steps
- Independent practice: seatwork, practice to overview learning, monitoring, and daily/weekly/monthly reviews
- Direct instruction sequence: this includes the teacher's presentation of content, teacher-directed review of presented material, additional content provision, student learner practice, teacher feedback, additional review, more content, further practice, additional feedback, and lastly teaching and reteaching

Indirect Instruction

This teaching strategy exemplifies the teaching of concepts, patterns, and abstractions. It is used for inquiry, problem-solving, and discovery learning experiences. These may be evidenced with students utilizing short answers and/or essays, where a good deal of thinking is required. This is opposed to the multiple-choice or fact-based responses customary to direct instruction techniques. Deductive and inductive reasoning are used simultaneously. The teacher presents initial instructional stimuli. *Student-centered lessons are the mainstay, with the teacher as a facilitator of these.*

This type of instruction may be in the form of content, materials, objects, and events, asking learners to go beyond the information given to make conclusions or generalizations or find patterns of relationships as they reason. The learner acquires a behavior indirectly by transforming or constructing the stimulus material into a meaningful response and/or behavior that differs from both the content used in the presentation and any previously given response.

Indirect instruction requires the learner to transfer facts, rules, and action sequences to concepts, processes, meanings, and understanding using his/her own reliance on who he/she is as a learner-teacher. The teacher's role, therefore, is to guide the discovery process, present contradictions, probe for deeper understanding, point the discussion in a new or different direction, and pass responsibility for learning to the learner, who will reference his/her own experiences, use examples to seek clarification, and draw parallels and associations, or find disassociations.

Discussion is a major component of the classroom for indirect instruction, as the learners will examine alternatives, make predictions, discover generalizations, prioritize, and project actions with decisions that encourage critical thinking and evaluation through reflection. The room design for indirect instruction, when possible, is usually informal with small groups, shared literacy, and learning cooperatively with collaboration (Schiering, 2000–2010).

Indirect Instruction: Strategies

- Presentation of material to be addressed
- Discussion-based inquiry with problem-solving and decision-making in whole-class, small-group, or partnership

formats—having *more* than two choices/options concerning decisions is imperative

- Student-centered instruction with generalizations leading to specifics
- Student-centered prioritizing
- Opportunities for inference and applied comprehension
- Using reflection and making connections to individuals' past experiences for comparison and contrast with others
- Applying critical and creative thinking for evaluating concepts and developing meaning

Indirect Instruction: Functions

- Content organization: providing advance organizers that serve as focus points
- Conceptual movement: inductive and deductive reasoning using selected events to establish general concepts and patterns (induction), and principles and generalizations that apply to specific events (deduction)
- Examples include introducing critical attributes that promote accurate generalizations, gradually expanding a set of examples, and heightening discrimination with noncritical attributes
- Questions that guide the search and discovery process, present contradictions, probe for deeper understanding, point the discussion in new directions, pass responsibility for learning to the student, and provide student empowerment
- Learner experience (one's experiential past results in comparison and contrast for problem-solving)
- Student self-evaluation includes asking students to evaluate the appropriateness of their own responses while providing cues, questions, and hints that call attention to appropriate and inappropriate responses

- Discussion includes promoting classroom dialogue that encourages students to examine alternatives, judge solutions, make predictions, make initial decisions, and discover generalizations that encourage critical and/or creative thinking

We recommend using both direct and indirect instruction when you're teaching!

Instruction Using Convergent Questioning

In order to initiate learners addressing reasoning as an active process, there need to be questioning skills that apply to provide this result. One type of questioning involves convergent statements that stimulate this form of thinking. This type of questioning involves recall and limits answers to questions to a single or small number of responses. It is referred to as closed questioning. There is no specified requirement for the learner to be involved in thought processes involving analysis, making a generalization, synthesis, prediction, or reflection.

Questions are customarily limited to those asking for "yes" or "no" answers, who, what, how many, and when. These are in reference to an experience, read material, or viewed material. Direct instruction, inductive reasoning (presented later in this chapter) and convergent questions go together with respect to having similar desired outcomes in that they are restrictive or limited and adhere mostly to fact-based instructional methods.

Examples of convergent questions:

1. What is the meaning of the word *now*?
2. Who are the characters in the book *James and the Giant Peach*?
3. What did you eat for breakfast today?
4. How many apples are in the picture?
5. Where is the tree?
6. When did you last see the dog?
7. Did you clean your room?

Convergent questions are discernable with reference to specific events and do not call for opinions and/or perspectives, or interpretation.

Instruction Using Divergent Questioning

This type of question encourages a general or open response of the learner. This relates to indirect teaching strategies. There is no single best answer. Nonetheless, there is the potential for incorrect answers to divergent questions. Subsequently, it is often appropriate and necessary to follow up divergent questions with more detail, new information, or encouragement regarding deeper thinking/reflection. In this sense, divergent questions become a rich source of lively, spontaneous additional material that can make a teaching and learning situation interesting.

A divergent question can result from a convergent one. An example would be asking the definition of the word *indecisive*. If the one answering the question has never seen the word, and arrives at the correct answer through generalization and inductive reasoning by thinking about the meaning of the words *in* and *decisive*, synthesizing these two words, and analyzing the meaning through the synthesis, then the divergent portion is evident, due to the question asking for a meaning of the word.

Examples of divergent questions:

1. What are some forms of the element sodium in our universe? This question requires the learner to recall, reflect, apply, and problem solve.
2. What would be examples of the kindness of James, in *James and the Giant Peach*? This question requires interpretation, analysis of content, and decision-making regarding the term *kindness*. The answer is subjective, with a personal set of values being used to determine the answer.
3. How does indecisiveness impact on your life, someone you know, or someone who is a family member?

To use divergent questions, you'd ask yourself about how something is perceived by the students and/or why you think it is perceived in a particular way, why something happened in your opinion, what your thoughts are about this, and address "what do you suppose"–type questions.

Receiving Answers to Questions

The teacher knowing how to create convergent and divergent questions is good and important. But, you being the recipient of answers by being aware of your reaction to students' answers is just as important. Why? Because how you respond will be a factor in determining the students' sense of ownership and comfort—what they think and feel about belonging in your classroom. And this will impact on classroom management. Both ownership and management were mentioned when classroom community was presented a few pages ago.

Students' answers need to be accepted in a manner that relates you are listening and interested in receiving responses. So what you want to do is be accepting in a way that relates that you acknowledge the answer that has been given by (1) nodding, (2) smiling, and (3) agreeing, (4) showing interest through praise, and/or (5) reinforcement of the answer by repeating it, and/or (6) asking for more information in an affable manner.

But what if the student gives an answer that you think doesn't hit the mark, lacks some component, or is completely out of context? Suggestions for this situation include that you (1) show interest through praise and acceptance and (2) follow this up with an idea for modifying the answer by (3) rephrasing the question and/or (4) stating an idea that will assist the student in thinking further about the answer and then (5) asking for any other idea he/she may have.

When you apply some or all of these ideas you are allowing the student to have a sense of success, which will encourage further sharing. If you respond with a "No, that's not right" and move to another student's answer, then you have limited the possibility of future responses from that first responder or anyone who might consider replying. Students think, "If the teacher discounted his/her answer will the same thing happen to me when I respond?" It's imperative that, as the teacher, you're in the act of being open to varied answers in a congenial way.

In a manner of speaking, you having a negative reaction may well mean that you've set the ball in motion for the student clamming up or not partaking in classroom discussion for fear of being marginalized or rejected. This is especially the case when you ask divergent questions that require the application of higher-order thinking skills. Looking back to when you were in earlier grades, how did you respond when asked questions? Did you have a good feeling, one of disinterest, or was answering something you were or were not eager to do? Why or why not? What were you thinking and feeling?

Direct and Indirect Instruction: Evidence of Reasoning

Have you ever seen a person enjoy eating a piece of pie, and the pie was a kind you personally liked, and the person eating it also liked it? If so, it was obvious to you visually. The person eating the pie was being watched by you, so you were a witness to the experience. Therefore, as you saw the pie being eaten, you may have inferred how it tasted and what it felt like, and drawn the conclusion that you'd like some. Using the cognitive collective, you may have asked for some pie, because the witnessed experience appeared logical to you, thinking-wise, in that you'd enjoy some of the pie. Feeling-wise you sensed the emotional delight of the delicious taste.

Your reaction was based on when you had not been the eater, but rather the pie-eating witness, and this caused you to surmise—draw the conclusion—that you'd like some of this pie and would enjoy it. This was because of the evidence being presented that the pie was fine. Good sense intuitively let you know that you were thinking coherently. That's an example of reasoning.

Now you're invited to take the same scenario of being a witness to the pie eating and the person enjoying it, but knowing from past experience it is a kind of pie whose flavor you don't like. Your good sense lets you compare and contrast, which seemingly leads to you intuitively knowing that you're thinking coherently, as you are directly witnessing this pie eating, but indirectly having the experience.

Your inference is twofold and/or multidimensional. First, the person eating the pie likes the pie, as they appear, through facial expression and continuance of eating, to be enjoying it. Secondly, you wonder how that is, because your past experience was not favorable. Logically you surmise—draw the conclusion—that should you be eating the pie, it wouldn't be enjoyable. As you continue watching, you may assume that you and this person have different tastes and in this area do not enjoy the same flavor. The result is that you do not ask for a piece of this pie. This is an example of reasoning.

Combining both of these pie-eating situations provides direct and indirect evidence. The direct evidence is when you experienced eating the pie and the indirect evidence is when you were the witness to the pie eating, but hadn't had this exact experience. At that juncture, you made an inference through comparison to your past experience. Reasoning was involved in the decision you made about the pie eating. In each preceding scenario you used direct and then indirect evidence.

Inductive and Deductive Reasoning for Instruction

When referencing instructional techniques, you may consider that there are two forms of reasoning. These are referred to as inductive and deductive. The former type of reasoning is considered an initiation or introduction, as in a prelude to the actual in-depth occurrence. It's a bringing about of reasoning where facts or instances are referenced so as to prove a general statement.

On the other hand, deductive reasoning refers to going from the general to the specific. This may be viewed as a transformation from logic moving progressively from basic premises to a valid conclusion. Therefore, inductive reasoning differs from deductive reasoning in that it is reasoning done from particular facts or individual cases to a general conclusion. Deductive reasoning involves inference and tracing the course or derivation of thoughts, or "reasoning out" something from known facts or general principles.

Inductive Reasoning

This is a thinking process that's used when a set of data is presented and individuals draw a conclusion, make a generalization, or develop a pattern of relationships from the data. It is a process in which one observes specific facts and then generalizes them to other circumstances. Inductive reasoning is similar to making inferences based on previous experiences.

Example of Inductive Reasoning

1. The professor tells stories and utilizes anecdotes to stimulate student interest. At the start of the next class, most students believe the teacher will utilize this method.

2. A student states, "I studied two hours and received an unsatisfactory grade on a chemistry exam this week. I am planning to study chemistry six extra hours a week for the rest of the semester." (The student's reasoning that there is a direct connection between amount of study time and the test grade. If the next test results are not better with the extra study time, the inductive reasoning will be challenged and modified.)

Deductive Reasoning

This type of reasoning proceeds from principles or generalizations to their application in specific instances. Deductive thinking includes testing generalizations to see if they hold in specific cases. Deductive reasoning follows these steps:

1. State a theory or generalization to be tested.
2. Form a hypothesis in the form of a prediction.
3. Observe or collect data to test the hypothesis.
4. Analyze and interpret the data to determine if the prediction is true, at least some of the time.
5. Conclude whether the generalization held true in the specific context in which it was intended or tested.

Example of Deductive Reasoning

As a result of severe storms causing damage to homes along the coastline of Florida, more storms and damage are to be anticipated this year. And as recorded by the National Weather Service, Florida's coastline has experienced two to five hurricanes during August for the past three years. Hurricane Theodore is scheduled to arrive this week. Suggestions are given to help homeowners secure their places of residence. It's predicted that this particular hurricane will cause tremendous damage if homeowners are not prepared.

Traditionally, these storms have received general news media coverage on each occurrence. Storms of this type and magnitude may be anticipated and result in home destruction or damage in accordance with past history, due to the tropical depressions in this area of the country.

It is suggested that homeowners be prepared for these storms and prevent damage to their houses by securing wooden window coverings that may easily be placed on the windows when a storm warning is announced. Additionally, it would be prudent to evacuate dwellings when notification is provided by the Weather Service.

In the past, it has been observed and recorded that doing this has prevented severe home damage 90 percent of the time, and moderate home damage was prevented nearly 100 percent of the time during hurricanes. It was noted, a few days after Hurricane Theodore struck, that extensive damage was evidenced where precautions were not made with wooden window coverings. The National Weather Service thanked people for evacuating their homes when asked to do this. (Homeowners, using the deductive reasoning steps, concluded that the final component of generalizing held true in the specific context in which it was tested/intended.)

Chapter Discussion and/or Journal Questions:

1. What are the three forms of classroom design?
2. What are two ways classroom design has changed over the past twenty years?
3. What was one cause of this change?
4. What is meant by formal and informal classrooms?
5. What are components of traditional and nontraditional classroom design?
6. What is meant by a teacher's style of delivery, and what is your style of delivery?
7. What is an example of direct instruction?
8. How would you explain indirect instruction?
9. What are examples of (1) convergent questioning and (2) divergent questioning?
10. What is one suggestion for receiving answers to questions?
11. What are the two forms of reasoning, and what are examples of each one?

CHAPTER TEN
PRACTICAL MODEL APPLICATION: LESSON-PLANNING

Central to the process of teaching is the construction and delivery of lessons. A model for academic and social cognition defines the various cognitive processes that individuals use and links these processes to the various factors that can influence thinking and feeling. In so doing, lesson-planning represents the thoughtful preparation and delivery of predetermined material or content that is deemed to be important.

The model's external factor of academics is addressed through the effectiveness of arranging lessons that benefit students' comprehension. Common social and societal realities and the students' belief and value systems are considered when planning a lesson by way of their impacting who students are in the classroom. In fact, the components of part 1 of this book are addressed in what is to be taught as much as how it's delivered and who students are as learners, along with the room design addressed in chapter 9.

The purpose of this chapter is to directly explore the impact of this model on teaching, using lesson-planning as an example. In so doing it specifically addresses this teacher process with whole-class, small-group, and individual instruction. Applying the model to lesson-planning and then examining it through a "new and review" overview by addressing all the components of it are given attention. What follows is (1) applying the model to the classroom with a checklist to aid in lesson-planning, (2) construction and delivery of lessons, (3) components of the Molloy

College Lesson Plan, and (4) culminating thoughts on lesson-planning with reference to the model.

A lesson chart for the four kinds of sentences in figure 10.1 relates the assignment, guides for presentation, and the purpose/relevancy of the assignment. A checklist to aid in lesson-planning and an example of a full written lesson plan on awareness and distinguishing these four kinds of sentences are presented. Lastly the model's cognitive collective in reference to the written lesson plan is explained, as the chapter culminates with the model's application of SOW, internal and external factors, a general assessment checklist for a lesson, and a personal note to teachers.

Key words: lessons, planning, differentiated instruction, objectives, learning standards, indicators, adaptations, developmental procedures, assessment, independent practice, academic intervention and enrichment, and declarative, interrogative, exclamatory, and imperative sentence types

Applying a Model for Academic and Social Cognition to Lesson-Planning

Do you remember the reference to the notebook of the mind in the previous chapter? This is where classroom design was discussed. This chapter is the second tab in that notebook, in which our conversation is on lesson-planning. In order to address the application of creating lessons you also need to consider the other chapters about the interior and exterior components of the model.

These components are interwoven, like a finely textured tapestry, into the fabric of valuable student-centered assignments for comprehension of curriculum. Experienced teachers know that careful and diligent preparation makes for effective learning. The lesson-planning components serve as an example of this industrious preparation.

This preparation increases greatly the chances that given content will be learned by an increasingly greater number of students. This will be to the level that is expected by the teacher and the school. Despite careful preparation, however, lessons often do not go as intended and sometimes do not result in the planned outcomes. Why?

It's because the process of learning is a complicated, multilayered, and fluid process that is highly individualistic and can be impacted by many factors. This comprehensive model attempts to combine these various factors into one holistic conceptual framework that can be used to better understand what is happening within the thinking and learning continuum.

Applying the model to the process of lesson-planning can help the teacher anticipate many of these factors and, as such, make for more effective and efficient student-focused/student-centered teaching. And you're invited to remember that good lesson-planning makes provision for whole-class, small-group, and individualized instruction.

It is important to begin one's comprehension of lesson-planning with awareness that students enter the classroom at the beginning of a school year with their own already formed, but alterable, thoughts, ideas, opinions, and judgments. The preconceived cognitive products, as mentioned by Dewey (1937; 1938) and other theorists, convey that new knowledge is reconstructed from existing knowledge. Subsequently, one of the teacher's responsibilities requires the connecting of new content to the already-existing understanding and ideas of the students.

There are many opportunities within the lesson-planning experience to do this, starting with the motivation and objective. These may be shaped so that the lesson is seen as important to the student today in his or her own life rather than *only* in the future, such as being necessary for the passing of a comprehensive exam next year. Also, there is the opportunity to relate the newly presented material to former curricular experiences of the students when creating lesson purposes.

Materials, strategies, differentiation of instruction, developmental procedures (student-based activities and questions to develop comprehension), intervention, and reinforcement activities can all be shaped in a similar fashion. They're being chosen to connect to what the learner brings into the classroom. This requires knowing students as individuals and what works best for them in the whole-class or group learning situations.

Applying a Model for Academic and Social Cognition to Lesson-Planning: New and Review

As you may recall, the learner's thoughts, ideas, opinions, and judgments are formed within the context of his or her belief and value systems. They're constructed and bolstered by family and social networks that can continually enforce the appropriateness of certain behaviors and perspectives.

Of course, there is a diversity of belief and value systems among the students. These, as such, are due to individual multiplicity.

Belief and value systems flow into the classroom, providing another context for variability. The teacher, therefore, needs to understand the variation of these and take them into consideration in lesson construction. Previously, we've presented information about common social realities, the sociology of the world, which may well provide the general ground for understanding of complex issues, including belief and value systems. Then identifying the differences and commonalities are viewed as essential tasks of the teacher. Basically, knowing *who* your students are and addressing this impacts on them being open to lessons.

You already are aware that feelings and emotions can and do impact learning. Feelings about self, as outlined by Bandura (1997) on the topic of self-efficacy, can influence how an individual approaches the task of learning. Related to this are feelings about the likelihood of success. In configuring the lesson, the teacher needs to look through the learner's eye to see if the tasks contained within the lesson will evoke positive feelings or strong negative ones that may prevent the desired learning.

You also know that the teacher needs to attend to, as well, the overall classroom environment/design to ensure that it promotes a sense of community, safety, and comfort that will enhance learning. It's imperative that lessons be configured and implemented to produce student success. Once this occurs and a student realizes his/her ability, then other successes follow. Create lessons using techniques that promote student success!

Thinking takes place at varying cognitive levels, employing a variety of cognitive processes. Often the learning objective is designed in part to enhance a particular cognitive skill, or to challenge the student to use higher-order thinking. Examples would be encouraging the students' use of "critical or creative thinking" through open-ended instruction. Or problem-solving skills may be addressed, with outlining of thought processes for accomplishing this.

If the overall goal of education is to challenge students to think rather than to recall and parrot back information to the teacher, then it is important that the teacher consciously identify what cognitive skill or process the student is expected to employ. He/she will then construct the lesson such that the student will use this process.

As described in previous chapters, effective learning happens best when the learner can identify the cognitive or metacognitive skills he or she is employing and can then move forward in developing these skills. The delineation of the cognitive skills contained within the three thinking phases of basic awareness and acknowledging, critical and creative thinking, and the metacognitive processes, as presented in chapter 5, has been an attempt to do just this.

The classroom does not exist in isolation from society. In fact, it is the place where society expects that the future generation will learn about what is important and how to think about these matters. As such, the constructs of society impinge on the classroom. The external factors of REAP can influence the success of each lesson. The teacher should know before the lesson whether any of these factors will impact the teaching/learning situation, as well as how this may be the case.

Do you recall that the encompassing component of the model is the process of reflection? All learning occurs through individuals' reflection on the material, content, and/or experience that is presented. This reflection operates within the context of already formed belief and value systems, as well as already formed thoughts, ideas, opinions, judgments, and feelings. To be sure, these can and do influence the learning that will take place in the classroom.

Consider reflection as a cognitive process which may, therefore, be enhanced using the lesson-planning process. You want to note that at times there are real opportunities to teach students how to reflect in ways that are more well grounded, appropriate, and critical. There is the opportunity, then, to ask, "Where in my lesson can I teach guided reflection, critical review, and scientific or philosophical inquiry?" Can reflection be taught? The answer is yes. Knowing what you and your students may be thinking and feeling gives the learner greater facility to succeed in this area.

Applying the Model to the Classroom with a Checklist to Aid in Lesson-Planning

1. What are some thoughts, ideas, opinions, and judgments the students bring into the classroom?

2. What belief and value systems held by the student or by student influences may shape the learning situation?
3. Are there strong feelings on the part of the students that may preclude learning?
4. Can these feelings and emotions be tempered through design of the lesson or classroom environment?
5. Are there external factors that could influence learning? If so, what are these, and how might they be mitigated?
6. Are there common social factors that can be used to bridge individual variations?
7. What thinking phase(s) and cognitive processes are being encouraged for use in the lesson?
8. What activities within the lesson are designed to encourage self-reflection?
9. Is the classroom physically and emotionally arranged to facilitate a sense of comfort?

Lesson-Planning: Delivery and Construction

Central to the process of teaching is the construction and delivery of lessons. Lessons represent the thoughtful planning and delivery of predetermined material or content that is deemed to be important. While the teacher is often given considerable flexibility in how the material in the lesson is taught, evaluated, and reinforced, the content is often decided by the school system and/or state/national learning standards. This content reflects agreed-upon learning objectives that are considered appropriate for a given age and developmental level. Increasingly, the school and the teacher are evaluated against the students' achievement of these goals.

The processes of lesson-planning often operates within constructs mandated by school systems, state incentives, and colleges of teacher education. These employ predetermined rubrics, which are considered to be essential for the construction of effective lesson evaluation. While there are variations in these rubrics, in general, the formal lesson plan includes written objectives for the lesson, aligned with learning standards that are utilized in the particular area of instruction. The following is a typical lesson-planning checklist that includes the components of the Molloy College Lesson Plan.

- Objective(s) of the lesson
- State, national, or discipline standards that apply to the lesson
- Indicators: evidence that these objectives have been met
- Motivation for the lesson: the catalyst to stimulate students' interest
- Materials to be used when teaching the lesson
- Strategies to be utilized: This section addresses kinds of instruction, whether direct or indirect, or the formation of groups and/or whole-class involvement.
- Adaptation(s): Primarily this refers to special needs of a student.
- Differentiation of instruction: creating diversity of instruction. Some considerations address students' pace and ability level, tier/scaffold lessons, kind of instruction, learning-style preferences, or interest groups. This section of the lesson plan stands alone, but is in conjunction with the lesson's objectives.
- Developmental procedures: These are the actual activities that will be presented with questions following each activity to stimulate students' cognitive skill development. Question types may be convergent and/or divergent, closed- or open-ended, and use literal, applied, and/or implied comprehension. Students may also be asked to address the common social realities of the lesson or feeling/emotional components of the provided activities.
- Assessment: These are evaluation processes that may include teacher observation, varied forms of testing, checklists, rubrics, or student performance through project-based or hands-on activities.

- Follow up: This is the homework assignment that addresses the lesson, and its completion is reported back to the teacher or the class and/or provides some way of realizing the work has been completed and referred to as a reporting alternative.
- Academic intervention: This is an activity or several activities for students who were unable to meet the lesson objective(s). Specific forms of differentiation may be employed to assist in students realizing the lesson's objectives/concepts.
- Academic enrichment: This is an activity or several of them designed for students who exceeded meeting the lesson objective(s). A reporting alternative is helpful for feedback on work addressed at this juncture.

Culminating Thoughts on Lesson-Planning: The Model

Even with the information in the preceding checklist, the classroom needs to be a place where learning is encouraged by the design of the lesson plan. You want to facilitate a relationship between those in the classroom to provide student learners with interest in what's to be presented. This may be partially accomplished by having the students aware of what's to be learned and the "purpose" and "relevancy" of this for their experience. Therefore, each of the factors related in the model are addressed with the following in mind:

1. What are things you want the students to learn and be able to do as a result of your teaching? (cognitive collective, reflection)
2. Is the material in the lesson relevant to what's happening in and around them socially and academically? (common social and societal realities, belief and values systems, external factors, sociology of the world)
3. The stimulus for the lesson is in direct proportion to interest areas, previous lessons' content knowledge, and needs of the students. Is the lesson designed to make this a reality through motivational techniques? (cognitive collective for differentiation of instruction)

4. Is the instruction engaging, and is there a need to differentiate and make accommodations for specific learners? What would these entail? (all interior and exterior components of the model)
5. Your style of delivery of material is such that it stimulates students' interest. (all interior and exterior components of the model)

A Lesson Chart: The Four Kinds of Sentences

One major component of lesson-planning is that the students are informed about the general assignment, procedural guidelines for presentation/ implementation, and, most importantly, the purpose of the lesson. This causes it to have relevancy in their combined and individual perspectives.

Assignment	Guidelines for Presentation	Purpose and Relevancy
Identify and then write each of the four kinds of sentences: Remember that: 1. Declarative sentences make a statement. 2. Interrogative ones ask a question. 3. Exclamatory sentences exclaim something in an excited fashion. 4. Imperative sentences give a command or order to do something. (The subject of the sentence—'you'—is understood).	1. Working in partnerships and using sentence strips, write an example of each kind of sentence. Be sure to have the correct punctuation. 2. Next, cut up these sentences by having each word separate from the other. 3. Place these words randomly on the floor. 4. As a whole class, create new sentences. Be sure to have at least one example of declarative, interrogative, exclamatory, and imperative types of sentences.	Your comprehension of how to identify and write the different kinds of sentences is important because: 1. They are in books and part of everyday conversations. 2. They make what is written or read interesting to the reader or listener. 3. You understand the thinking and feelings of yourself and others by using a variety of sentence types. 4. You become an effective communicator.

Figure 10.1. Lesson Chart for the Four Kinds of Sentences

Example of a Written Lesson Plan

The following example of a lesson plan is from Schiering's first-, third-, fifth-, and sixth-grade classrooms in Ohio, North Carolina, and New York. It was presented between 1965 and 1999. The topic of the lesson is the four kinds of sentences. Since 2000 it has been used in the Childhood Education course EDU 504: Interdisciplinary Methods for the Diverse Learner at Molloy with the use of the Molloy College Lesson Plan format.

(When reading the developmental procedures section and those others that pertain to student involvement in the lesson, you'll note that there is attention given to each of the four modalities, with auditory, visual, tactile, and kinesthetic perceptual preferences being addressed. Additionally, there's direct and indirect instruction with convergent and divergent questions, as well as inductive and deductive reasoning.)

Objectives

Following the students identifying interrogative/question-asking-type sentences, the students will be introduced to the three other kinds of sentences, which are found in oral and written/literary formats. Then the students will identify these as they orally share and then write two examples of each sentence type.

Learning Standards

New York State English Language Arts #1, language for information and understanding: Students will listen, speak, read, and write for information and understanding. As listeners and readers, students will collect data, facts, and ideas; discover relationships, concepts, and generalization; and use knowledge generated from oral, written, and electronically produced texts. As speakers and writers, they will use oral and written language that follows the accepted conventions of the English language to acquire, interpret, apply, and transmit information.

Indicators: This will be evident when the students are introduced to the four kinds of sentences in oral and written formats and identify these as they orally share and then write two examples of each sentence type.

Motivation

The teacher will write the words to the "Four Kinds of Sentences" (Schiering, 1965) song on the board. Then the students will sing the song with the teacher.

"The four kinds of sentences . . . they are as follows: declarative, interrogative, exclamatory, and imperative. Declarative it states. Interrogative it asks. Exclamatory exclaims. Imperative it orders. Declarative, interrogative, exclamatory, imperative." Repeat three times with your voice getting softer each time.

Materials

Handout of the "Four Kinds of Sentences" song, sentence strips, markers, masking tape, and storybook containing the different sentence types.

Strategies

Direct instruction, indirect instruction, small groups, partnerships, hands-on instruction, collaborative groupings.

Adaptations

For the learner with an auditory disability, the lesson activities and components within them will be provided on an overhead projector and/or Smart board.

Differentiation of Instruction

Since all learners do not learn in the same manner, the students will be separated by learning-style perceptual preferences.

- The tactile learners will create a Velcro matching game with the names of each sentence type and examples of each of these.
- The visual learners will create a PowerPoint presentation of the four sentence types.
- The auditory learners will create an audiotape of the sentence types, with definitions provided on the audiotape.
- The kinesthetic learners will role play the four different types of sentences and ask to have the audience identify each one being presented.

Developmental Procedures

1. The students will be introduced to the four types of sentences: declarative, interrogative, exclamatory, and imperative. This will be followed by the students selecting a partner to give an oral example of each of the sentence types, as the partner identifies each one. Facial expressions, voice modulation, and gesturing will be used to accomplish this task. *(What are the four types of sentences? What does a declarative sentence tell you, and what punctuation is used at the end of this sentence? What does an interrogative sentence do and what punctuation is used at the end of this sentence? What does an exclamatory sentence relate, and what punctuation is used at the end of this sentence? What does an imperative sentence state, and what punctuation is used at the end of this sentence? What types of facial expressions do you use for each one? How do you think this activity helps you identify the correct kind of sentence?)*

2. The students, still working with a partner, will write on sentence strips one example of each kind of sentence. This will be without the punctuation marks at the end of the sentences. Sentences will then be tacked on the wall and one student will come forward, read a sentence not of his/her making, identify the kind of sentence, and add the punctuation before calling on another student to do the same thing with another sentence that's on the wall. *(What was the sentence you selected? Were you able to identify the correct kind of sentence, and if so, why do you suppose that was possible? What were the types of sentences placed on the wall? Were you able to place the correct punctuation at the end of the sentence? If so, why do you think you were able to do that? Did you enjoy this activity, and if so, why, and if not, why not? How many sentences were on the wall in total?)*

3. In small collaborative groups, the students will remove their sentences from the wall and then cut the individual words from each sentence and scramble these on the floor. *(What does it mean to scramble the words? What type of perceptual preference were you using to do this activity? Is this one that you use to learn*

best? Why or why not? How many new sentences do you think you can make from the words on the floor?)

4. The students, working together as a whole-class collaborative group, will create as many new sentences from the words on the floor as possible, in fifteen minutes. *(What does it mean to work collaboratively? How many new sentences do you think you'll be able to create? Which sentence, if any, did you think to create? What type of ending punctuation did most of the sentences require? Was each sentence type presented in the new ones created? Why or why not? What was your opinion of this activity? How many sentences were actually created from the words on the floor? [Which cognitive and/or metacognitive skills did you use to do activities 1–4? Which reciprocal thinking phases were represented in each activity?])*

5. The students will form a line, and the teacher will give instructions for different hand gestures for each type of sentence she reads aloud as the students go to the school gym. Later, they will record their answers to the following questions in their English notebooks. *(What is the gesture for a declarative sentence? What is the gesture for the interrogative sentence? What are the gestures for the exclamatory and imperative sentences? Was this an easy task as we walked to the gym? Why or why not? How many sentence types do you suppose you identified correctly?)*

Assessment

The teacher will observe and note, on a teacher-created checklist, (1) the students working collaboratively in partnerships, (2) their ability to create new sentences correctly that represent each sentence type for the wall activity, and (3) their ability to make new sentences from former ones.

Independent Practice

For homework, the students will write a paragraph or two on a topic of their choosing. Sentences are to be used, with at least one representing each of the four types provided in class. These will be shared with the teacher the following day.

Academic Intervention

For the students who did not meet the objective, the teacher or teacher assistant will provide one-on-one instruction time. This review will be accompanied by a worksheet that has examples of the sentence types and a space for filling in the name of the sentence type.

Academic Enrichment

The students who exceeded the objectives of the lesson will be given the opportunity to write a short story using the four sentence types for in-class sharing.

Addressing the Model through the Four Kinds of Sentences Lesson Plan

When assessing students, the teacher takes into consideration the internal and external components of the model by addressing the students' cognitive collective for social acceptance and interaction. Here are some suggestions for examining the lesson's intent and content.

The Model's Cognitive Collective Application in the Lesson

In the lesson plan on the four kinds of sentences, the model is addressed with regard to the objectives of the lesson and the developmental procedures activities. Reciprocity of feelings occurs with teacher realization of students being comfortable when working collaboratively as a whole class or in partnerships. And individualization takes place through coming to the wall to identify the sentence types and punctuation as well as walking in the hallway to the gym and responding with gestures to read sentences of each type.

Classroom implementation and application of cognitive and metacognitive skills in the reciprocal thinking phases of basic awareness and acknowledging, critical and creative thinking, and metacognitive processes is evident when students answer the questions in activity 4 and partake in:

1. Recognizing the topic of the lesson and the developmental procedures when they respond kinesthetically to read sentences.

2. Realizing the different types of sentences and classifying them in accordance with how they're written and verbalized.

3. Comparing and contrasting through practicing configuring different types of sentences on sentence strips, as well as orally giving examples of sentences in partnerships.

4. Communicating these different types of sentences verbally and in written formats in each of the developmental procedure activities.

5. Generalizing that all sentence types are present when talking with others and in textbooks, as well as informal/pleasure reading.

6. Sequencing sentence types when talking and writing so that there's interest created in conversations and reading what one has written, whether one is the author or someone else is.

7. Inferring and "initial and advanced deciding" is experienced when sentences are spoken in partnerships with examples of declarative, interrogative, exclamatory, and imperative. Additionally, the type of ending punctuation that goes on the sentence helps students become aware of deciding the difference between declarative and imperative sentences. Placing proper punctuation at the end of a sentence, as in the second activity, allows for students to make decisions on the kind of sentence, and later on the ones written in activity 4.

8. Actively listening occurs when relating the sentences to one another as depicted in the developmental procedure's first activity.

9. Initial problem-solving when students cut up their sentence strips to reconfigure new sentences representing all of the four kinds of sentences.

10. Evaluating each other's sentences for correct punctuation and sentence type.
11. Organizing the sentences on the floor with appropriate wording for scope and sequence and good sentence structure.
12. Critiquing one another's sentences when listening to them and trying to decipher through facial expressions and voice intonation and modulation which sentence type is being delivered.
13. Advanced deciding occurs when students practice writing sentences in paragraph format.
14. Inventing occurs throughout the lesson as students configure their sentences verbally and in written formats representing each kind of sentence.
15. Synthesizing occurs with the creation of new sentences of activity 4.
16. Recalling and reflecting are addressed when students refer back to the definitions of the different kinds of sentences and apply this through creating new ones of each type.
17. Self-actuating is evidenced throughout the lesson's activities, as the students are going forward and doing by verbalizing the different sentence types, applying appropriate punctuation, and practicing these during and following the lesson in conversations and writing.

The Model's SOW Application in the Lesson

1. A world sociology is realized in this lesson when students interact to create sentences reflecting and revolving around common social and societal realities and belief and value systems. These demonstrate their thinking and feelings being in accord with the varied modes of instruction utilized in the lesson.
2. The questions that the teacher asks during the assigned activities in the developmental procedures adhere to the social struc-

ture of the classroom. This involves what students are thinking and feeling/the cognitive collective in the classroom as well as outside of it. It's accomplished by directing attention to common experiences/social and societal realities that are held and evidenced through partnership endeavors and construction of sentences both on the wall and later on the floor.

3. An example of SOW would be comprehension of what are acceptable sentences to write resulting from common social and societal realities, and what is accepted behavior concerning working together as a whole class or in partnerships, as well as when walking in the hallways.

The Model's Internal and External Factors Application in the Lesson

1. The subliminal and overt discourse that encompasses a classroom is continually reflective of circumstances and situations that impact students' lives in and outside the classroom. The model's internal and external factors then come into play as a means of expressing thoughts and feelings about these, as evidenced in sentence construction.
2. The social realities of a classroom and belief and value systems are evidenced when the four kinds of sentences are used to express feelings, thoughts, ideas, opinions, and judgments.
3. The students' experience with creation of sentences, as these frequently depict current or past events in their lives, which represent each of the external factors of the model.
4. The students conversing and then writing, at the end of the walk-to-the-gym experience, the answers to activity 5 questions in their English notebooks. Attention is called to subject matter that impacts sentences read and comprehension of the interconnection of all the model's components. Being a reflective practitioner is realized when students form ideas from previous experiences and share these using the different sentence types.

5. In fact, sentences are used all the time, and students' knowing which types they are using helps to empower them in creating viable and interesting conversations and/or writings. These ultimately reflect influences of religion, economics, academics, and politics.

A General Assessment Checklist for the Teacher

Having completed an example lesson plan, the teacher may want to evaluate his/her work with the following question checklist, to be attentive to meeting the criteria of generally planning a lesson, and its connection to the model.

1. Is the objective stated, and does it apply to the topic?
2. Is the lesson done sequentially in accordance with the accepted plan format?
3. Are descriptive data adequately provided?
4. Do the lesson objectives and developmental procedures include application of reciprocal thinking phases skills?
5. Is the plan content grade/age-level appropriate, and is it appropriate for the objectives?
6. Does the lesson involve activities connected to a world sociology in that they will be utilized in everyday situations?
7. Have the internal factors of belief and value systems been addressed?
8. Are there common social and societal realities present in the lesson?
9. Are some or all of the external factors evidenced in applications of the lesson?
10. Are students involved in being reflective practitioners?
11. Is there sufficient motivation that will engage the students in learning?

12. Is there interaction, and are the activities developmentally appropriate for the intended students?
13. Are the assessment and the content appropriate for the lesson?
14. Are there culminating activities that include follow up?
15. Does the material bridge to other disciplines for optimal learning?
16. Are the standards clear, and is the evidence clearly stated?
17. Is there adequate closure to the lesson?
18. Are there comments and/or suggestions on appearance, voice stress, modulation, expression, juncture, articulation, knowledge of topic, and general presentation style provided by the teacher?

A Personal Note for Teachers

What is true for the student is true for the teacher as well. Knowing what you, the teacher, are thinking and feeling is essential to successful teaching. What belief and value systems do you bring into the classroom? How do these allow you to connect to the students or prevent you from doing the same?

Similarly, what thoughts, ideas, opinions, and judgments about our subject matter do we bring with us? To be sure, our enthusiasm for subject matter comes from these and what we believe to be important information for student learners. And conversely, we should note that these can also preclude us from teaching certain items or at least doing so without any great love.

Feelings shape the world of the teacher as well. These same feelings of self-efficacy and self-esteem are present in the beginning teacher as well as the most experienced. Math or science anxiety, for example, can be present in the teacher as well as the student. The content expressed in the lesson plan is shaped as much by teacher self-confidence in the subject matter as by the school's required curriculum and/or set of objectives.

As with our students, we all want to operate within areas of security where we have high degrees of self-confidence, minimizing risk-taking.

Knowing and being able to name these feelings, as they relate to the lesson, helps the teacher to be most effective. This is due to an infinite awareness of one's self.

External factors clearly influence the world of the teacher. The religion, economic, academics, and politics of the community and the school shape what is considered appropriate to be taught and how it is taught, impacting as well the materials that are available to the teacher. The challenge for the teacher is to do what is best for the student despite these constraints.

The mastery of teaching occurs over time, and as with all cognitive processes, relies at its core on effective and ongoing reflection. We improve teaching when we engage in ongoing refection—reflection, of course, on the effectiveness of a given strategy, adaptation, motivational technique, or evaluation process, whether it worked, why it worked, and how it might be improved.

Also, reflection on our students—what they bring into the classroom; their feelings, thoughts, attitudes, and belief and value systems; and the way in which these impact learning—is vital. Furthermore, reflection on our own thoughts, feelings, and value systems and their impact on the learning-teaching enterprise serves to impact a lesson plan most profoundly.

As teachers we are engaged in a noble undertaking, wrestling with the vastly varying dreams, hopes, and beliefs of individuals and society, helping to fashion anew each day a different but connected reality. It is a complex task that requires the insight of numerous models and conceptual frameworks. Each, like that of a model for academic and social cognition, is aimed at improving this task of learning and teaching.

CHAPTER ELEVEN

APPLYING THE MODEL IN THE CLASSROOM: DIFFERENTIATED AND INTERACTIVE INSTRUCTION

Recognizing the diversity and experience students bring into the classroom, the act of teaching involves utilizing the cognitive collective. This is to provide different ways for students to learn the same material. This paradigm within the model recognizes the reciprocity of thinking and feelings, which ultimately leads to using varied instructional strategies.

These strategies address how students may learn by engaging them in differentiated instruction, as well as using interactive techniques. Ultimately these strategies inform students of who they are as learners. This is done by constructing new meaning about their lives with respect to beliefs and values, as well as common social and societal realities, and developing new concepts also ensues.

There are many situations that impact students' daily lives both inside and outside the school setting. You probably remember this when you reflect on your years in elementary, middle, and high school. We think that structuring the content of learning in our classrooms so that it is useful and applicable to the learner's present situation is vital! This chapter recognizes the need for teachers to provide students with alternative paths to obtain success in meeting lesson objectives through differentiated teaching.

The basic concept of differentiated instruction, we think you'll agree, is that since students don't learn the same way, we need to teach them the way they learn (Dunn and Dunn, 1992). Differentiated instruction provides this opportunity to structure lessons to meet the learning needs of your students. This chapter is the third in the notebook of the mind tabs.

Two schools of thought regarding whether to have or not have differentiated instruction begin this section of the book. A definition of what it means to differentiate with respect to content, process, and product follows, with attention to teaching and reasons for differentiation. Types of differentiated instruction (pace, ability level, kinds of instruction, learner's interests and needs, learning styles, and tier lessons) with examples are provided. The model's connection to this type of information dissemination follows.

Graphic organizers are given attention, with general requirements for their construction along with their relevancy. These include story maps, sequences of events, cause-and-effect maps, and character analysis. There's a narrative explaining their content with directions on how to configure each one, as well as the purpose for each presented type of organizer. Connections are made to the model. The decision-making graphic organizer is provided in an illustrated format (figure 11.1) with directions for its construction and explanations of how it assists in decision-making and problem-solving for all age groups.

The trifold board (Schiering, 2005) as a form of differentiated instruction is presented in figure 11.2 and serves as a means for engaging students in self-empowerment, social cognition, and comprehension of reaching an objective or goal. A photograph of one board addresses the topic of recycling (S. D. Schiering, 2006). Then this board's interactive instructional resources are addressed in detail.

Interactive instructional resources/educational gaming (Schiering, 1974; Schiering and Taylor, 1998) conclude this chapter. Explanations of these are given with accompanying computer-generated illustrations for the flip chute, pick-a-dot, wraparound, puzzle task cards, electro-board, and mathematics addition and subtraction floor game are provided in figures 11.3–11.8.

These illustrations are accompanied by the applied thinking skills from the reciprocal thinking phases that each one develops. In figure 11.9, a Velcro fill-in cloze game is provided, and then some final thoughts on interactive instructional resources are presented before the Chapter Discussion/Journal Questions section, which as you know ends each chapter in this book.

Key words: differentiated instruction, content, process, product, pace, ability level, kinds of instruction, tier lessons, perceptual preferences, interest areas, learning styles, interactive instruction, graphic organizer, trifold boards

Two Schools of Thought

How we teach what we do brings up two areas for consideration when addressing differentiated instruction. Let's think about this: Do you think we should we teach all lessons the same way to the same children at the same time? Why or why not? Or do you think we should we teach lessons using varied forms of instruction? Why or why not?

You may have experienced, during your kindergarten through college years, instructional strategies that focused on telling you what was to be done and how to do it. Or you may have been given information on what was to be learned and provided latitude on the implementation. Those are two schools of thought on teaching.

They're diametrically opposed to one another. Whether we should teach all lessons the same way focuses on whether we think all students learn the same way. If you think this is *not* the case, then differentiated instruction is what would be utilized in your classroom teaching. We recommend it, as today's classrooms have students of diverse backgrounds and languages, with some having learning difficulties and others excelling with giftedness.

Differentiated Instruction: Definition

You're asked to focus now on the concept that if all children do not dress or act alike we may surmise that they also learn differently from one another. Hall refers to Tomlinson's work (2001) on differentiation by relating, "Not all students are alike. Based on this knowledge, differentiated instruction applies an approach to teaching and learning so that students have multiple options for taking in information and making sense of ideas. This requires teacher flexibility in their approach to teaching and adjusting the curriculum and presentation of information to learners rather than expecting students to modify themselves for the curriculum" (Hall, 2002, p. 2).

And Tomlinson (2000) relates that "differentiation consists of the efforts of teachers to respond to variance among learners in the classroom.

Teachers can differentiate by giving attention to content—what the student needs to learn, process—activities in which the student engages in order to make sense of or master the content, and product—culminating projects that ask the student to rehearse, apply, and extend what he or she has learned in a unit." Therefore, "teachers varying lessons to create the best learning experience possible, exemplifies differentiating instruction" (p. 2).

Differentiated Instruction: Teaching

When teaching, what does "differentiation of instruction" mean? To answer that, let's first look at what it means to differentiate. This is defined as "to distinguish and/or set apart." Set apart from what, you may ask? In designing a lesson, it separates this section from the developmental procedures, adaptation, academic intervention, and academic enrichment sections, which all call for specific activities. Simply stated it means that the differentiation of instruction section stands alone.

Differentiated activities adhere to the theme and general objective of the lesson, as the activities you design would not be repeated elsewhere in the lesson. Differentiating a portion of the lesson plan is for the entire class or several groups of students and not just one student with a specific problem—that's adaptation, and is given explicit attention in appendix A. Differentiation is specifically applied to learners who would most benefit from this type of instruction.

Differentiated Instruction: Reasons

First think about how you like to learn. What's the best way for you to comprehend material that's part of a curriculum? Do you prefer memorizing by reading alone, in groups, or learning in a partnership? Do you like project-based learning? Are creativity and interaction important to you? Where do you like to learn: at home, in school, with someone, alone, at the beach, at the library? What time of day do you think you're most attentive? And what do you suppose causes you to remember things you are supposed to learn?

All of these questions' answers, along with the following pages addressing types of differentiated instruction, come into account when thinking about students' instructional needs. This is because each of us has learning preferences that need to be met in the school setting. Simply stated, we are all different and do not learn in the same fashion.

In the academic setting, some reasons for using differentiated instructional strategies are the overall individuality and/or small-group learning experiences they provide, with consideration and opportunity for meeting learners' preferences. Realistically, as a teacher you have your preferences, just as do the students in your classroom. Overall, the use of differentiated instructional strategies fosters the chance to interact as much as working individually for taking in information. Information that is pertinent, germane, and significant in a fashion to arrange and plan for the learning situation, so it meets students' needs, is necessary.

At the most basic level, some students would prefer listening to a teacher explain something, while others would want to see it, be able to touch it (tactile), or be kinesthetically (whole body) involved. We believe that varying the instructional modalities or use of students' perceptual preferences is important.

You might not teach the same topic with lessons repeating the material in *each* perceptual preference. However, you may definitely vary lessons by using different modalities/perceptual preferences for different content material. Modality preferences are just one form of differentiating instruction and have most frequently been associated with learning styles.

Other forms of differentiating instruction are those that consider the pace at which students work best, their ability level, and kinds of instruction. We provide a few more by addressing students' interest areas and needs and, finally, scaffolding or tier practices. Each type of differentiation is explained below with examples for the teacher serving as the learning facilitator.

Types of Differentiated Instruction: Content, Process, and Product

Learning by Pace

This involves the time on task that best accommodates learners. While some learners need a good deal of time to complete an assignment, others may require less time, or a small extension of time, in order to address the material presented. Your lessons need to take this into consideration by providing some students the opportunity to work for longer, shorter, or intermediate periods of time on the same assignment.

Example of Learning by Pace

Writing examples of the four different types of sentences, declarative, interrogative, exclamatory, and imperative, have been assigned. Those that work at a slow pace will be allotted twenty minutes to complete this, while those who are able to complete work quickly or at a medium speed will be given ten and fifteen minutes, respectively.

Learning by Ability Level

This refers to the general expectation of student performance and competency at a given grade and/or age. Student learners may function at what has been determined as above, at, or below grade level. More specifically, achievement level may vary from one discipline to another, so that grade or age level is acceptable, but content adeptness within a subject area may differ.

Determining differences in ability levels is often facilitated through scores on standardized tests. These serve as the determining factor for what is considered "on level" and what is above or below it. Also, classroom pretests in varied disciplines' topics provide pertinent information for differentiation by ability level. These pretests let the teacher recognize what areas need to be addressed. A posttest or alternative means of evaluation (see graphic organizers and interactive instructional resources in this chapter as well as appendix A for further information) will assist in determining what has been learned—the product.

Example of Learning by Ability Level

The students have been assigned the creation of an acrostic poem using a word associated with the winter season. Those who have English as a second language or other learning differences may have difficulty with this exercise. For those who are proficient, *snowstorms* would be a suitable word.

Those who were less adept would have a word of shorter length, such as *snow*. Those with a lesser ability level might be asked to use the word *ice.* The idea of using shorter words is to have the students working at their levels with their language acquisition and implementation being such that feeling secure with the assignment, as opposed to working at a point of frustration, is evident. This enables the end product to be of a formidable nature.

Kinds of Instruction

This refers to instructional techniques or methods. Passive recipients of knowledge would be diametrically opposed to the instructional strategy in which students are actively engaged in the process of acquiring information. The Socratic, behaviorist, experientialist, and constructivist methods, as presented in chapter 2, are a few of the methods practiced in schools and considered to be kinds of instruction.

Learning through discussion, examples, types of questions, inductive or deductive reasoning, and emotional components are considered when addressing this type of differentiation. Lessons are flexible, in collaborative groups or through whole-class instruction, with varied end products (Tomlinson, 2001). Providing students with choices as to how things will be done for the end product is another operative.

Examples of Kinds of Instruction

The students have been assigned to conduct research on community helpers for later reporting to the class. Some would use the now popular Internet medium to gather this information. Others might seek an interview with a community helper and take notes. Some might work passively and use their experiential past encounters with someone practicing this job to form an information sheet for later sharing.

Still others might watch a video that provides information, or simply read the textbook, with or without a buddy, taking notes on important points, or for general information gathering and later reporting. Reporting styles would also vary in accordance with the kind of instruction to be utilized when disseminating information to peers, as the final product for this research assignment.

In the final reporting, some students might prefer the use of PowerPoint slides to show what's been learned, while others create an educational game. Those who favor lecturing might read their information to the class. Still others might ask students to contribute their experiences with community helpers to add to a presentation, or create illustrations with commentary, while others conduct a role-playing scenario of a community helper practicing his/her job, or relate a real-life experience related to these persons.

Learners' Interests

This refers to the areas where students are focused due to intentness, concern, curiosity, importance, consequence, and variations of thinking or feeling regarding learning fields. Some learners may want to gain information about sports, while others are not even mildly concerned.

Simultaneously, one may have curiosity about how to get from one place to another while others are simply interested in another taking care of that circumstance. Interests are emotionally and/or cognitively based. They might involve using varied kinds of instruction, which correspond to modality preferences, or construction of materials to facilitate learning.

Example of Learners' Interests

The teacher suggests that students create a chart to examine the similarities and differences between two characters in a selected piece of literature. Some students may be interested in creating a Venn diagram to illustrate these. Others may choose to, as with kinds of instructional reporting, conduct a mock interview or make an audiotape or videotape.

Some other interest areas for acknowledging differences between story characters would be to configure slides for a presentation or make a mobile with a picture of a each character and words hanging from them representing differences. Then an illustration of them together would show the things they have in common.

Then again, the students might be interested in conducting scripted role-playing or using excerpts from the book's dialogue to show where the characters are in agreement or disagreement. Then again, as explained later in this chapter, some interactive instructional resource that conveys the similarities and differences of the characters might be an interest area to address.

Learners' Needs

This is the subjective and/or objective evaluation component regarding instruction. While some students' needs are obvious, as in the hearing-impaired student requiring an amplification system in the classroom, or students needing enrichment activities to stimulate them, others are not as apparent.

Student needs vary as much as individuals themselves at any given time. Emotional components, assessment tools, achievement in one area and not in another, students' sense of security, and stress factors are all considered when determining learners' needs. Also addressed in this category are students with language backgrounds other than English, physical and/or mental disabilities, giftedness, culture, experiences, and aptitudes (Mulroy and Eddinger, 2003).

Determining, through subjectivity, the needs of a student, is feeling-based. Determining the needs of a student through objectivity is based on a comparison and contrast of students' performance, as in results on an assessment. Most importantly, learners' needs should be met by the teacher's emphasizing students' areas of strength. Interestingly, a study by Affholder (2003) revealed that teachers employing higher levels of differentiated techniques experienced increased feelings of self-efficacy and demonstrated greater willingness to try new instructional approaches. We relate that this sense of self-worth may also be experienced by students.

Example of Learners' Needs

A story has been assigned for reading enjoyment. Comprehension questions are on a handout with fill-in responses. The teacher notes that several students in the classroom have hearing impairments. As a story is orally presented, these students may have copies of the story to read silently. Visually impaired learners would have an audiotape of the story as backup. If learners have difficulty with fine motor skills, then the written fill-in comprehension questions portion of the assignment would have the teacher providing assistance with a buddy or teacher assistant filling in the answers.

Learning Styles

This is attention to the way individuals process and retain information. Brain dominance with respect to one's being field-dependent or field-independent, and emotional, sociological, psychological, and physiological factors are referenced when addressing learning styles (Dunn and Dunn, 1978; 1992; R. Dunn and Blake, 2008).

Within these areas are student learners' preference or nonpreference for (a) sound (present or quiet); (b) light (soft or bright); (c) temperature (warm or cool); (d) room design (formal or informal); (e) working alone, in pairs, in teams, or in small groups with authority figures present or absent; (f) structure; (g) motivation; (h) responsibility; (i) persistence; (j) mobility; (k) wanting intake or not; (l) taking frequent breaks, or remaining on task until a single assignment/project is completed or not completed; and (m) sequencing or simultaneously working on several projects, as well as being reflective or impulsive.

Example of Learning Styles

The instructional part of this form of differentiation involves having the students make a floor game about the life cycle of a butterfly. The field-dependent students (global) would work with a partner or in a small group in a portion of the room with an informal design, such as a comfy corner.

These students would prefer to have soft illumination and sound present when working on the game. They'd need to see the entire picture, as opposed to the structured sequential order of constructing this game. They may take frequent breaks and want a snack time while working, in order for their attention and persistence to be formidable.

Conversely, the field-independent (analytic) learners would show a preference for working alone in a high-intensity-lit area with no sound interfering with their concentration. They would want to work on this project to completion before beginning any other assignment, and they would want a formal room design.

No snacking or taking of frequent breaks would be acceptable, as they demonstrate a high level of responsibility for completion of the task at hand. And in both of the brain-dominant situations, the instruction adhering to these differentiations would include students' personal modality/perceptual preference(s) being met with any of the aforementioned activities in the students' interest area.

Tier Lessons

These are lessons in which the assignment begins at a basic level and builds in complexity. The instruction is designed to add layers for greater cognitive skill application and comprehension. Tier lessons and/or scaffolding are implemented like the rungs of a ladder, moving from lower to higher levels of understanding. Varying levels of achievement may be noted as students work in small-group format for problem-solving and decision-making about the assignment.

Example of a Tier Lesson

The teacher has assigned the construction of a three-dimensional flower for a classroom "garden." The students first discuss what it means for something to be three-dimensional. Then they decide on a type of flower they want to construct. Materials are gathered for this construction. The flower is put together, with a means for having it stand freely. The flowers are put together to form a garden on a table in the back of the classroom.

The Model's Connection to Differentiated Instruction

As stated previously, differentiated instruction, at its foundation, realizes all persons do not learn the same material in the same way. Yet there are other reasons for using this strategy, which a model for academic and social cognition displays through its comprehensive configuration. Students' life experiences are taken into account as they come to share these in the classroom through discussion or teacher observation when realizing likes and dislikes.

Common social and societal realities and belief and value systems, as well as the cognitive collective, are considerations regarding differentiated instruction. This is related through reflection on students' past experiences in previous years' work in school, or during this year. The external factors move inwardly and outwardly in overt or subliminal ways to influence these interior components and are addressed by knowing your learners' cultural mores, habits, and held beliefs and values.

In the classroom the teacher becomes the facilitator of learning, moving from the product of information provider. Inside and outside of school, through reflection on these life experiences, we become aware that differentiated instruction explores and allows for choices to be made about material that is presented and, very importantly, how it is presented.

How exactly is differentiated instruction a further connection to this model? It's connected because the model relates to the present time with references to one's experiential past, which is relevant. It relates to *who* you are as a learner and teacher and what you're thinking and feeling. As you know, these are intertwined, and being cognizant of the learner makes it possible to better teach him or her. As Bogner stated in 1990, "Structuring the content of learning so that it is useful and applicable to the learner's present situation is vital. This is best facilitated with the use of differentiated instructional strategies" (p. 130).

You may ask, "Why?" The answer would be because you know who your students are in totality by the behaviors they exhibit through expressing their preferences, or demonstrating success when these are used in the classroom, or realizing the common social and societal realities that bring you together or separate you and the beliefs and values you hold dear.

Over fifty years ago, Dewey addressed the idea of the relevancy of reforming education to make it something to which students could relate when he stated, "If I were asked to name the most needed of all reforms in the spirit of education, I should say 'cease conceiving of education as mere preparation for later life and make of it the full meaning of the present. . . . An activity which does not have worth enough to be carried on for its own sake cannot be very effective preparation for something else'" (Dewey, 1893/1972, p. 50).

In alignment with both of these educators' statements (Dewey and Bogner), relate that all too often education is separated from learners' experiences because of the types of teaching that are implemented in the classroom. In separating or "divorcing content from the learner's present experience the teacher minimizes the content's impact on learning" (Bogner, 1990, p. 129). It is more difficult to form connections when the content is removed from current experience. In a similar vein, Dewey, in *How We Think* (1933/1986, pp. 141–50), as also cited within Bogner's writing in 1990, relates, "By removing content from applicability to the present, the teacher negates an important motivation for learning. If the content is immediately useful, then the motivation to learn the facts and information is extremely high. Conversely, if the only motivation is a grade or a possible usage of the material, then the motivation to learn will be much less. Furthermore, there's a suggestion that choosing content that is useful and applicable to the learner is important" (pp. 129–30).

Along with all these aforementioned reasons for using differentiated instruction is providing students with the opportunity to think about how they best learn. This is accomplished by using strategies that provide new learning techniques or former ones that have been modified. Not all students learn when information is given to them in a lecture format—talking at them. Yet many teachers use this method exclusively, especially in the high school and college settings. A few means of using differentiated instructional strategies are presented in the remainder of this chapter, with respect to varied and interconnected modalities being utilized.

Differentiated Instructional Strategies: Graphic Organizers

The use of graphic organizers to promote student learners' decision-making, problem-solving, story creation and review, and sequencing, as well as character personality analysis and comprehension of cause-and-effect relationships, is presented. Are you questioning whether the use of graphic organizers does all this? If you are, this is answered simply with the notion that creating these organizers addresses the cognitive collective with beginning cognition and feelings as much as critical and creative thinking and the metacognitive processes.

At the same time, the topics of these organizers provide an interdisciplinary opportunity to arrange thinking sequentially or simultaneously for comprehension. Graphic organizers are designed to create visual stimuli for those constructing or reading them. Generally, they serve as a means for recording known information, as well as speculative responses to specific categories represented within or on the organizers. And they allow the student to construct new material with use of their imagination and critical thinking.

Graphic organizers foster the use of creativity, reflection, conversation, risk-taking, initial decision-making, synthesizing of material, prioritizing, and self-actuating. This forms solid inductive and deductive reasoning for present-time implementation. Additionally, applying this newly gained information for later subtle and informed addressing of life experiences is plausible.

This would be the case whether the learners are in a social or academic setting. Most important, activities which are designed to develop, apply, and implement effective teaching are those which adhere to the needs of learners through the differentiated strategy. A simplified list of (1) types of graphic organizers, (2) general construction requirements, and (3) their purpose and relevancy follows. After this section, each listed type of graphic organizer is addressed with respect to its configuration and how it may be used for learning.

Types of graphic organizers:

- story map
- sequence of events
- cause and effect
- character analysis
- decision-making

General construction requirements:

1. Use thirty-six-inch by twenty-four-inch poster board, oak tag, foam core, or card stock.
2. Design and create these five different types of graphic organizers.
3. Have boxed sections bordered.
4. Use theme-related decorations and good color contrast for all sections.
5. Print on light-colored backgrounds.

Purpose and relevancy of graphic organizers:

- Discovering components of organizational design elements
- Developing creativity, imagination, and invention strategies

- Linking thinking and feelings of characters
- Connecting disciplines
- Assisting in goal setting, developing theme, or concept comprehension
- Providing application and implementation of the cognitive collective
- Realizing common social realities
- Recognizing and applying social literacy through sharing belief and value systems
- Addressing one being a reflective practitioner

The Story Map Graphic Organizer

The story map graphic organizer addresses a piece of literature's six story elements. These are the character(s), setting(s), mood(s), events, problem(s), and solution(s). Each one is addressed in a separate section of the organizer, with connecting lines depicting the linkages of elements in a story. Boxed sections surround a center circle. This has the story title and author in it. The boxed sections placed from left to right on a poster board provide information as follows:

- The first section on the left is titled "Characters," and should include the name of the character, as well as a personality trait and/or how the character is related to others in the story, or serves as protagonist or antagonist.
- The setting relates to where the story took place and at what time period. This could be present-day, in the past, or in the future. This section is connected by a horizontal line to the story character section.
- The mood section of the graphic organizer is placed underneath the character section and is connected by a line to this part. It relates the different feelings evoked in the reader of the story and/or those thought to be intended by the author when specific events occurred in the story.

- The events section provides, in chronological order, the key situations in the story. These involve ascending and descending actions. This section is to the right and across from the moods section. It's connected by a vertical line to the setting section.
- The problem is the last boxed section on the left side of the organizer. It's connected by a vertical line to the moods box. The problem relates what main character(s) consider as causing dismay, conflict, and/or confusion in that an action needed to be taken to alleviate the situation. It's connected by a horizontal line to the solution section, which is the last one on the right side of the organizer.
- The solution section, which is on the right side of the organizer, is connected by a vertical line to the events above it. This section addresses what led to a culminating circumstance that resulted in solving the story's problem.

Overall, depending on the story theme, the students will learn about new situations that address thinking and feelings in social situations or in school situations, along with an opportunity to reflect on what they might have done in a similar situation. Also, attention may be given to discussing with classmates the story's overt and subliminal intent, as perceived by the reader of the story.

Interestingly, the story map may be used for creating a story as much as reviewing one. In this instance, the six elements are provided to give writing guidance and organization of thoughts, ideas, opinions, judgments, and feelings. This type of graphic organizer provides one with links from the characters to the setting, moods, and events/rising and descending actions, which lead to the climax of the story/situation and result in a solution to a posed problem.

Sequence-of-Events Graphic Organizer

The sequence-of-events graphic organizer is designed to have four or more events of the story listed in their order of occurrence. Events may include character experiences relating to what happened at a particular place or at a certain time. Events may include a culminating problem and/

or solution as it/they occurred in the storyline, with rising and descending action. Or the sequence of events may be a personal experience and just contain what led up to that moment without a final event or solution.

Regardless, the main focus of this graphic organizer is to place, in order, from beginning to end, what events occurred that were of particular relevance in a story, situation, projected encounter, and/or problem. The primary purpose is to illustrate the connection between one story's situational event leading to another one.

Story sequence-of-events organization: events are presented vertically in boxed sections or some other shape in the following manner:

1. Story title and author
2. First event: This section has a narrative about the beginning event the character(s) experience in the story. This begins the social cognition connection.
3. Second event: This section has a narrative about the next major event the character(s) experience in the story. This is the beginning of the life event of the story problem the characters face. If desired, more boxed sections may be added for more events; customarily there are four used for this type of organizer.
4. Third event: This section has a narrative about the problem the story character(s) experience in the story.
5. Fourth event: This section has a narrative about how the story problem was resolved by the character(s). This provides the solution to the life event problem for social cognition.

Cause-and-Effect Organizer

A cause-and-effect graphic organizer is designed to illustrate, in narrative and/or picture format, the events of a story or real-life circumstance. This is where actions were taken or things were said by the main storybook character(s) and/or real-life person(s) that resulted in particular effects/events. The main requirement is that the cause of specific actions or words spoken are first presented and then related to the next set of actions or words spoken. These convey thoughts and/or emotions for scope and sequence. Generally there are three to four causes and resulting effects.

The cause-and-effect graphic organizer relates singular, dual, or multiple effects through a set of sequentially labeled rectangular boxes going vertically down a page next to one another. Or these may appear horizontally across a page. In either case, an arrow goes from each cause to its corresponding effect. A narrative is presented in each consecutive boxed section with the titles "Cause" in boxes 1, 3, 5, and 7, and "Effect" in boxes 2, 4, 6, and 8. The relationship between the cause and effect may result, when seeing the flow of these, in changes or modifications in actions or words spoken, or neither of these. Nonetheless, through reflection, other causes and effects will most likely emerge.

One of the most significant components and purposes of this type of graphic organizer is that it provides an opportunity to make connections to real-life situations—common social and societal realities in the areas of the external factors of a model for academic and social cognition. This is accomplished while visualizing the scope and sequence of these events, as well as the impact on one's life.

Character-Analysis Organizer

Each character of a story, or person in our lives, has a specific role which forms the overall content theme of the story/our social reality of that person. We're witnesses to this experience, although we may not be in it. The personality traits of the participants are supported by situations that occurred, or dialogue that took place at specific times.

The character-analysis graphic organizer lists personality traits and then supports these with events or dialogue with information that has been provided from the book or individual circumstances being addressed. While there are often several character traits, there may be more than one event to support each one selected. One character trait is placed in a boxed section and connected with a line to one or several situations that verify that trait being present in the represented story character/person's life. Then two to three more personality traits are given and connected by a line to the corresponding events.

The purpose of this type of graphic organizer is to involve the learner in reflection, analysis of discourse, evaluation of personality traits, and making connections between actions and/or expressed thoughts and feelings, as well as recognizing, realizing, comparing, and contrasting while synthesizing.

Decision-Making Graphic Organizer

From the time we're little and exploring things around us, we're involved in making decisions. However, our reflection on this reveals that our decisions are frequently limited to two things. This is first imposed, most often, by parents. Examples would be that we can wear sandals or sneakers, a green shirt or white one, go to visit a relative or friend, play one particular computer game or another, and the list could continue.

What's been established is a pattern of having two choices. This pattern carries over to the beginning and ensuing school years, in which the two choices may not be present at all. Primarily, this is due to teacher-imposed lessons and conformity to classroom schedules, to name two examples, but there are more of these.

One way of limiting choices that is continually provided for students in the classroom, and you undoubtedly experienced this at one time or another, is preparation for an assignment. The materials with which one works have been laid out, or everyone is told what to have at the ready. It's been decided whether work is to be done alone or with another/others. We're informed about amounts of time to do this assignment, where this will take place, and the specifications that lock it into not being of our own design.

With this process, the ability to make decisions becomes clouded. In fact, we suggest that an *inability* to make decisions becomes apparent, especially as the years transpire and students become accustomed to this routine. Just in thinking about teacher-to-student schedules, one becomes extremely aware that individuals are told exactly what's to be done at a given time on a given day in a particular manner. This results in fewer, if any, student decision-making opportunities. So we're patterned to think of decisions being "either/or" opportunities. However, differentiated instruction through the decision-making graphic organizer's implementation eradicates that.

The decision-making graphic organizer requires a statement of the problem or decision topic. Then, three or more choices are to be posed, with three possible positive and negative outcomes imagined and listed. These lead to a final decision, with reasons for this decision being stated. A line is drawn from this choice to the final decision box.

Then again, the students may choose to leave this final connection blank and have classmates decide the best choice for the problem presented. Given the information on the graphic organizer, they'd be involved in discussing which would be their "final decision." If doing that, the class becomes involved in decision-making and reasoning, with convergent and divergent questions being asked, or their suppositions examined.

This graphic organizer leads one to realize multiple possibilities for solutions to problems for everyday situations that require thinking and feelings being evidenced. And the situations are those that revolve around the external factors of the model in that these are the places where we come to develop our beliefs and values, as a result of our nuclear family's influence and/or those of friends, relatives, community, peers, and neighborhood, being places and persons with whom we experience common social and societal realities.

At the onset, the purpose of this type of graphic organizer is to recognize the steps taken for one to make a decision that's within a piece of literature or personal circumstance. The problem and solution are related to those instances. The use of critical thinking is evident. Analysis of the decision-making process is heightened when analyzing *why* a particular decision was formulated. Children benefit from seeing this process's scope and sequence by examining their own thinking and feelings as they prepare to make decisions. Applied comprehension is evident, with cognitive awareness leading to self-actualization, the highest level of metacognition. (The figure that illustrates this concept, as well as other figures appearing throughout this chapter, were created by M. Schiering.)

Differentiated Instruction: Trifold Boards

Trifold boards (Schiering, 1974; 2005) are preconstructed stand-alone approximately three and a half feet high by five feet wide boards that have a center section and two foldout side pieces. Interactive instructional resources, presented later in this chapter, and/or the previously presented graphic organizers are placed on each of the board's sections. But most fre-

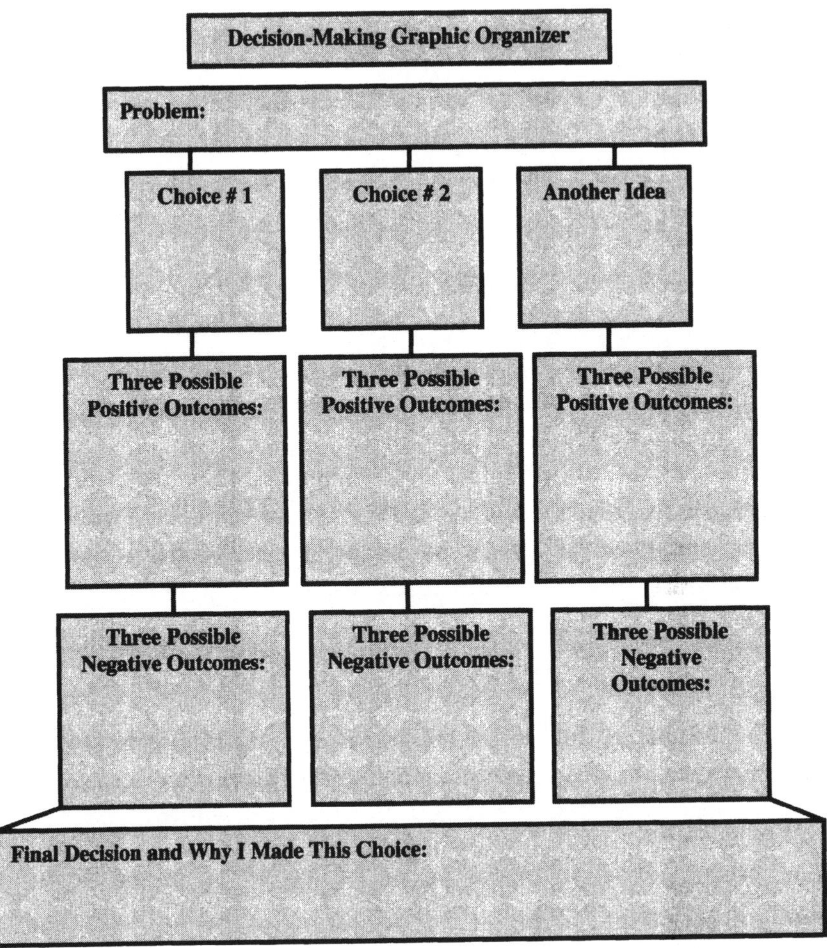

Figure 11.1. Decision-Making Graphic Organizer

quently they're on the side panels. They serve as vehicles that require "playing," where material involving a piece of literature or thematic unit topic may be newly presented and/or reviewed. The connection to a model of academic and social cognition resides in the subject matter being addressed.

Trifold Board: Connection to the Model

If the subject matter addresses a piece of literature, there's material on the board that calls attention to the interaction of characters and their social realities, beliefs, and values, as well as thinking and feelings. One way of doing this would be to have a "Who Said That" match of characters and quotations. The board may also present vocabulary, math word problems using the characters' names, or social studies–related information from the literature piece.

Each of the side panels may be addressed for comparison to the student's own reactions or experiences regarding the literature's theme. Primarily, the side panels of the board are designed for some form of interaction, either through discussion or playing with the resource (see the interactive instructional resources section of this chapter). Either way, the reciprocity of thinking and feelings are given attention when the students use the resource and develop cognitive and metacognitive skills through practical application via these interactions.

If the trifold board addresses a specific unit to be studied, the model is utilized with explicit reference to the topic of the unit on the board. For example, a unit on ecosystems might have the students comparing and contrasting their knowledge of vocabulary and the interaction of living and nonliving things in a, let's say, land environment. An opportunity to realize the interconnection between these thus impacts common social realities.

As the students are learning about the specifics of this type of ecosystem, they come to be engaged in knowing their place in such an environment. They come to address their common social and societal realities within it. They may also address their beliefs and values with respect to the external components of the model by realizing where they fit in within the ecosystem.

Trifold board discussions might find the students talking about how they feel when walking in a woodland environment. The model's external factor of academics may refer to a preference for studying there, or what's to be learned in such a place, or ecological concerns, places that are politically permitted for them to visit.

Then, economically, there's the affordability of going to national visitor attractions, vacation homes or such, in this type of ecosystem. There is the opportunity to address not only the external factors of the model, but the internal ones as well, with respect to thinking and feelings about similarities and differences concerning beliefs and values and/or common social and societal realities.

Trifold Board: Purpose

Generally, the trifold board's purpose is designed to develop students' cognitive and metacognitive skills through educational game playing (Schiering, 1974). Activities are presented on the board's sections, which adhere to students' use of precise thinking skills with the use of graphic organizers and/or interactive instructional resources. These develop student learners' cognitive skills (reciprocal thinking phases) relating to a specific topic in a discipline or interdisciplinary endeavors on a topic which demonstrates the linkage between subject matter (REAP), and/or a piece of literature.

The board's interactive portions, which are self-corrective, provide the student learner with a viable means for self-efficacy and empowerment as a learner. The trifolds, when utilized in the classroom, also serve as a means for social cognition (SOW: common social realities, belief and value systems) and comprehension of reaching an objective and/or goal.

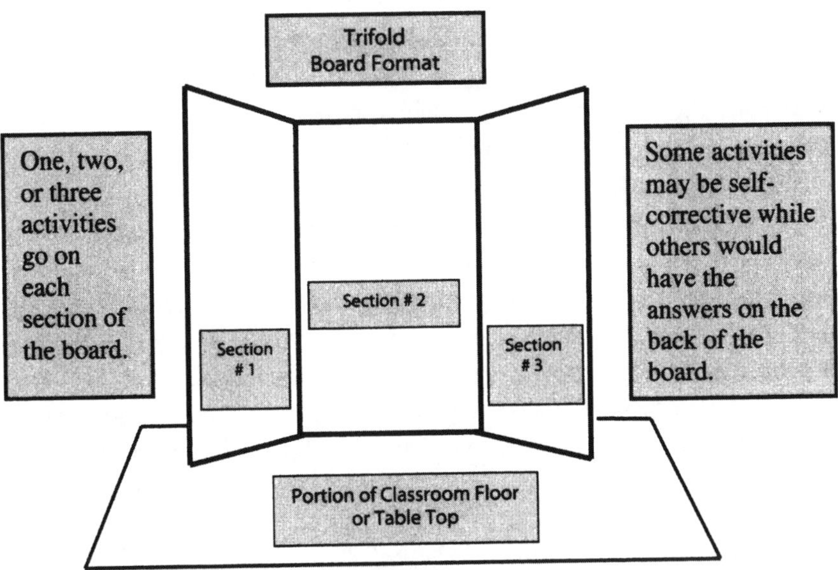

Figure 11.2. Trifold Board Illustration

Steps for Creating a Trifold Board

Step 1: Select a white or dark trifold board. The board color is important as you want to be sure you have good color contrast with the items to be placed on it. This means if the board is dark blue, you should use light borders and/or sections, having internal sections with white and then dark print.

Step 2: Decide on the piece of literature or discipline to be addressed. Have the center of the board provide information about the main point of the literature, or if a specific discipline, the vocabulary or key concepts of that unit of study. For example, if the unit to be addressed is about weather, then the center section would represent different types of weather with appropriate labeling. The center section of the board has the main theme represented. For literature, this might be a large story map or character-analysis graphic organizer.

Step 3: Select interactive instructional resources (see photo 11.1) or graphic organizers to enhance student learners' conceptualization of the content in a piece of literature or specific discipline. Construct these so one, two, three, or four, depending on the size of the item selected, are on each section of the board, or just on the side panels.

Place explanatory instructions on each section of the board that addresses the actions to be taken to use or play this interactive resource. On the back of the board, list the cognitive and/or metacognitive skills that are being developed for each activity. And if the activity is not self-corrective, then place the answers for each activity on the board's reverse side. Or, if a matching game, then put the answers on the back of the matching cards.

The trifold board, on the following page, in photo 11.1 is from Dr. Rose Marie Iovino's EDU 341.04 course, which is an undergraduate college course addressing the topic of interactive learning centers. The work is that of teacher candidate S. D. Schiering (2006), who used a second- through fifth-grade topic on recycling. Each section, either at the top or bottom, presents the content area being addressed on that section with pertinent information as to how this is the case. The top of the center section of the trifold board picture uses the international symbol for recycling.

The Board's Interactive Instructional Resources on Recycling

Velcro tab matches: The bottom portion categorizes six different types of recyclable items. These include aluminum, tin, wood, paper,

Photo 11.1. Photographic Example of a Trifold Board

glass, and plastic. Pictures of each of these with the name of the object are in hard plastic Velcro sleeves. Three Velcro bins appear under these cards with each containing the symbol of metal, wood, and glass on them. The interaction occurs when the student approaches the board and places the correct picture above the recycling bin in which it belongs by using the Velcro tab pieces located above each bin.

An Earth Day vocabulary match on the left section of the board relates that our environment is special. We need to be sure we don't pollute our Earth. The students are exposed to the words *conserve*, *recyclable*, *landfill*, *waste*, *toxic*, *composting*, and *resources*. The words and their definitions are placed in hard plastic sleeves and fastened with Velcro to the board. Each word is then matched with its corresponding definition. "This 'matching game' activity will help you to build your science vocabulary for keeping our world safe with respect to words used when talking about pollution" (S. D. Schiering, 2006: Instructions for Using the Trifold Board).

Word search: On the right side of the board is a packet of word search sheets placed in a page protector. The interaction occurs when students either approach this board section or remove it from the trifold board to work at their desk and find the words. These words are placed vertically, horizontally, or diagonally in correct order or backward on the word search sheet. The words are circled with erasable marker if one is not removing the sheet from the page protector, or if the sheet is done at one's seat, and removed from the acetate cover, a pencil or pen may be used to circle the words.

Electro-board: This is on the board's right section under the picture of "road signs" having the words *reusable*, *recyclable*, *durable*, *repairable*, and *less packaging*. This section is not removable, as it's attached to the board. The student uses a continuity tester and touches the brass fastener by the appropriate road sign and to the pictured items that may be recycled, are recognized as durable, and so on, appearing underneath the road signs. If the light on the continuity tester lights up, then the student knows that the answer is correct. This activity is self-corrective.

Since this trifold board is primarily a set of matching games, which are presented in different interactive formats, the cognitive and metacognitive skills include acknowledging and realizing what needs to be done to complete the task, comparing and contrasting the possible answers, analyzing the information provided, evaluating the possible answers, recalling information from the book or other resources while reflecting on the story content, risk-taking when selecting the answer, deciding on what match is probable, and self-actuating when making the decision to problem solve with the electro-board, Velcro match, dry-erase word search, or categorizing recyclable items.

For this particular trifold board, it's interesting to note that New York State learning standards for the science and social studies disciplines are presented on the reverse side of the board, along with the four important points that students are to glean from playing the different sections of the board. These include "Recognizing the international symbol used to represent recycling, identifying vocabulary related to recycling along with definitions of these words, categorizing them, and recognizing the concept of recycling being a means for saving resources."

Using the reciprocal thinking phases, you're invited to ask yourself or discuss with others, "What cognitive and/or metacognitive skills do you think are being used by the student when playing each of the interactive instructional resources on the trifold board?"

Differentiated Instruction: Interactive Instructional Resources/Educational Games

Interactive instructional resources apply to all components of the model in that social interaction adheres to collaboration, conversation, and social literacy through the interplay of the activity. The cognitive collective is a main focus area for development of these skills. However, the model's foundation is equally realized, as well as the umbrella term of reflection, in that the subject matter is addressed through student learners' conversations as they pertain to these resources by playing them. Recalling is also realized in order to answer posed questions.

Educational gaming has been around for a long while. And it has been proven time and again that the socialization allows for a different way to learn material that provides self-efficacy, as well as a sense of individual and group empowerment. While auditory and visual modalities are commonly addressed in classroom instruction, interactive instructional resources provide for tactile and kinesthetic involvement as well.

As Cafferty (1980) related, students were able to reach educational goals more efficiently when instructional procedures were adapted to their individual differences. Employing educational gaming is a way to accomplish that. Schiering and K. Dunn (2001) stated, "Through the use of educational games or tactile/kinesthetic instructional materials and 'interactive resources' (Schiering, 1974) that learning is stimulated, that a child discovers himself or herself" (p. 46).

The outcome of using interactive instructional resources promotes autonomy with respect to one's own learning (Deighton, 1969). As Piaget (1968) noted, most educational games or interactive instructional resources engender both social and cognitive development. The process involving action and the ability to use self-regulating mechanisms or cognitive monitoring that ensure the success or completion of a task (Wilen and Phillips, 1995) and promotion of positive attitudes toward learning (Takata, 1969) is apparent.

Another component is that the learning situation is simply fun when educational games are employed! Over the past two decades we've experienced video and computer games in greater numbers. The forerunner for these advanced educational games could be considered classroom board games and student involvement in utilizing other types of interactive instructional resources.

Koster (2005, p. 46) relates, "Games are excellent teachers and fun in using them is just another word for learning. Depending on what a game is targeting Gardner's Multiple Intelligences (1993, pp. 5–12) apply with linguistic, logical-math, bodily-kinesthetic, spatial, interpersonal, and intrapersonal intelligences being addressed when educational games are experienced." Gardner himself advises using multimedia techniques and hands-on approaches combined with teachers being capable of extending skills and understandings in new ways to motivate and stimulate learning through use of multiple intelligences.

Think for a moment how much information is taken in when you play a board game or sport with others. The actions and reactions of those with whom you participate are very strongly intermingled. Feelings about playing the game, thoughts and ideas you have about competition, and games that allow for cooperation and collaboration when teams are created add to the fun and your own knowledge. Sometimes even toleration is required as each one conceptualizes how the game should/must be played.

On the next few pages are seven illustrations of interactive instructional resources/educational games. The first six of these, over the past thirty years, have been associated with those in Dunn and Dunn books on learning styles. They specifically adhere to individuals' perceptual preferences.

Explanatory paragraphs addressing the activity and applied thinking skills are provided prior to the illustration of all seven of the interactive instructional resources. In appendix B, there's information given with respect to (1) uses of specific interactive instructional resources, (2) the materials need for their construction, and (3) directions for the construction of them.

Additionally, in this appendix there's a list of graphic organizers, other learning tools, and interactive instructional resources. This is provided along with some of the cognitive and metacognitive skills from all three reciprocal thinking phases that these resources help develop. It should be noted that, most importantly, each interactive instructional resource may be utilized, depending on the level of intricacy or topics addressed, for any grade: kindergarten through postsecondary.

Instructional Resource: Flip Chute

This is a "question in" and "answer out" activity. An empty and dry one-half-gallon milk container is most often used, although other top-opening containers of varied sizes are just as effective. The size of the flip-chute card would vary depending on the size of the container. The container has top and bottom slots, which are interiorly connected with two pieces of card stock paper. These form the chute portion of this learning tool.

Flip-chute cards are notched in the upper right corner. The card's reverse side appears when the card is flipped over from top to bottom. Now the notch appears in the lower right section. Information or questions may be placed on the top of the card, with more information on the other side (see appendix B, p. 263, for more ideas on card material). The front/top side of the card is placed into the top slot. The answer comes out of the bottom slot. This activity is self-regulatory and corrective, as the student says the answer mentally and then decides when to release the card to discover if his/her answer was correct.

Applied thinking skills: acknowledging, recognizing, realizing, classifying, comparing, contrasting, inferring, initial deciding, recalling, inventing, generalizing, reflecting, and self-actuating. The flip chute may

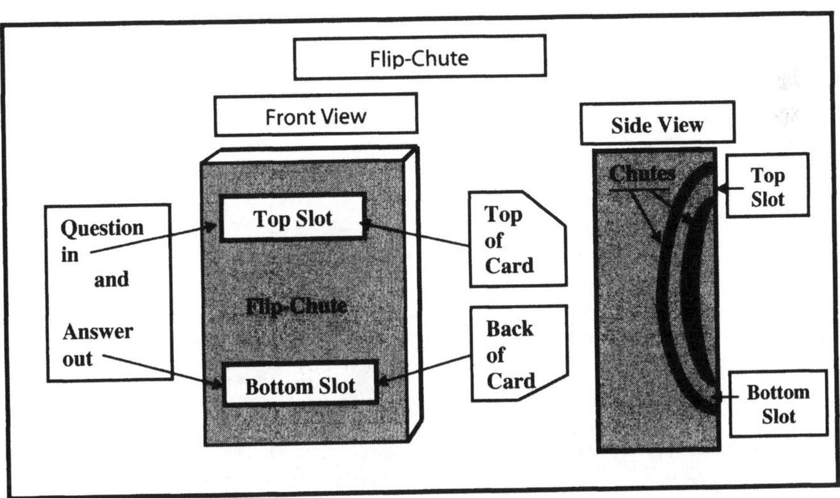

Figure 11.3. Flip-Chute Illustration

be used at any grade level in any discipline. Learning foreign language vocabulary or one's multiplication tables are just two examples. The flip chute is a comprehension-gaining strategy for developing one's cognition.

Instructional Resource: Pick-a-Dot

This activity requires learners to make a correct answer selection from several provided answers. A pick-a-dot holder is configured to contain approximately five to twenty laminated question cards. Two to three possible answers are written on the bottom of the card, with holes punched into it that align with those on the holder. The correct answer hole is punched all the way to the bottom on the pick-a-dot statement/question card. The card is inserted into the holder. Using a pen, the student places it in the dot which is thought to be the correct answer. Then the card is pulled from the top, and if it pulls out, the correct answer has been selected.

Applied thinking skills: recognizing, realizing, classifying, comparing and contrasting, organizing, synthesizing, predicting, risk-taking, initial and advanced deciding and problem-solving, prioritizing, analyzing, evaluating, recalling, reflecting, self-actuating

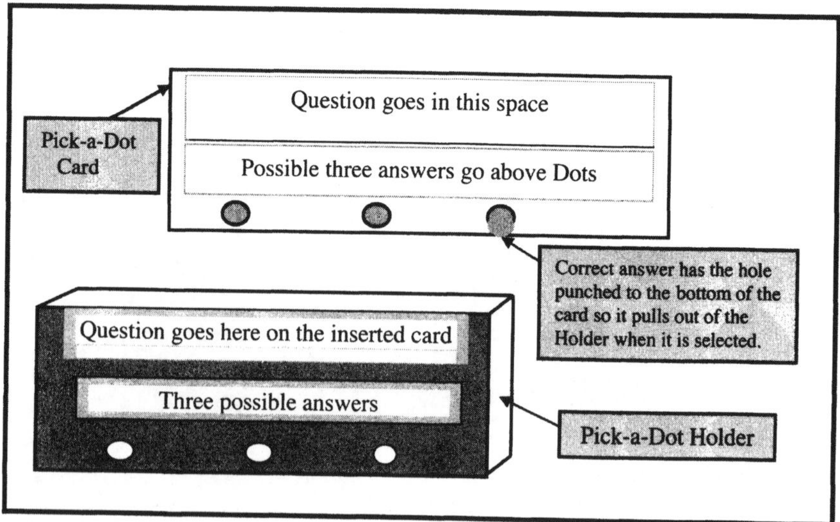

Figure 11.4. Pick-a-Dot Illustration

Interactive Instructional Resource: Wraparound

This activity requires use of laminated card stock paper, yarn, and a hole punch. There are numerous ways to use this resource. One idea is to have quotations on the left side and the names of the people who said them on the right side. Punch half a hole by each listed item on both sides of the paper.

Use the yarn wraparound-fashion to match the quotes with the people who said them. Then, on the reverse side, draw a line under the yarn. When the students turn the paper over, they'll see if their lines match those presented. Answers should not be directly opposite the names. This is a self-correcting activity for cognitive skill development.

Applied thinking skills: recalling, reflecting, classifying, comparing and contrasting, initial and advanced deciding, organizing, risk-taking, initial and advanced problem-solving, sequencing, evaluating, and self-actuating

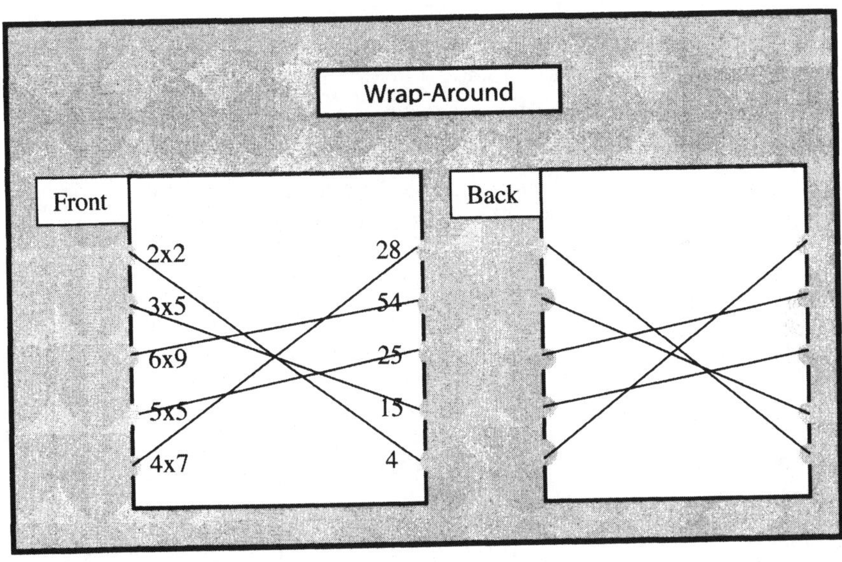

Figure 11.5. Wraparound Illustration

Activity: Puzzle Cards/Task Cards

These are puzzle pieces that are the same color and designed as a shape match. Laminated five-by-eight index cards are customarily used. Students put the pieces together by specifically matching the shape. A

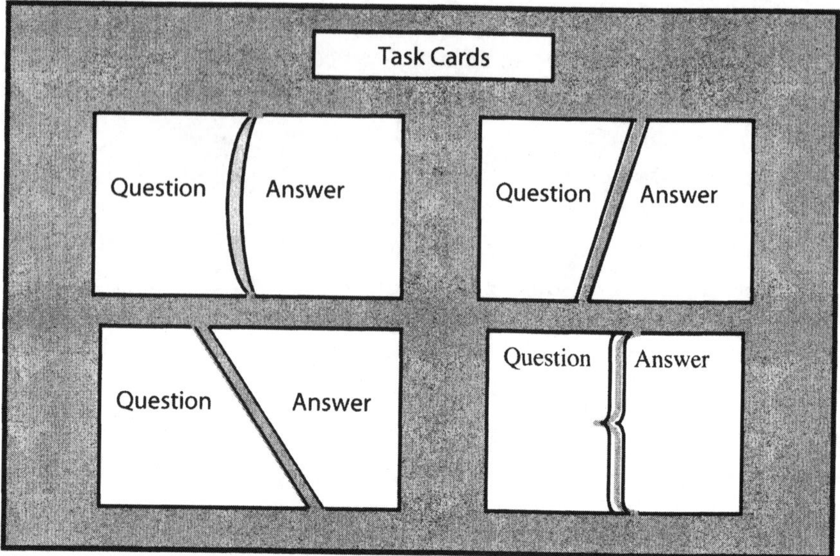

Figure 11.6. Task Cards Illustration

question is placed on the left side and the answer is placed on the right side. When the pieces are put together, they create one whole card. This activity is self-corrective.

Applied thinking skills: recognizing, prioritizing, comparing and contrasting, inferring, synthesizing, initial and advanced deciding, problem-solving, generalizing, sequencing, evaluating, and self-actualizing

Interactive Instructional Resource: Electro-board

This is a learning tool that requires an electrical connection having been made. A continuity tester is used for this purpose. On the front of the board or card stock paper, there are the brass fasteners beside the questions and the answers. On the reverse side, the brass fastener's wings are opened and connected with a thin strip of aluminum foil. The fastener's wings and aluminum foil are completely covered with masking tape. Then the entire back of the board is covered with another sheet of card stock paper, so students may not see these connections.

The game player, using a light-producing continuity tester, then places the pointed tip of it on the question and the other end on the answer. The other end of the continuity tester for making the electrical connection may be a clip or one's finger. If the light lights up, the answer is correct. If the light does not show, then the answer is incorrect and the student tries again to find the answer. This is a self-correcting activity for cognitive development.

Applied thinking skills: classifying, recognizing, realizing, initial and advanced deciding, critiquing, comparing and contrasting, predicting, synthesizing, organizing, advanced problem-solving, risk-taking, recalling, reflecting, and self-actuating

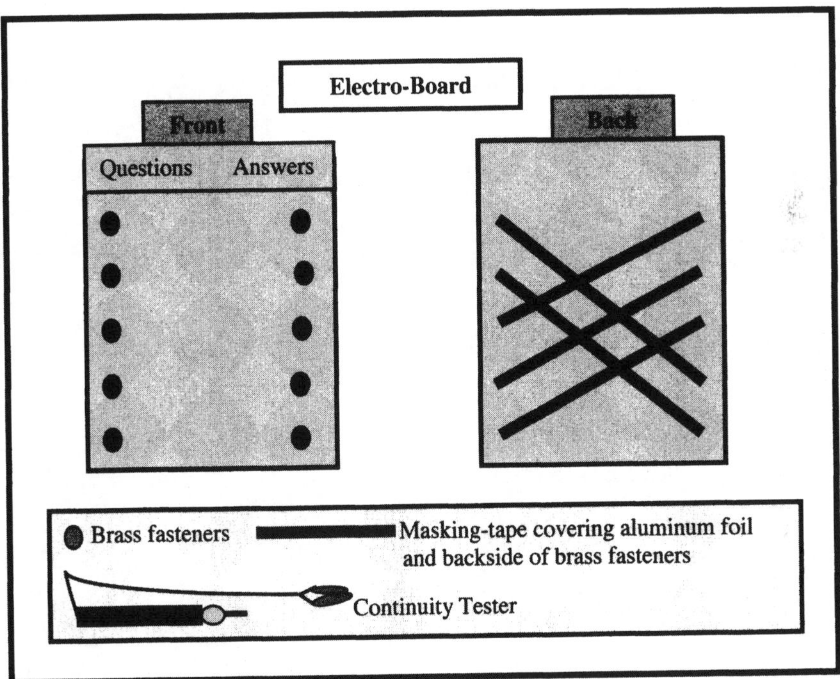

Figure 11.7. Electro-Board Illustration

Interactive Instructional Resource: Floor Game

This activity uses a shower-curtain liner, which is placed on the floor. It's subject/discipline-specific in design. Students remove their shoes to play this tactile and kinesthetic game, moving sequentially from one numbered shape to the next one. This is a partnership, two-to-four-person, or small-group activity. A series of question cards are made with the question on one side and the answer on the reverse side. A correct answer to the question provides the move from one space to another. Players move sequentially from one space to another.

The design of the shower curtain should be attractive and inviting, with the use of bold outlining and varied bright color shapes. One might draw the design of the game or use this in conjunction with five-by-eight index cards or larger card stock paper pieces. Velcro to the liner. This game may also be used as a wall game, with a beanbag used for tossing at the spaces and questions being addressed in accordance with the numbered space.

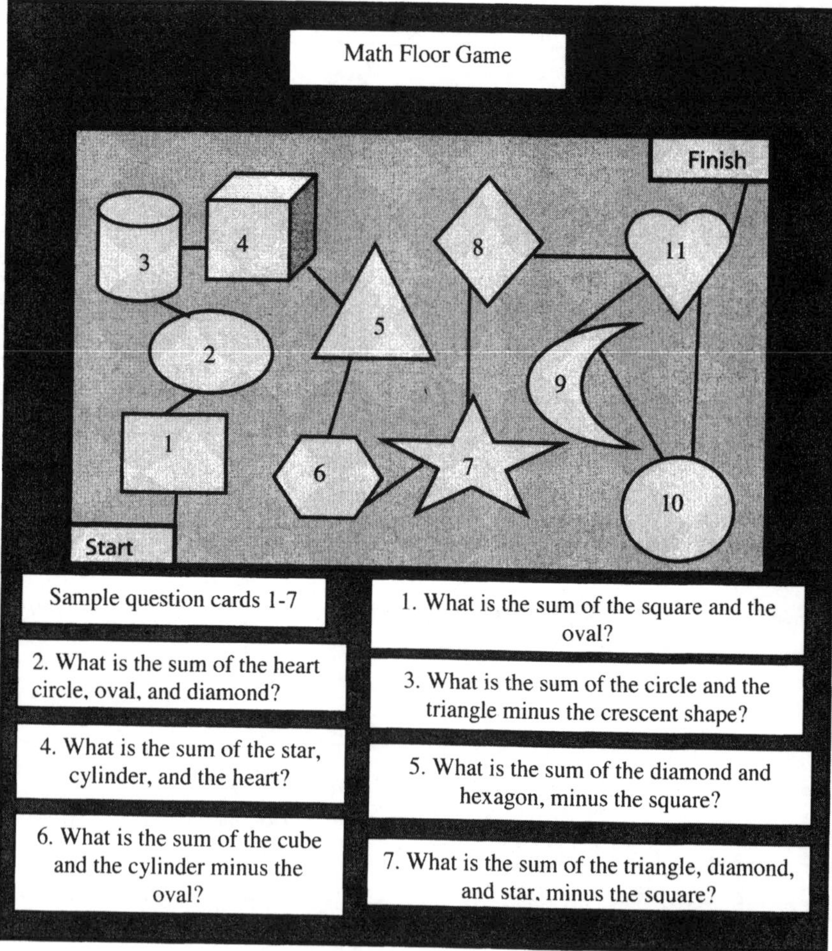

Figure 11.8. Math Floor Game Illustration

Applied thinking skills: classifying, recognizing, comparing and contrasting, prioritizing, inventing, communicating, inferring, predicting, generalizing, initial and advanced deciding, active listening, initial and advanced problem-solving, tolerating, recalling, reflecting, and self-actuating

Interactive Instructional Resource: Velcro Fill-in Cloze Game

On a large piece of poster or foam core board, there is a paragraph with missing words. The students select cut-out Velcro tabs, which have words on them that correctly fill in these spaces. These words are placed either alongside the text in random order or at the bottom of the selected board type.

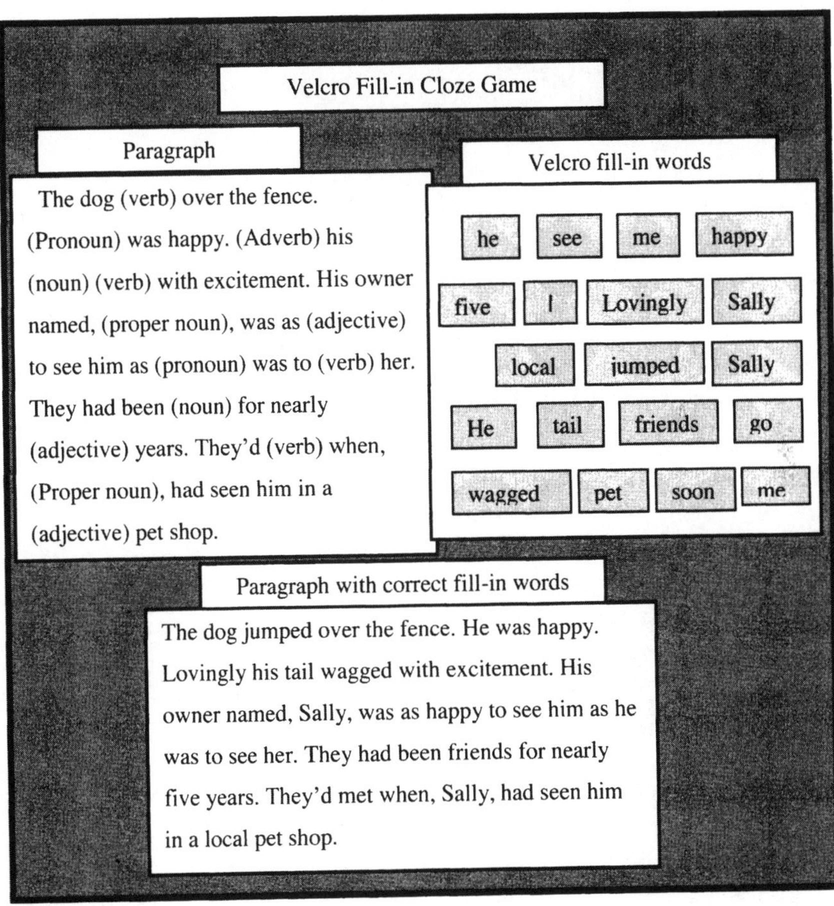

Figure 11.9. Velcro Fill-in Cloze Game Illustration

On the reverse side of the board, the paragraph is repeated and the words that fill in the blanks are provided. Sometimes extra words may be used to ascertain if the students are able to select the correct "cloze" word. This activity primarily serves to develop vocabulary awareness and paragraph comprehension. Identifying parts of speech may be provided. If so, on the reverse side of the board where the filled-in words are provided, there would be parentheses around the parts of speech that fill in the space. These would be placed next to the words that complete the sentences.

Applied thinking skills: recognizing, classifying, comparing, contrasting, inferring, sequencing, initial and advanced deciding and problem-solving, sequencing, evaluating, organizing, analyzing, reflecting, and self-actualizing

Some Final Thoughts on Interactive Instructional Resources

We've covered many ways to differentiate instruction with the use of graphic organizers and seven examples of additional interactive instructional resources. Each serves a purpose for addressing students' needs by varying instruction to meet the needs of students. You might question whether there are more of these educational games. The answer would be, "Certainly!" Just as importantly, there are others you'll discover, even ones you invent as you teach and learn.

What has been attempted in this chapter is exposing you to different instructional methods taking into consideration that students do not learn the same way and teachers need to be attentive to how they learn as well as who they are as learners. From this chapter, it's hoped you are refining your comprehension of new ways to teach a lesson and/or concretizing those of which you were already aware. Teaching is an art and a craft that encompasses learning—our learning what is best for our students by realizing all of the components of a model for academic and social cognition.

Chapter Discussion/Journal Questions

1. What is meant by *differentiated instruction*?
2. What are five ways to differentiate a lesson?

3. How would you explain each type of differentiation?
4. How do graphic organizers serve to involve students in the differentiation of instruction process?
5. What is a story map graphic organizer, and how may it be used to review and create a story?
6. What is a sequence-of-events graphic organizer?
7. What is a cause-and-effect graphic organizer, and what cognitive/metacognitive skills does it address?
8. What is a character-analysis graphic organizer, and how do you think it could it be used in a classroom?
9. What are five types of interactive instructional resources, and how might these be used in a classroom?
10. What are five reasons that establish interactive instruction being important?

CHAPTER TWELVE

PRACTICAL MODEL APPLICATION: CHARACTER DEVELOPMENT

Character development serves as the underpinning for a classroom community. It recognizes differences of students while respecting these through demonstration of the six international traits of being a person of good character. These involve one's being fair, kind, caring, responsible, trustworthy, and a good citizen.

A model for academic and social cognition represents each of these. They're in the belief and value systems through best teaching practices, as related in the preceding chapters (3–11) with regard to the overall design of the model. This design incorporates the foundation, its interior and exterior components, and reflection, which serves as the umbrella for the model.

How we teach one to be a person of good character is exhibited in the lessons we plan, our room configuration, types of instruction, questions we ask and the way we answer them, and style of delivery. The latter represents meeting the needs of all students, with the cognitive collective being important.

When the classroom environment is conducive to learning, one is aware that the instruction is being defined and modeled with these six character traits at the forefront of what's vital for the practice of the model. Following a poem about being positive in one's demeanor, this chapter has a historical overview of character development. This serves as the lead-in to a story that began a workshop. Initially created and presented by Schiering at Molloy

College in 2000, she began presenting it internationally in 2002, first in Europe and then in South America (2008). What follows are means for teaching character development with connections to the model.

Steps for implementing the topic of this chapter are provided through activities that focus on the six international components of being a person of good character, as well as stress factors that impinge on these. Home and school skills for character development are provided. These demonstrate how one might diminish stress, for appropriate classroom behavior, demeanor and dispositions to be displayed.

The idea of a classroom being a place where there's a "comfort zone" serves as a major theme of this final book chapter, which is the fourth and culminating tab in your notebook of the mind. Closing comments connecting all the book's chapters and a poem by A. G. Walton (1865) titled "Our World" complete these twelve chapters.

Key words: character development, respect, kind, trustworthy, fair, responsible, good citizen, behavior, stress factors, and comfort zone

One Life/Classroom Rule
(M. Schiering)

In my twelfth year of classroom teaching
Out of a career spanning nearly forty-two
I came across a situation
That was affecting both the home and school

No matter where one went
It brought a loss to everyone's needs
This was "negativity" taking over
In people's thoughts, words, and daily deeds

So I reflected for a period of time
About a variety of classroom rules
Like no gum chewing and how to sit
As well as overt and subliminal cues

The one rule that I wrote and implemented
Was first written in the front of my mind

Then I posted it on the classroom wall
And it worked, well, really quite fine

Honestly, it was undoubtedly very simple
And it impacts individuals feeling good
About their personal self-worth and value
If all used it . . . it surely would

Create a community of caring
One that promotes with incessant reason
A sense that there is thoughtfulness
In our sharing . . . regardless of the season

It's a rule for daily living
Without bias being displayed
With positive self-esteem the result
And it demonstrates a good "give-away."

Here's the rule for living
The best way that one can
To care about what one is saying
Without sarcasm . . . we'll really be trans-

Formative in what we're doing
With getting/giving a very big plus
The rule to which I refer is
"NO Put Downs . . . Only Lift UPS!"

Connecting the Model to Character Development

This model adheres to the concept of a classroom being an environment that enables constructive and affirmative social cognition for academic excellence. As you know, it's important to create a positive-based environment in order to teach most effectively and have students learn. This is because the magnitude and impact of being a person of good character by knowing oneself fosters constructive or upbeat behaviors. "Knowing about oneself, or for that matter knowing another in a positive way, enables individuals to be proactive with matching dispositions in the learning and teaching environment" (Schiering, 2000a, p. 6; 2009a, p. 3; 2009b, p. 29).

Also, "Teaching and learning should be a function of social change and should be an effective tool in developing critical and unbiased understanding, and thereby greater educational, political, economic and cultural justice" (McLean, 1999, pp. 55–91). Finally, "critical pedagogical approaches can help students construct an engaging knowledge, based on their realities and also help them to use their background experiences as a self-empowerment tool" (Freire and Macedo, 1995, pp. 377–402).

The connection of the model to character development is in the teaching of *how* to be a person of good character. This is accomplished by addressing the topic in the classroom, defining it, and practicing the components—modeling it—addressing four most important factors of character development.

1. A basic awareness that character development comprehension may be recognized as a process that might encompass the early childhood, preadolescent, adolescent, and adult years.
2. Character development is a learned response that becomes more natural as one practices it.
3. Life experiences upon which one can reflect, synthesize, and analyze may well result in character building.
4. There are certain crucial life experiences that all cultures embrace. These are birth, death, success, failure, tradition, and love (Dewey, 1937).

A Need for Character Development

In this chapter, it's noted that the nuclear family unit provides initial belief and value systems. Generally, it contributes to affirmative social cognition in that setting. Oftentimes, this carries over to schools and their classrooms. The resultant behaviors add to one's scope and sequence regarding possibilities that may provide reestablished or new constructive sociosocietal norms wherever one goes.

Think about it: character development is vitally necessary in today's schools, because in the past fifteen years the beliefs and values taught in homes are not essentially what was previously experienced. Repeatedly, there have been reports regarding moral and ethical standards waning on an international plane. And the prevailing response remains one of denial and acquiescence at home. As Brooks and Goble explained in 1997, "Schools point to parents, parents at schools, and society in general points at everyone else when it comes to who's responsible for problems in school" (21–38).

A study conducted by O'Neil (1996) revealed that boys in the second grade who are always getting into trouble are six to eight times more likely than other children to be violent in their teens and commit crimes. *USA Today* magazine in 2004 reported on school-related bullying resulting in violence with twenty-seven children killed by schoolmates, and an equal number injured, in the past ten years.

Furthermore, 74 percent of student learners reported cheating on homework, with 38 percent having stolen something and 43 percent believing one had to cheat or lie to get ahead in life, with a 27 percent diminished parent interest or involvement rate in character development between grades K–5 and 9–12.

Strangely and conversely, 95 percent of twelve thousand school-age children thought it was important to be trustworthy (Josephson, 2002). With statistics like that and more recent reports on school violence and bullying being in newspapers, on television, and on the Internet, a question arises: do children who are lying, cheating, and stealing anticipate, from the character traits they profess to have, others being trustworthy?

Regardless of this, multiple media sources continue to inform an international public about disgruntled socially rejected individuals killing classmates and/or disrupting instruction at colleges, universities, and elementary-grade, middle, and secondary institutions. Gaul (2010) cited the Josephson Institute of Ethics report relating that 28 percent of high school students thought school violence was okay.

Researchers on the topic of character development refer to it being needed as a result of ongoing and substantive violence and bullying in schools. They continue to cry that there's a critical call for developing both cognitive and social skills—this, along with the necessity for providing an equitable balance between these attributes, as they are essential for ethical growth in children (Brazil, 2004). Britzman and Hanson (2005, n.p.) sum up the current state of affairs: "While our present society places enormous academic pressure on children, this is often at the expense of character development."

Schools, as stated in an earlier chapter, are the neutral meeting ground for varied cultures, dispositions, and belief and values systems. They are often recognized as being far less than that, as enjoying learning dissipates. What do you suppose caused this? The answer may be, "This situation is due to numerous reports on lack of ethics and moral substance within the public and private sectors" (O'Connor-Petruso and Schiering, 2005, p. 4).

The role of academic success in educational settings is not the only factor concerning individuals being successful in this arena. Feelings existing there play just as important a role. As Dr. Martin Luther King Jr. stated as far back as 1947 regarding the purpose of education, "We must remember that intelligence is not enough. Intelligence plus character—that is the goal of true education. The complete education gives one not only power of concentration, but worthy objectives upon which to concentrate. The broad education will, therefore, transmit to one not only the accumulated knowledge of the race but also the accumulated experience of social living."

Our not remembering this has exacted a price far too overwhelming and resulted in our great awareness of the need for social change. This is part of growing up too fast. As David Elkind relates, "This is because, the real danger of growing up fast is that children learn the rules of social license before they learn the rules of mutual respect" (Schiering, 2009b, p. 68).

Partially due to the aforementioned negative perspectives that result in antisocial behaviors, bookstores are filled with literature addressing character development. This literature focuses on ethical behaviors, including bullying prevention, tolerance, friendship, feeling special, overcoming setbacks, and strengthening relationships with others, friends, family, and/or a higher power, as well as integrity. The goal is to promote self-awareness and self-esteem by providing information that will create amicable relationships, resulting in persons of good character and, ultimately, creating peace within an individual and in a community.

Social Cognition and Social Change

When referencing the dynamics concerning reflection on one's economics, academics, and political situations earlier in this book, there was mention of common social and societal norms. It was repeatedly pointed out that an individual's meaning is constructed with reflective reactions to one's thoughts, ideas, opinions, judgments, and feelings, as the cognitive collective is addressed. The importance of social cognition to institute social change relies on these reciprocal and symbiotic processes. They need to be held on to, and serve as the guardian of individuals' modified or newly evidenced experiential responses to situations being of a positive nature—your positive nature.

However, all too often, we note that this is in opposition to the present-day reality of students' test scores being compared to ascertain who one is as a learner, which is smarter than the other, and who will probably be academically and, subsequently, socially, an achiever of significance. Supplementing, creating, or designing experiences in the responsible classroom relies on societal and social cognition being centered on changing what is presently being evidenced to being uplifting and optimistic for future endeavors.

The baseline in all too many classrooms is the emphasis on what's wrong instead of what's right. In every part of one's daily encounters there's a pervasive importance placed on what has not been done, accomplished, and/or addressed, rather than on accepting what is achieved with added encouragement to progress. There appears to be an establishment of a mental patterning with respect to the negatives being given more importance than the positives. Is this is a present-day way of life or just a happenstance? As educators we need to be concerned with techniques that bring one to realize who one is in social-academic environments being of a formative and constructive nature.

It was mentioned that the physical design of a classroom serves as an invitation to learn and teach oneself by having a place that connotes comfort and acceptance. While this belief is adhered to by many teachers, it is also conceptualized as being important to realize that creating this physical setting is enhanced by what transpires within that place, giving attention to what is occurring intellectually and emotionally.

The ideas of accepting one another are reliant on there being not just an arrangement of desks and chairs in formal or informal configurations, traditional or nontraditional teaching, but positive social cognition for everyday classroom interactions. These include open-minded conversations addressing topics that promote student learners and teachers demonstrating caring and concern for one another.

Exhibiting a pleasant disposition, realizing the strengths of oneself and others, accepting varied viewpoints, and adhering to this chapter's poem's last line of "NO put downs . . . only lift UPS," provides an overall sense of classroom security, safety, and well-being. How this can be accomplished serves as the foundational structure of the remainder of this chapter.

A Story that Began a Workshop in Character Development

(The following story that began a workshop in character development and the steps for creating it are from Schiering, 2000a; 2000b; 2008; 2009b.)

It was 1999 and a sixteen-year-old, 250-pound athlete stood before a classroom of doctoral students at an eastern university. His mother, the class's professor, had invited him to speak about the impact of self-perception on a person's life. The young man looked the part of the self-assured football player and track star. However, the class learned his attitude had been much different in previous years. He told the students how he had seen himself as a failure. He explained, "I failed tests, didn't do homework, stayed back in school, and was considered an oddball. I could do well in sports but not in much else."

Although his parents praised him, assured him of his intelligence, and offered him money, trips, and/or special privileges for good grades, nothing seemed to help. He told the class, "I saw myself as a failure and believed I was a failure and accepted myself as a failure, except at sports." This constituted his major belief system from the time he was in elementary school.

Of course, this impacted his social life. He hung out with like-minded kids. He gained accolades for his athletic prowess, but he simultaneously felt separated from most people. "Good grades weren't everything," he said. "But not having them sure kept me from being accepted, or people listening to me. Guess they thought I was a great jock, but not too bright."

"What made this self-perception of being a failure change?" a doctoral candidate inquired at the end of the presentation. "What caused you to see yourself as a success, after you refused to accept the incentives that were presented to you?"

"What made me change was the ability to challenge myself, to see if I could be successful on an exam in my ninth-grade English class. I earned a grade of 100 percent. It was my first real academic success. I realized that if I had achieved this one success, I could achieve two, three, four, and as many as I wanted. One success led to another."

Another student, a woman in her mid-forties, asked how teachers could get teenagers to be respectful. The young man sauntered forward and stood very close to the woman as he answered, "How do you get us to be respectful to you teachers? Well, how do I give you something I don't have for myself?"

An audible gasp could be heard throughout the room.

The student elaborated, "If you are asked for an apple and you have one, then you can give it away. But if you don't have an apple, you can't. If you do not have self-respect, then you cannot give respect to another. You cannot give someone something you yourself do not possess."

(The dialogue in the preceding story occurred in 1999 [M. S. Schiering and S. D. Schiering]. In the aftermath, a workshop was created for teaching character development to teacher candidates and student learners, whether in a home or academic setting, in kindergarten through advanced-degree college classrooms, both nationally and internationally.)

Teaching Character Development: Areas of Commonality; A Review

While we've been told there are six degrees of separation between humans, in fact we are all interconnected; we are joined by the fundamental cognitive and emotional aspects of the shared social realities that influence our thinking and feelings. Do you recall from chapter 5 the writings of renowned educator John Dewey, in which he noted that all people from all cultures share six common areas with respect to feelings and emotions?

These are birth, death, success, failure, tradition, and love. We related that the overall thoughts and emotional responses to such situations are reasonably constant and similar; new life, the passing of a loved one, doing well in school or achieving a high salary for work, being unaccepted due to poor grades or losing a job, celebrating holidays, caring about a significant other, or the feeling of parents for a child and vice versa. They've been repeated here because these six areas of commonality impact greatly on the formation of our character.

Character development is influenced by these aforementioned six areas in their effect on beliefs and values that begin in a family or home, regardless of its physical or social configuration. As the individual matures and enters school, new societal realities are imposed that affect the family's mores.

Character is formed as an individual is exposed to this array of thoughts, ideas, opinions, and judgments in common social-societal realms. Changes of beliefs occur when there is a shift from familial social realities to an individual's comprehension of what he/she wants and needs in terms of current social and societal trends.

A Workshop on Character Development: Steps 1 and 2

In an imagined high school corridor, the presenter asks the audience to imagine two teenagers bumping into one another and being profoundly rude. The presenter(s) then ask the audience what took place. The disrespect that was demonstrated is discussed and examined as a list is created of words that connote respect. After over 150 workshops, the following is the list that most often appears: A respectful person is one who exhibits being kind, a flexible thinker, caring, trustworthy, considerate, tolerant, accepting of others, polite, compassionate, encouraging, pleasant, an active listener, responsible, fair, empathetic, thoughtful, conversational, helpful, encouraging, positive, upbeat.

Following this list being presented on a chart, each individual is then asked if he/she exhibits each of these words to every person met every day. Then, the question is posed if he/she exhibits each of these words to herself or himself every day. The idea is presented that in order to be each of these words that connote respect to another, one must first be this to oneself. Also, in order for one to understand being respectful, the words that appear on the chart need to be defined and modeled.

If a student says he/she does not exhibit each of these words to himself or herself, the course leader asks, "Why?"

Discussion follows about the overall negativity in our homes, schools, and other settings that are experienced on a daily basis. Why do we remember negative things that are said to us, as opposed to positive statements? It is not necessarily the case that there are more of one than the other. Yet, as individuals, we hold on to a negative comment and can recall it more readily than a positive statement.

A Workshop on Character Development: Step 3

To demonstrate this idea of negativity taking the forefront of our emotions, a paper heart which workshop attendees had earlier placed their names on is displayed. The group is asked to repeat at least one negative statement they've used or that they've heard another use. It could be something a child, adolescent, or adult said. Examples include: "I don't like you." "You're dumb." "You take the short bus to school." "I hate you." "You're gay, stupid, ugly." "Poor test results, shut up!" "Your mom is dumber than you and you're really dumb." "I can't read what you wrote." "You stink at sports."

As each negative is given, the paper heart is folded.

The heart-folding is followed by asking the audience to repeat positive statements that they might have said, or heard someone else say, to another. Examples include: "I like you." "I love you." "You're the best." "Nice work." "You're smart." "Come over for a play date." "Your mom's the best." "You did that well." "You look nice today." "Wow, what a fantastic picture." "I'd like to be like you." "You're talented." "Those are great sneakers." "Nice driving."

As each positive statement is given, the paper is unfolded.

Even if there are more positives than negatives, the unfolding of the heart reveals creases on the paper as it's shown to the audience. The audience is told, "We call these, scars on the heart. Although you gave more positives than negatives, the scars do not go away. If you gave one hundred positive statements the negative ones remain with you and are recalled, even reflected upon from time to time. The 'scars on your heart' are remembered!"

Why do you suppose we (learners and teachers—everyone) hold onto the negative comments and question ourselves about these character traits? And how can we change this?

A Real-Life Explanation

We hold onto the negative due to modeling of negativity which surrounds and encompasses our daily lives. People often use sarcasm to mask negative statements, but the recipient is hurt. Participants in the class were told that the Greek definition of sarcasm is "to tear at the flesh." With this definition in mind, why do you suppose one would find this type of humor funny?

"How can this negativity in our talking be changed?" the instructor asks the students. "It can be changed by you," they are told, "because you are a change agent. You are in control of what you say, and the actions you take. An act of your conscious will is needed to be engaged and practiced with positivity."

There's one classroom and life rule which I wrote and instituted in 1976: "NO put downs . . . only lift UPS!" Try using that to live by and see what results. Interestingly, that one classroom rule has spread. In the late 1980s, in an elementary school where I was teaching, it extended over five years to include each classroom in the school and many home fronts. What it brought about was a sense of a caring community of individuals. Character development was/is "in action."

Remaining Steps for Teaching Character Development

During this three-hour workshop, interactive components are realized in a small-group format. One activity involves recording and sharing examples of the six international components of being a person of good character. These are then discussed in whole-group format. A handout on the definition of these six character traits is distributed to assist one in realizing the meaning of each term/word. These are presented here and are followed by the small-group activity worksheet. (Source: The Josephson Institute, Michigan Model Partnership for Character Education, Mt. Morris Schools in New York [Schiering 2000a].)

Six International Character Traits and Their Definitions

- Trustworthy: This involves being honest, which incorporates being sincere and loyal. Sharing important information in relationships of trust is contingent upon your not being deceiving, misleading, devious or tricky, a cheater, or a thief. Standing up for your beliefs about right or wrong is necessary. Being trustworthy involves keeping your word, honoring your commitments, paying attention, returning what you borrowed, keeping a confidence, and honoring the integrity of others. Also, supporting and protecting your family, friends, community, and country are signs of being trustworthy.
- Respect: This involves being courteous and forthright. Don't say one thing and mean another, or be two-faced by saying one thing to someone and the opposite to another on the same topic. Respectfulness requires being tolerant, appreciating, and accepting of individual differences by not abusing, demeaning, or mistreating anyone.
- Responsible: This calls for accountability by thinking before one speaks and being answerable for one's actions. One considers the consequences for everyone who will be affected by one's words or actions. The responsible person is one who doesn't offer excuses and sets a good example for others by being present and/or not blaming others for his/her mistakes. He/she gives credit for others' achievements. Being responsible means having self-control of one's actions, words, and attitudes, and being diligent in trying one's best.
- Caring: A caring person is one who shows interest in others through kind and compassionate actions. This is also done for oneself. Those who care are aware of or question in a concerned manner how another is feeling. This person shares with others and is not selfish. Such a person treats others the way he or she would want to be treated.

- Fair: This person listens to others and realizes that fairness means each person getting what they need, but not everyone getting the same thing. Demonstrating this character trait requires listening to others while trying to understand what they are saying, thinking, and feeling. Sometimes it's necessary to ask for clarification so comprehension can occur. Fairness requires honoring others and being concerned that one is not doing something for one's personal gain.
- A good citizen: This person is involved in playing by the rules. He or she supports being a good sport by taking on a reasonable amount of responsibility while showing respect for others. He or she stays informed about the world around him or her, votes when able to vote, protects neighbors and community, helps his or her school by volunteering, shows concern for the environment, and conserves natural resources.

Character Development Activity: Being a Person of Good Character

1. I think a person of good character has the following qualities:

   ____

2. Small-group directions: Working in groups of six, but not less than four, decide which character trait you will address and complete the steps listed below:

   a. Reflect on and select a time when you either observed a person demonstrating this term through his or her behaviors, or when you personally demonstrated the selected term.
   b. Describe, in writing, this scenario on the lines next to each character trait listed at the end of these directions. Please be specific and select a particular incident with setting, conversation, and actions taken that denote utilization of the term in a real-life situation.
   c. Share what you've written with the other group members.

d. Allow time for group members to share a time when they saw someone address or personally addressed the same term.

e. At the completion of each member having shared, there will be a whole-class discussion regarding behaviors and values associated with being a person of good character. This includes why you selected the particular scenario, what cognitive skills were involved, and emotions experienced at the time of the actual incident.

Character Traits

Caring: ______________________________

____

Respectful: ______________________________

____

Trustworthy: ______________________________

____

Fair: ______________________________

____

Responsible: ______________________________

____

Good citizenship: ______________________________

____

(Portions of this activity are from Mt. Morris School District in upstate New York.)

Factors that Impinge on Being a Person of Good Character

Common social and societal realities are such that while they may be pleasant experiences there are also situations that bring about a sense of feeling unsafe and insecure. This is most commonly evidenced when a life pattern is altered or there's a social cognition shift from what's previously been happening and/or anticipated. Experiencing fast-paced societal norms leads to stress.

Subsequently, stressor situations may happen at any age at any location at any time, just by something taking place that's not expected or is negative, threatening, intrusive, disquieting, dubious, or favorably or unfavorably out of the ordinary. Stressors impinge on or interrupt one's being a person of good character. There's a heart-mind reality that affects individuals' behaviors.

Stressors may cause a sense of feeling isolated, rejected, or uncared about, which at one time or another happens to many individuals. This feeling can wash over one like a heavy rain so that when experiencing stress one's ethereal self is saturated with grief and the overflow is channeled into the physical body. A sense of lethargy is evidenced. There's a physical emptiness and longing which may be transmuted into feelings that often cannot be put into words. Mending a difficult situation can seem a task so monumental that one dare not attempt it for fear of damaging oneself further.

Nonetheless, like all emotions, stress falls under the spell of individuals' conscious influence. Implementing character development in classrooms, with evidence of kindness, caring, and mutual respect, may well be the best way to relieve stressors and may even eradicate them. This would be due to the classroom environment providing a safe haven where it's reciprocally understood that each of us goes through difficult times.

How one emerges from a place and/or situation that served as the cause of stress is reliant on the positives and uplifting nature of the classroom environment. Some of these stress-causing, heartbreaking circumstances that affect behaviors in a negative fashion at home or in the school setting are listed for course/workshop participants.

Activity: Stress Causes Behavioral Changes

Directions: From the list of stressors, in small groups of four to six, reach consensus on the five you think are most likely to impact people experiencing them. You may add to this list if you so desire. Then, through your group discussion, list the reasons why you think these cause the most stress.

Stressors: death of a family member, relative, or friend; sibling or personal serious illness; divorce; parent traveling; loss of responsibility; fear of abandonment; personal or friend moving to another school/city/state; addition of another adult or child to the core family; teacher change; theft of personal possession; discord with family member/stepparent/guardian; home arguments; change in family financial condition; tests; failure; birthday parties; bullying; cliques; social estrangement; developmental transition stages; feeling different/unaccepted/alone/unwanted/rejected/helpless; authority figure demands; eating patterns compromised and/or loss of freedom/privileges/game/sports event/treasured item/means of transportation/favorite toy or pet; shyness; family financial problems; alcohol or drug abuse.

The Five Most Common Stressors

1. Death of a parent or family member
2. Divorce
3. Bullying
4. Moving from one area to another
5. Change for the worse in home financial situation

Reasons Why These Are the Most Stressful Experiences

Each of the situations listed above may cause a person's (1) loss or distortion of his or her sense of security. This is due to a change in his or her established patterns with previously experienced social cognition. Attention is called to the operative word regarding stress stemming from (2) change. This is because change, in whatever form, is underscored as incorporating a (3) fear of the unknown.

Home and School Skills for Stress Reduction and Character Development

The following are suggestions for being a person of good character regarding social cognition. Some of those listed are from the New York State Project SAVE curriculum in Albany (2000):

a. Read books to stimulate conversation about good character.
b. Hold discussions and have a sharing time.

c. Listen to children's problems.
d. Establish family rituals.
e. Give children responsibilities and chores.
f. Prevent scapegoat attitudes.
g. Avoid one child competing against another.
h. Help reinforce children's empathy by asking about how they feel and sharing your own feelings on this topic.
i. Help use constructive criticism, which is interpreted as being helpful by first calling attention to accomplishments.
j. Emphasize good sportsmanship.
k. Create opportunities to work together.
l. Model and promote kindness through appropriate language.
m. Lead by example.
n. Teach and model courtesy.
o. Admit your mistakes and seek to correct them.
p. Give sufficient feedback when evaluating.
q. Talk about the need to care for all living things.
r. Regularly weave the questions for social cognition interactions and feelings into discussions: What are the common social and societal realities of those in the classroom? What are the stressors for individuals and/or the economic, academic, and political circumstances? What's the right thing to do? How are you demonstrating being a person of good character?

Culminating the Workshop on Character Development

This program ends with the concept of our life being focused not on forgetting things that happen to us, but forgiving them. "Our life is not forgetting, but forgiving" (Million, 2007–2008). In order to be a person of good character, one may examine this following concept: our life is not *for getting*, but *for giving*. When we reach out to others and ourselves with forethought about being positive in speech, demeanor and actions, we are building a person of good character and inviting others to do likewise. The end result is, hopefully, each of us realizing we're human beings: humans in the act of being who are doing our best to promote a community of good citizens who are responsible, caring, respectful, kind, trustworthy, and fair people.

Chapter Discussion/Journal Questions

1. What are the six international qualities of being a person of good character?
2. What is social cognition?
3. What are the two components for having a classroom comfort zone?
4. What are five stressors that impinge on being a person of good character?
5. How does change affect people, and what are two fears concerning change in one's routine?
6. How do you think stressors may be reduced in the classroom setting?
7. How might a model for academic and social cognition relieve stressors?
8. What are five home and school skills for character development?
9. What are two classroom rules for positive social cognition?
10. How do students know what respect means if there are so many different definitions?
11. What do you suppose are two immediate results of one's being a person of good character?

Closing Comments

The idea of our lives, as learners and teachers, being *forgiving* and *for giving* has been presented in this chapter and the eleven that precede it. By utilizing *Teaching and Learning: A Model for Academic and Social Cognition* within the academic and social settings, a comprehensive means for being person of good character is evident.

Relieving one's "fearing the unknown," dealing with stressors, or accepting change by giving conscious thoughts to the components of the model, are other accommodations. Simply stated, this is accomplished by the model's practitioner having knowledge of who one is as a learner and teacher resulting from attention to the model's components of belief and value systems, common social and societal realities, the cognitive collective, SOW, and REAP being affected by individual's reflection—everywhere and every day.

With each person having this knowledge of himself or herself and others, it is possible to create classroom social literacy situations that address behaviors, personalities, and dispositions, as well as all the other factors that are part of the classroom. It also makes it possible to create an atmosphere which encourages a sense of belonging, well-being, cooperation, and safety. Of course, as the chapter relates, this requires a good deal of attention and reflection on daily situations, and it is thoughtfully time-consuming.

However, the end result is that teaching and learning are achieved most successfully for the benefit of the students and us as educators. Today's experiences become part of one's experiential past a moment from now. As we stated in the beginning of this book, "Go forward and enjoy the read!" We hope you have, as we invite you to "Learn and teach effectively!" And with those thoughts we culminate with this poem by A. G. Walton written in 1865.

Our World
We make the world in which we live
By what we gather and what we give
By our daily deeds and the things we say
By what we keep or cast away . . .
We make our world by the life we lead.
By the friends we have,
By the books we read;
By the pity we show in the hour of care;
By the loads we lift and the love we share.
We make our world by the goals we pursue,
By the heights we seek and the

higher view.
By the hopes and the dreams that reach the sun, and a will to fight
till the heights are won.
We gather . . . We scatter . . . We take and we give . . .
We make this world and here we live.

We invite you to make our world a good one by practicing a model for academic and social cognition!

AFTERWORD

Did You Know?
(M. Schiering)

I have been teaching for quite a few years,
And that I am concerned about my students learning?
Did you know?
That I am brilliant in the classroom?
Did you know?
That I think about students' learning
Even when I'm not in school with them?
Were you aware?
That sometimes I think I'm smarter and/or less
Informed than others in my field?
I think that this depends on so much—
Like what teaching methods I use
Or who I am as a teacher and learner.
Did you know?
That I am basically a thoughtful person,
and like the willow tree I can bend?
Did you know?
Over the years I have developed
A comfortable level of tact and patience.
Did you know?
When I left college someone told me
I couldn't count on teaching being an exact science.
I've wondered if the knowledge of that truth

caused me to, now and then, doubt myself.
Did you know?
I sometimes question if I'm successful
in meeting my students' needs.
Did you know?
I have taken graduate courses,
Postgraduate courses, and
Professional Development classes.
Did you know?
I have been evaluated, staff-developed, and work-shopped.
I have been evaluated in each of the aforementioned.
I have been defined as disorganized and creative,
or, structured and responsible.
Did you know?
This depends on who's doing the assessment.
I have been praised and also have not received recognition
When I thought a pat on the back was deserved.
Not so long ago I looked in the sky
And saw geese heading south.
I wanted to follow them,
And the next morning I didn't feel like teaching
Did you know?
I think am in control of so much, so little,
So great, so small a task.
And, simultaneously, I think I am in control of nothing.
Did you know?
Someone who is not a colleague, but a person
who matters to me
Said something that upset me the other day.
The person used finesse, but the words hurt.
Did you know?
I didn't think I was as effective in the classroom
On that day and felt disappointed in myself.
Did you know?
The very next afternoon
Two of my students commented on
How they like the different ways I teach.
This meant their being engaged in their learning
And my not just talking at them.
Did you know?

This was acknowledgment from students
About "How" I teach.
Did you know?
This is the meaning of Teaching for me.
My using differentiated instruction.
My using ideas from other educators
To create my own teaching style.
Did you know?
A fellow teacher came into my classroom today
And commented on how she liked the projects that
My students were doing.
Did you know?
She wanted to collaborate on ways to implement
These projects in her teaching.
I had wings . . . I could fly.
I felt good.
Did you know?
I am brilliant in the classroom!
Did you know all these things?
Do you know me?
I am YOU
I Am A Teacher!

APPENDIXES OVERVIEW

These appendixes, A–C, are written to add clarification and/or extended information on initially addressed topics of this book. This edification serves to assist you in being the most informed comprehensive educator on the topics surrounding a world sociology with beliefs and values, common social and societal realities, the cognitive collective, reflection, and the external factors of a model for academic and social cognition.

Appendix A
- Topic 1: Definition of Reciprocal Thinking Cognitive Skills with Examples
- Topic 2: Adaptations for a Diverse Student Population

Appendix B
- Topic 1: A List of Instructional Resources with Potential Cognitive and Metacognitive Skills They Develop
- Topic 2: Interactive Instructional Resources; Information and Uses, Materials, and Construction Directions
- Topic 3: Definitions and Examples of Team Learning and Circle of Knowledge
- Topic 4: The Art of Storytelling
  - A. An Overview of Storytelling
  - B. Directions for a Storytelling Assignment
  - C. One Teacher Candidate's Story
  - D. Questions to Extend the Story

E. Reciprocal Thinking Identification Chart for the Story

Appendix C

Topic 1: Suggestions for Evaluating Students' Work:

Topic 2: Samples of Rubric Criteria and Evaluation Comments for:

A. Storytelling

B. Story Map Graphic Organizer

C. Partnership-Written Lesson Plan and Teaching Performance Demonstration Lesson

D. Decision-Making Graphic Organizer

APPENDIX A

We now examine, in detail, some of the components mentioned in the text chapters. Appendix A specifically calls attention to the ways for individuals and groups to realize what thinking is involved in situations that occur throughout one's day—whether this is goal setting, using steps to make a decision for reaching an objective, realizing behavioral patterns, or realizing why one acts the way one does, as much as varying a perspective due to addressing what one is thinking.

Think about this: by knowing the definitions of cognitive and metacognitive functions, the opportunity to have a multitude of thinking implementations and applications in the academic setting becomes possible. But first it's important to know—to internalize these definitions of—the cognitive and metacognitive skills involved in the reciprocity of thinking.

Realizing, being aware of, and recognizing these functions, whether inside or outside the classroom, prepares each of us for self-actualization. Subsequently, this appendix begins with the definitions of the cognitive and metacognitive skills presented in the reciprocal thinking phases, with examples of each one. These examples are for adding clarity to the definitions.

The next section of this appendix addresses the definition of adapting a lesson to specific student needs of the diverse learners you may have in your classroom. Since many schools, nationally and internationally, are geared toward the concept of inclusion schooling, adaptations for a diverse student population are good information for you to have.

Topic 1: Definition of Reciprocal Thinking Cognitive Skills with Examples

Phase 1: Beginning Awareness and Acknowledging

1. Recognizing: To be aware of, be familiar with, acknowledge, or identify from previous experience.

   Example: The person knew that the car was new.

2. Realizing: To become conscious of something or comprehend it.

   Example: The girl knew/understood there was danger when the fire alarm rang.

3. Classifying: To arrange, sort, or order things into groups according to established criteria.

   Example: There were five green apples on the table with one next to the other.

4. Comparing: To examine, judge, link, or evaluate two or more things in order to show how they are similar.

   Example: The audience noted that each performer had red hair and all were women.

5. Contrasting: To show the difference, distinction, or disparity between two things being compared.

   Example: The peach tasted sweet, but the lemon was sour.

Phase 2: Critical and Creative Thinking

1. Prioritizing: To deal with or list something in order of its importance or level of concern.

   Example: Before going to see the movie, the tickets first had to be bought.

2. Communicating: To converse in oral, written, or sign formats. A means for sharing, making a statement, passing along information, or publicizing.

   Example: The driver yelled out the words on the sign, which read, "Do not park here."

3. Inferring: To suppose, deduce, surmise and/or form an opinion based on information one has.

   Example: The bird prints in the sand caused the group to believe a bird was walking there earlier.

4. Active listening: To be engaged in hearing what is being related by being attentive to the discourse.

   Example: The student heard every word being spoken and demonstrated interest in the topic by being able to discuss it.

5. Inventing: To discover, think up, devise, or fabricate in the mind, to think out, produce something new, or originate through experiment.

   Example: She originated the idea of having student-need times for snacking during the school day.

6. Predicting: To forecast, envision, guess, and/or calculate that something will happen before it actually occurs.

   Example: The townspeople foretold the arrival of a storm.

7. Generalizing: To form an opinion or take a broad view of something.

   Example: Everyone simplified the importance of the car on the lawn.

8. Sequencing: A series of related events, actions, or the like that happen or are done in a particular order/progression—placing in specific order.

   Example: The links of the chain were in a red, green, blue, and pink series.

9. Initial deciding: Beginning choice, resolution, or judgment about something, as in making up one's mind concerning how to handle a situation.

   Example: Initially there were three possible choices provided for the best gymnast award.

10. Initial problem-solving: Beginning thought, dealing with, and/or providing explanation about a difficult situation or

person. To find the correct answer to a question, or the explanation for something that is difficult to comprehend or considered a predicament.

Example: The dilemma of the dog chasing the cat seemed to have no immediate resolution.

Phase 3: The Metacognitive Processes

1. Evaluating: To judge or determine the quality of something, as in to assess or appraise its worth.

   Example: The teacher estimated the grade for the student's essay.

2. Organizing: A systemization of categorizing things, whether this is being objects, thoughts, or feelings. To make into a whole part with unified and coherent relationships or to arrange things in an orderly fashion.

   Example: The students systematized the list by sorting out and classifying the nouns.

3. Critiquing: Thoughts, judgments, or accounting as to whether something is favorable, unfavorable, has both of these components, or resides in between these. A level of degree is applied to critiquing. Analysis, examination, review, and appraisal are part of critiquing.

   Example: After the diamond was examined, the appraisal was very high.

4. Collaborating: To work together with another person or groups in order to achieve or produce something. This is done in a cooperative manner, as to team up and/or pool resources.

   Example: The two boys teamed up for the basketball competition.

5. Tolerating: To abide, endure, or put up with by accepting it.

   Example: She permitted the purchase of the new puppy, although she didn't want a new dog in the house.

6. Advanced deciding: Reaching a high degree or level of difficulty by providing choice, judgment, explanation, and/or resolution to a situation.

   Example: The final resolution was to have the class elect a new leader.

7. Risk-taking: Action requiring grabbing a chance without knowing the outcome of that action.

   Example: It was a gamble to go in the door without knocking.

8. Analyzing: The careful examination of something in order to comprehend it, or to examine the thought and feeling components to ascertain its general composition for comprehension.

   Example: The investigation seemed to produce positive results.

9. Synthesizing: To form by bringing together separate parts of a situation in a concise manner, such as to compact its various components.

   Example: She blended the important life events from ages five through twelve into a six-page essay.

10. Advanced problem-solving: To find a solution to a problem when there's requirement to do this by there being a high degree or level of difficulty concerning one's thinking. This may be by providing explanation about a nonsimplistic situation or person or something that is considered difficult/challenging to comprehend, or explanation for something that is considered comprehensively difficult.

    Example: After reflecting for some time, the final solution was to try the roller coaster ride, even though it was challenging and difficult to comprehend why one made that choice.

11. Recalling: To bring back to one's mind something from the past, as in reference to a memory, whether a moment earlier or a longer expanse of time.

Example: The girl reminded herself that she was due at the birthday party by noon.

12. Reflecting: To realize something after giving it thought or contemplation by pondering and considering it, as in going back in time to examine a previous circumstance.

    Example: Tom contemplated the wonderful time at the gym as he realized it was a positive experience.

13. Self-actuating: Going forward and taking action; doing something as opposed to remaining stationery.

    Example: She activated the plan by moving to a different house.

Topic 2: Adaptations for a Diverse Student Population

Questions and Answers about Adaptations

1. Q: For whom is the adaptation portion of a lesson plan?

   A: The adaptation portion of a lesson plan addresses one student with one specific problem in learning, or one who is "learning different." Basically, the idea of making an adaptation for a student refers to "the three ones." This means:

   One student with

   One problem, and

   One remediation technique applied to instruction for this student.

2. Q: What is the most important consideration regarding adapting instruction for learning-different students?

   A: The most important consideration is that you be thoughtful regarding the student's needs. At all times when teaching, practice being kind without calling attention to an individual's problem area. Generally, as the teacher, it's important to be accepting of each student in the classroom, and that's without exception. Make the adaptation one that recognizes that the student is part of the classroom community, as he/she is an individual who thinks and feels.

3. Q: How is an adaptation different from differentiation of instruction?

   A: The adaptation of a lesson addresses "the three ones." However, differentiation of instruction is primarily for the whole class or small groups of students.

4. Q: What is the most important thing to know about an adaptation?

   A: The teacher should work toward a student's area of strength, as opposed to an area of difficulty. This is especially true with respect to the four modalities used when presenting material, which are:

   - Auditory: A student learns best by listening to the material.
   - Visual: A student learns best by seeing the material.
   - Tactile: The student learns best by touching the material, such as with use of interactive instructional resources.
   - Kinesthetic: A student learns best by having whole-body involvement with the material, such as in role-playing or a floor/wall game.

   Let's say a student has a visual impairment. A lesson relying on reading would find the teacher *adapting* the reading of a book by having an audiotape of that piece of literature. Another example would be a child having a hearing impairment having an adaptation of material presented in a visual format. The hands-on type of instruction is especially applicable for those with visual and auditory difficulties, as for those with fine or gross motor skill impairments.

5. Q: What are some types of learning disabilities?

   A: "Aside from perceptual impairments (auditory, visual, tactile, and kinesthetic), these may include emotional problems (ED), attention deficit disorder (ADD) and attention deficit hyperactivity disorder (ADHD) or primary focusing impairments, dyslexia, socialization inabilities, developmental aphasia, brain injury, environmental, cultural, or economic disadvantage" (Salend, 2004, pp. 104–12). Additionally, there are learning problems concerning "memory, attention, and organization" (McNamara and Wong, 2003, pp. 394–406).

6. Q: What oftentimes constitutes the need for adapting a lesson's content to a specific learning problem? A: When the student has an IEP (Individualized Education Program) that requires particular intervention strategies, or when you observe a student repeatedly struggling with a particular exercise, then the adaptation of lesson content is necessary. Also, if you observe that a student excels in several or some areas and is continually ready with work that goes beyond the anticipated outcomes, an adaptation assists with reinforcement or extension of the lesson to be taught. This would be something that creates added interest for that student.

7. Q: What are general accommodations, as opposed to adaptations that may be used in the classroom regularly for the whole class, or small groups?

   A: Accommodations enable students to do their work independently by changing the setting, requirements, demands, and expectations of the lesson. These include such things as:

   1. Talking distinctly and slowly
   2. Allowing for increased response time
   3. Arranging special seating
   4. Placing fewer problems or questions on a page
   5. Giving alternative directions and having alternative means of assessment
   6. Asking for oral feedback on directions or information
   7. Pointing out what seems obvious, but may not be such to the student(s)
   8. Providing frequent review of material
   9. Reducing paper-and-pencil tasks by incorporating a multimodality means of presenting material
   10. Allowing for experiential learning
   11. Encouraging collaborative peer activities

12. Previewing vocabulary words
13. Encouraging computer use for written assignments
14. Using graphic organizers with design
15. Taking the time of day into consideration when presenting new material
16. Allowing for self-correction and review of material presented
17. Providing positive feedback and reinforcement
18. Using rubrics that address several components of a lesson, such as grammar, spelling, paragraphing, design, and overall content
19. Extending time for tests and assignments
20. Allowing for classroom mobility, as opposed to being continually stationary
21. Being flexible and open-minded with respect to offering encouragement and motivational strategies (these listed adaptations and those in the following bulleted areas are by Schiering, 2000–2010, and refined by Salend, 2004)

8. Q: What are some categories and characteristics of learning disabilities and accompanying remediation strategies?

A: The following are some specific categories of disabilities that may evidence in a classroom.

- Students with physical and health needs: This category includes those with fractures, burns, a congenital disorder, perhaps limited strength and/or vitality, asthma, heart conditions, Tourette's syndrome, diabetes, and/or autism. When providing an adaptation for students with one of these physical or health needs, first, it's important to establish communication with family and medical providers.

  Also, be aware of the educational rights of students with special healthcare needs. Specific adaptations would include providing more time on task, allowing extra time for verbal responses, providing two copies of books so one may be used at school and one at home, and easy

LD Categs

access to classroom supplies. Overall, it's vital to be patient and offer praise to enhance self-esteem.

Other considerations for this category include provision for a quiet location to take tests, using alternative means of evaluation, and having a structured environment where assignments are listed in sequential order and given in advance of the lesson. Graphic organizers may provide this, with experiential learning being the mainstay, and with emphasis placed on key concepts. Students frequently respond to small-group activities with prompts. Also, you would want to have workstations or learning centers for specific assignments.

- Attention deficit disorder (ADD) or attention deficit hyperactivity disorder: Students with these types of disabilities have difficulty focusing, while being easily distracted and seemingly disorganized. Since they're known to daydream or be forgetful, while some are gifted in specific areas, it's good to have clear and concise step-by-step written and verbal directions for assignments. Vary the types of learning activities while minimizing schedule changes and limiting distraction. Examples of what's to be done should be provided in a list or with graphic organizers.

  Motivation is a key factor with these learners, as they require a stimulus. A multiperceptual preference approach is good, with auditory, visual, tactile, and kinesthetic accommodations being provided simultaneously. Assistance with organizing would be beneficial for ADD and ADHD students and ample feedback assists in affirmation of their work efforts. You would want to monitor their performance while on task, as they tend to easily go off task. Lastly, incorporate alternative means of assessment such as them making interactive instructional resources to demonstrate their acquisition of various disciplines' content.

- Perceptual motor disabilities: The students in this category might experience problems with recognizing;

discriminating, such as copying from the blackboard; and/or adhering to multiple-step directions. Sometimes poor balance is evident along with an inability to use fine motor skills, such as in drawing, cutting, pasting, and holding writing instruments.

Remediation would include practice in doing these aforementioned fine motor skills to build self-confidence and develop their abilities in these areas. Providing varied ways to do an assignment would be beneficial, with emphasis on perceptual strengths, moving to practice in weaker areas. Being supportive of their endeavors is very important, with provisions made for their having practice exercises, and demonstrate what's to be done in a concise manner. Teach using the facilitator role.

Emotional, behavioral, and social-emotional behavioral disorders: Students in this area may be those who are schizophrenic or have oppositional and defiant behaviors. They may resist requests of authority figures, are nonconforming, manipulative, vindictive, and/or demonstrate obsessive-compulsive behavior or anxiety. They may demonstrate irrationality along with an inability to get along with others in the classroom. As the teacher you want to avoid situations that trigger any of these areas.

Adaptations for these students would be to provide choices, as opposed to limiting the way something is done to strict conforming instructions. Offer support to this type of student by acknowledging the problem in an empathetic manner with sensitivity to the student's unique learning needs.

Other considerations include working with the family and professionals who have situational expertise and encouraging participation with roles for the classroom and consequences for following and not following these. You would want to emphasize acceptable behaviors by continually addressing components of character development with definitions and modeling of respect, responsibility, kindness, fairness, caring, and good citizenship.

When adhering to these, provide opportunities to exhibit collaboration and communication through role-playing that depicts these character traits.

Expressive language disorders: Students with this learning difficulty have trouble with responding orally in a classroom. They may demonstrate reluctance to participate in verbal activities and have speech problems including articulation, voice modification, and/or fluency in speech. Oftentimes, there are word substitutions or omissions with distortions and additions when presenting orally. For the teacher, it's most important to respond to what the student says rather than how it's configured.

It's good to maintain eye contact and pause before responding, staying calm. Criticism, hurrying the student, or correcting speech or forcing him/her to speak in front of others should be avoided. Do not call on the student to read something on the spur of the moment, but rather provide the student with ample in-school or at-home practice time for an in-class oral reading or presentation. In other words, tell the student which passage he/she will be called upon to read several days in advance of the oral reading. This prepares the student for being successful.

Oftentimes, having a unison speech presentation works for this student. Do this in conjunction with establishment of a learning environment that promotes positive thinking regarding how to respond to classmates who have expressive language difficulties. You will want to serve as a good speech model by using a slow and relaxed speech rate, pausing at appropriate times when speaking, and using simplified language and grammatical structures. Hands-on activities, as presented in chapter 11, are a plus. One final consideration is to place students in groups instead of row seating while using applied comprehension strategies.

APPENDIX B

This appendix is designed to bring you, the reader, some exposure to different means for developing students' cognitive and metacognitive skills. This is accomplished at the outset by listing activities and corresponding cognitive and metacognitive skills for potential development when using and/or creating these activities. Several interactive instructional resources and the Decision-Making Organizer Poster Board are given attention with regard to information and uses, materials needed to create these, and construction directions.

Next, team learning and circle of knowledge activity definitions and examples are provided. These have been selected due to involving the whole class at all grade levels. These activities are ones that oftentimes unify the classroom setting by being fun, developing creative and critical thinking, and recognizing student engagement in positive attitudes toward learning.

The art of storytelling is addressed, as we consider storytelling to be a mainstay in a classroom for building a sense of community. It also encourages social literacy, providing one with awareness of common social and societal norms, realizing beliefs and values through stories shared and fostering a sense of camaraderie for the students and teacher alike.

First, an overview of storytelling is provided with a historical component. Then, one teacher candidate's story is presented, along with questions to extend the story topic to encompass literal, applied, and implied comprehension, and making connection to today's empirical experiences.

Finally, a Reciprocal Thinking Identification Chart is provided to realize the cognitive and metacognitive skills given attention in the story.

Topic I: A List of Instructional Resources with Potential Cognitive and Metacognitive Skills They Develop

(Schiering, 2005; Schiering, Buli-Holmberg, and Bogner, 2008)
Story map graphic organizer: classifying, reflecting, analyzing, organizing, comparing and contrasting, prioritizing, sequencing, synthesizing, recalling, reflecting, and self-actualizing

Sequence mapping: organizing, prioritizing, deciding, classifying, comparing and contrasting, generalizing, sequencing, initial deciding, initial problem-solving, analyzing, and self-actualizing.

Who said that—matching characters and quotes: recognizing, realizing, recalling, reflecting, comparing and contrasting, classifying, predicting, communicating, initial and advanced deciding and problem-solving, analyzing, and self-actualizing

Math word problems: realizing, recognizing, recalling, reflecting, prioritizing, initial and advanced deciding with problem-solving, inventing, reflecting, synthesizing, comparing and contrasting, and self-actualizing

Cause and effect: recognizing, classifying, analyzing, critiquing, deciding, initial and advanced deciding with problem-solving, inventing, recalling, realizing, and advanced problem-solving with deciding, analyzing, risk-taking, evaluating, and self-actualizing

Word search: deciding, generalizing, acknowledging, comparing and contrasting, recognizing, generalizing, initial and advanced deciding, organizing, critiquing, sequencing, predicting, analyzing, evaluating, synthesizing, and self-actualizing

Food pyramid: classifying, comparing, organizing, advanced and initial problem-solving, contrasting, generalizing, inventing, and self-actualizing

Role play: classifying, deciding, communicating, active listening, organizing, initial and advanced problem-solving, critiquing, inventing, evaluating, synthesizing, inferring, tolerating, organizing, and self-actualizing

Fill in the blank: inventing, evaluating, synthesizing, organizing, and self-actuating

Team learning: realizing, recognizing, collaborating, communicating, active listening, comparing, inferring, contrasting, predicting, initial and advanced deciding, evaluating, analyzing, problem-solving, self-actualizing

Circle of knowledge: collaborating, communicating, active listening, inventing, predicting, generalizing, initial and advanced deciding and problem-solving, reflecting, tolerating, recalling, critiquing, evaluating, risk-taking, comparing and contrasting, recognizing, and self-actualizing

Self-designed pages: inventing, comparing, risk-taking, inferring, collaborating, and, in many cases, all of the cognitive skills are utilized

Matching and multiple-choice games: problem-solving, deciding, inferring, generalizing, organizing, predicting, sequencing, communicating, prioritizing, synthesizing, recalling, reflecting, and self-actualizing

Students creating audiotapes, transparencies, Venn diagrams, and tri-fold boards; programmed learning sequences; and brainstorming activities are involved in most of the cognitive and metacognitive skills from each phase of the reciprocal thinking phases.

Topic 2: Interactive Instructional Resources and Decision-Making Organizer Poster Board; Information and Uses, Materials, and Construction Directions

The directions for these resources of the (1) flip chute, (2) pick-a-dot, (3) wraparound, (4) task cards, (5) electro-board, and (6) floor game have been taken from chapter 14 of *Practical Approaches to Individual Staff Development for Adults* by Schiering and Taylor (1998, pp. 131–42). The decision-making board is a teaching technique used by Schiering since 1976 in her elementary, middle school, and college courses.

Flip Chute: Information and Uses

This is one of the most often used and beneficial self-corrective interactive resources for tactile learners. This particular learning game is designed to assist students in gleaning information by placing a question card in the top slot and receiving an answer in the bottom one, as the card flips over, going through the chute.

The student has control of this device by determining when to let go of the card as the answer is said to oneself as the card goes through the chute. A pile of correct answer cards is made, as well as a pile of incorrect answers, with the latter being revisited until mastery is achieved. This learning device is appropriate for all age/grade levels. College students have been successful in learning foreign language vocabulary, while elementary students have found the flip chute instrumental in learning their times tables.

Suggestions for the flip-chute cards with answers on the flip side include subject-specific vocabulary with definitions; math problems involving addition, subtraction, multiplication, and division, as well as fractions; identifying character quotations, cause and effect, and even fill in the blank for vocabulary or sentence structure, word opposites, or parts of speech. Another idea is to have a picture on the front/top side of the card with the word on the flip side. Or one might have consonant blends on one side, with the "cl" letters in the word *clown* underlined, with a picture of a clown on the flip side of the card.

The flip chute is highly versatile and provides for a fun way to learn new material or review previously studied topics. Many flip chutes are made from half-gallon empty milk or juice cardboard containers, but other sizes of boxes are easily adapted to this learning device with a few changes in chute opening measurements and chute width and height being adaptable to size of the box selected. (In chapter 11, figure 11.3 is an illustration of the flip chute.)

Materials for Flip Chute and Flip-Chute Card Construction

half-gallon milk or juice container
two 5" by 8" index cards
1"-wide masking tape
ten 2" by 2½" cut index cards
razor cutter, X-acto knife, and/or box cutter
scissors and 12" ruler
contact paper and thematic stickers for container decoration

Directions for Flip Chute and Flip-Chute Card Construction

1. Pull open the top of the milk or juice container.
2. Cut the side fold of the top portion down to the top of the container;
3. On the front face, measure down from the top 1½" and then 2½" and draw a horizontal line that is ¼" in from each side.
4. Cut out that opening with the box cutter (razor knife or X-acto knife), and repeat the same procedure at the bottom of the container.
5. Using your 5" by 8" index cards measure one 6½" long by 3½" wide, and using the other card, measure 7½" long by 3½" wide, then cut out these pieces.
6. Score the longer card ½" up from the bottom and the shorter card ½" up from the bottom and ½" down from the top.
7. Insert the smaller strip into the lower opening and attach it with masking tape to the upper part of the lower opening and lower part of the upper opening. It should form the letter "c" backward, if one is looking at it from the side.
8. Insert the longer strip with the scored part going over the lower part of the bottom opening and tape it. The upper portion of the strip is taped to the back of the container. At this point, you now have the chutes in place.
9. Using one of the 2" by ½" cutouts, put a notch in the upper right corner and write on the card a math equation, such as 2 × 2 =. Now turn the card upside down so the notch appears in the lower right corner, and write the answer to the equation.
10. Place the flip-chute card into the upper slot of the flip chute. This is done by having the equation showing with the notch in the upper right corner of the card. The card will flip over once it's placed into the upper opening/chute, and the answer to the equation will appear in the bottom slot of the flip

chute. Make as many cards as you choose and have students make these in any discipline. With each student having his or her own set of cards and flip chute, he or she may exchange cards with a classmate to learn new material or review previously presented topics. Laminating the flip-chute cards is recommended, as they'll last longer than those not laminated.

Pick-a-Dot: Information and Uses

This is a multiple-choice type of interactive self-corrective learning tool. The same types of uses as were mentioned for the flip chute apply to this interactive resource. However, the main difference is there being the concept of three possible answers and students having to make a choice regarding the correct one. This activity may be used for any discipline. Laminating the pick-a-dot cards is recommended. (In chapter 11, figure 11.4 provides an illustration of the pick-a-dot.)

Materials for the Pick-a-Dot

one two-pocket folder
fifteen 5" by 8" index cards
a one-hole hole puncher
masking tape
12" ruler
scissors

Pick-a-Dot Holder and Pick-a-Dot Card Construction Directions

1. Using a two-pocket folder, cut this in half vertically down the center.

2. Choose one half of the folder and place the other half off to the side.

3. Addressing the pocket, use your ruler to measure and mark ½" in from each side and 2½" down from top of the pocket. Cut out this U-shaped section (see illustration for visuals of areas to be cut out).

4. From the bottom of the pocket measure upward and mark 1" and 2½" in from each side. Cut out this rectangle.
5. On the bottom strip of the pocket, punch one hole on the left, middle, and right sides.
6. Place one 5" by 8" index card in the pocket. Trace the top opening outline, and each of the hole-punch circles. Remove the index card from the pocket and punch the holes out. But for where you will place the correct answer, punch the hole out all the way to the bottom of the card. (This is the pick-a-dot holder.)
7. Place the index card back in the folder. In the outlined open space at the top, write a question. Example: The boy had four apples and bought two more for one dollar. How much did he spend on apples in all?
8. Just above the hole-punch areas write three answers. Example: $3.50, $4.00, $3.00.
9. Insert the golf tee and/or pen point into the hole that has the correct answer and pull the top of the card. If it easily slides out, then the correct answer has been selected.
10. Make as many pick-a-dot cards as you choose and have students make these in any discipline. With each student having his or her own pick-a-dot holder and cards he or she may switch cards with a classmate to learn new material or review previously presented topics.
11. Fold the top of the pocket folder down over the pick-a-dot and secure it with a Velcro tab to hold the pick-a-dot cards in place and form a completed pick-a-dot holder for these.

Wraparound: Information and Uses

This tactile/kinesthetic self-corrective device is a matching game with questions on the left side of a paper and answers on the right side. However, answers are not placed directly across from the questions or statements. The size of the paper may vary. This interactive resource may be used for vocabulary with definitions, syllabification, and aligning characters with their personality traits or an event in a story. It might also be used for sequencing events.

Other uses for this interactive instructional resource include identifying parts of speech, noun-verb agreement, singular and plural verb forms, math equations and answers, word problems involving multiple computation skills, word opposites, colloquiums, different language/English vocabulary words, and the ideas mentioned for the preceding interactive resource. Laminating the wraparound allows for years of use, making this more durable. (In chapter 11, figure 11.5 provides an illustration of this interactive instructional.)

Materials for the Wraparound

one piece of card stock paper (8½" by 11")
scissors
12" ruler
yarn, string, or ribbon contrasting with the paper color
Magic Marker

Wraparound Construction Directions

1. Using the 12" ruler, create a 1" margin around the card stock paper.
2. Place a topic title on the top margin, such as "English/Spanish Wraparound."
3. Select the vocabulary or other criteria for the left-hand side and make a notch on the outside edge next to this word.
4. Select the vocabulary word definition, or the same word in another language, or other criteria, for the right-side "answer." Be sure the match is not directly across from the word or what you have on the left side.
5. Notch the card stock paper on the outside edge of the right side.
6. Placing a hole at the top center of the card stock paper, string a 3½' piece of yarn through this and knot at one end.

7. Swing the yarn in back of the board and into the first notch.
8. Put the yarn into the notch on the right side that provides the answer/match for the first notch on the left side. Swing the yarn around back and go to the second notch on the left side, repeating the process.
9. When finished, trace on the back of the card stock where the yarn appears. Use a marker or pen to do this. Now undo the wrap.
10. The students wrap the yarn beginning with the first left notch to the correct answer on the right side until the wraparound is completely wrapped. This is a self-corrective activity because the student turns the wraparound over and checks to see if the marked lines match where the yarn is located.

Task Card Information and Uses

This puzzle-piece self-corrective game calls for a shape match only, as the print on the cards, as well as the color of the cards, is the same. These either form a rectangle or some geometric shape, or a configuration representing the theme of the topic being addressed. The reason for the shape match only is to direct the student to rely not on print format or font, nor color of the cards, but rather completing the puzzle shape.

The identification of information with the left side having a partial statement and the right side having the completion of this is realized when the puzzle pieces are put together. Or one side of the card may have a picture and words to identify it on the matching side. And yet another idea is to have a math problem on one side and the answer on the other part.

Also, task cards need not be put in a left-right pattern shape match, but top-bottom, if desired. Furthermore, the task cards may form a time line if there is a three-way match, with the top portion having an illustration of an event and the bottom two pieces shape matching the date and event. If more detailed explanation is desired, then one might have this three-way shape match with the top piece being the event, the bottom left being the date, and the bottom right shape being the description of the event.

Task cards may be laminated before the cut is made. Lamination allows for use of this game over an extended length of time. (In chapter 11, figure 11.6 provides an illustration of two-sided task cards.)

Task Card Materials

one half of a two-pocket folder
a package of 5" by 8" blank index cards, or color card stock paper 5" by 8" size
scissors (regular or pinking scissors shapes)

Task Card Holder and Task Card Construction Directions

1. The task card holder uses one half of a two-pocket folder. The task cards are placed in the folder in nonmatching style. The top of the folder is folded down to cover the pocket and decorated with the topic of the cards represented. An example would be a task card holder having different colored geometric shapes for cards that had geometric shapes on one side and the name of the shapes on the other side.

2. Take ten 5" by 8" index cards and cut them in half using different shapes. Examples may be seen in chapter 11, figure 11.8. Further explanation of this process would include cutting one card straight up the center, the next one would have a diagonal cut, and the remaining ones a combination of these cuts, and/or half-circle shapes.

3. Task cards may also be done in whole shapes that match a theme of the topic being addressed. For example, task cards for vocabulary about the book *Charlotte's Web* might be in the shape of Wilbur, the main character, or the Zuckermans' barn. Then the shape would be cut in half as explained in step 2 above.

4. In random order, place the task cards in the pocket folder and then invite students to take these pieces out and match the cards by shape.

Electro-board Information and Uses

This is a very popular self-corrective tactile and/or kinesthetic interactive instructional resource. It's kinesthetic when it's made poster-board size. One of the most interesting things is that this interactive instructional resource does not have a specified order for the match that's to be created. The connection between the question, such as a vocabulary word and its definition, may be anywhere on the electro-board.

Naming parts of an object, such as a flower, house, car, or animal, may have the part listed on the bottom of the board and a drawing of the object on the top portion. The student uses a light-type continuity tester and places one end on the question and the other on the thought-to-be answer. If the light glows, the correct answer has been selected, and if not, then it's time to try again.

Such things as math problems in word or numerical formats for addition, subtraction, multiplication, division, money equivalents, and/or time of day in digital and analog styles; word jumbles, vocabulary and definitions, or English words matching with objects of foreign-language words of the same object; Spanish (or any other language)/English vocabulary; identification of systems such as respiratory, circulatory, or sequence of events; and life cycle of the butterfly or frog or stages of human development might be topics for the electro-board. Other topics include synonyms, antonyms, figures of speech, character and personality traits, authors and books, land forms and illustrations of these, varied types of ecosystems with descriptors, and types of weather with corresponding names. (In chapter 11, figure 11.7 provides an illustration of the electro-board.)

Electro-board Materials

poster board
colored markers
aluminum foil
hole punch
¾" masking tape
continuity tester
scissors

Electro-board Construction Directions

1. Begin with two pieces of poster board of exactly the same size and shape.
2. Section the left side of the electro-board to correspond to the number of questions you will be asking. Section the right side similarly for the answers.
3. Using the hole punch, make one hole at the point where each question will appear on the left side of the poster board, or randomly. Corresponding holes should be placed where the answers will appear.
4. Print the questions and answers on the poster board next to the punched holes. (If you desire, a brass fastener may be placed in the punched holes, with the wings on the reverse side opened fully.) Answers should not be directly across from the questions.
5. Turn the poster board over. Place a ¼"-wide strip of aluminum foil in a line, connecting a question with the correct answer. The foil should begin at the hole for the question and end at the hole for the answer. Cover the foil strip with ¾" masking tape so that there is no foil (brass fastener) exposed.
6. Using a light-style continuity tester, purchased in a hardware or automotive store, check the circuit by touching the aluminum foil hole and/or the brass fastener with the clip and the pointed end of the continuity tester on the question and then the thought-to-be answer on the electro-board.

Floor Game Information and Uses

This interactive resource is used primarily for kinesthetic involvement. However, tactile, visual, and auditory modalities are also addressed. This interactive instructional resource usually requires two to six players. A shower-curtain liner or plastic tablecloth is customarily used for creating this interactive resource. Drawing on one of these with a permanent magic marker is used to create a picture of an object or general shape(s).

Question/answer cards using heavy paper or index cards are used, having questions on the front and answers on the back. One person is designated to ask the questions and ascertain if the responder was correct. A correct answer provides movement from one place to another on the floor game.

The students would best be advised to remove their shoes to protect the floor game during multiple uses. Interestingly, the floor game may be designed to represent a sequence of events, time line, character similarities, and differences from a story in Venn diagram style; parts of speech identification columns with the question cards having words representing these; identification of parts of animals and/or plants; food chain; varied types of life cycles; matching game; cause and effect; or who said that, to name a few.

Basically, a question is asked which is read from a question card. Then a correct answer allows the student to move to a particular space on the floor. An incorrect answer means remaining in the same place as another game participant tries his/her luck/knowledge. Question/answer cards may be laminated for extended durability. (In chapter 11, figure 11.8 provides an illustration of the floor game.)

Floor Game Materials

shower-curtain liner
package of different color markers
twenty 5" by 8" index cards for questions and answers

Floor Game Construction Directions

1. Place a shower-curtain liner on the floor. The liner should be of a solid light color.
2. Design the liner to match the topic of the game. For example, see chapter 11, figure 11.8. Another example might be to create three columns headed, respectively, nouns, verbs, adjectives. Then, have a pile of 5" by 8" index cards with an example of either a noun, verb, or adjective on one side, and the part of speech on the other side. The student(s) select(s) a card, places it in the correct column, and checks to see if this is correct by turning the card over.

   There are many ways to design a floor game, and another idea is to have photographs of story characters attached with

Velcro to the liner. These would be from a selected piece of literature. Then, have a bubble shape or circle shape where a quotation could be placed leading from the character's head. The student is read a question card that has a quotation from a particular character. The student goes to the bubble and puts the quote in the bubble to relate who said that.

3. The first person to answer all the questions correctly is the winner of the game. A player may move from one place to another on the floor game, or place identifying objects in appropriate spaces on the game board, or identify parts of an object by standing on that space.

Decision-Making Organizer Poster Board

The Decision-Making Organizer Poster Board was first used by Schiering in the mid-to-late 1970s at the fifth- and then sixth-grade levels in the North Rockland Central School District in Stony Point, New York. Since the year 2000, it has been used in EDU 506A at Molloy College. This has been one of the assignments for teacher candidates' later student learner instruction and implementation in the K–6 classroom. However, many teacher candidates have commented on how this decision-making process has assisted them in the problem-solving process long after the course assignment has been completed.

Decision-Making Poster Board Information and Uses

This activity is a large graphic organizer and allows for individuals at any age to apply the reciprocity of thinking in the process of decision-making. This primarily phase two and three cognitive/metacognitive skill activity, with initial and advanced types, provides students the opportunity to first learn how to make a decision and then experience it unconsciously as it becomes part of their daily experience. Originally used during the 1970s in Schiering's elementary and then middle school classrooms, it later became a mainstay in many teachers' high school English and social studies classes and some Molloy College Division of Education courses.

Sharing these boards in a classroom setting provides for social literacy with awareness of the problems that cause one concern. Also, means for comprehension of possible ways to solve problems, should they arise, in another person's experience now or in the future allows for academic and social cognition on a variety of topics.

The first step regards recognizing a problem exists that requires a decision to be made for a solution to the problem. Next is awareness that there are more than two solutions to the problem. Then, there's the realization of the decision-making process taking in all of the cognitive and metacognitive skills on the Reciprocal Thinking Phases Chart, as well as more thoughts, ideas, opinions, judgments, and feelings on the topic being evidenced.

As explained in the decision-making section of chapter 11, individuals are used to realizing/imagining only two possible choices for a solution to a decision. Subsequently, when teaching the process of the decision-making graphic organizer, it is suggested that students confer in a collaborative fashion with classmates and/or adults to receive suggestions beyond these two possible choices.

This also applies to the sections under each choice where there are three possible negative and three possible positive outcomes for each projected choice. The final decision will take these into consideration, with the user weighing the positives and negatives in personal reflection before stating the final decision and why this one was selected. (In chapter 11, figure 11.1 provides an illustration of this activity.)

Decision-Making Organizer Materials

- poster board measuring approximately 3½' high and 2½' across (this may be smaller or larger as desired)
- color construction paper
- various color markers
- stickers or other forms of decoration (these are for the purpose of connecting the board's topic in an illustrative fashion to the theme of the board)

Decision-Making Poster Board Organizer Construction

1. At the top center of the board, place a rectangle, and in the left corner the word *Problem.* Then, using a large font or neat large hand-printing state the problem with some detail sentences.

2. Border this section so there is a color contrast with the color of the board.
3. Under the "Problem" section have three boxes horizontally placed next to one another and labeled "Choice #1," "Choice #2," and "Choice #3." There may be more choices, but a minimum of three are required.
4. Under each "Choice" section, make two bordered boxes, again for color contrast. One box is under the other. In the top box place the words *Possible Negative Outcomes.* In the other one write *Possible Positive Outcomes.*
5. Then, in these boxes, in large font or large hand print, first list a minimum of three possibilities of negative outcomes for "Choice #1," and then a minimum of three possible positives that may result from this "Choice #1" idea.
6. At the bottom of the poster board place a rectangle and write in the far left corner *Final Decision and Why.* Using large font or large neat hand-printing, state the final decision and why this has been made, in your opinion.
7. Decorate the board so it connects with the theme or provides a good color contrast with the background color of the poster board. Connect each choice area with the possible outcomes beneath it with a thick line. You may choose to draw an additional line from the appropriate choice section to the final decision section. Or you may leave it blank and have those reading it take a guess as to which choice was selected and then read the final decision to ascertain if their decision was correct.

Topic 3: Definition and Example of Team Learning and Circle of Knowledge

Team Learning Activity

This is a small-group activity where students read a selected passage and then answer questions about this passage. The questions are designed to address all three types of comprehension (literal, applied, and implied).

An additional component is added with directions for students to create a poem, interactive resource, drawing, role play, or inventive means of conveying the synthesized information from the read paragraphs of the selected passage.

Example: Team Learning—Benjamin Franklin

Directions: Record the names of your group members above the passage to be read. Then read the paragraphs about Benjamin Franklin orally in your group. One person may read or you may take turns reading the information. Underline or mark in some fashion the areas you think are most important, as the reading occurs.

When the reading is complete, answer the questions presented. Do this in a collaborative manner. Be sure everyone in the group agrees that the answers are correct. Then the last portion of this team learning is to work together to create something that presents the information from the paragraphs, or a portion of that, in a manner that represents your group's interest. We will go over the answer to questions in a whole-class format and then each group will present their "creative" portion of the team learning.

Source for team learning—Benjamin Franklin: This individual was known to be an inventor, scientist, and leader. The team learning exercise was created for this book by Schiering with synthesized material from Time Magazine, *Benjamin Franklin: An Illustrated History of His Life and Times*, 2010.

Names of Team Learning Members:______________________________

A Story about Benjamin Franklin

Benjamin Franklin was a founding father of the United States. He was a scientist and inventor and his accomplishments made him a famous American of his time. He was also a diplomat with achievements as a key figure in an alliance with France and the American victory regarding the Revolutionary War. He was known to be an easygoing person and one who could associate easily with everyone.

Benjamin was born in 1706 in Boston, Massachusetts. He was the fifteenth child born to his father's two successive wives. They all lived in a modest house on Boston's Milk Street until he was six. It was then that the family moved to a larger place in the same town. Ben was an athletic boy and a gifted swimmer at a time when being involved in this sport was unusual. In his memoirs he recalled a time when he was flying his kite by a mill pond when he decided to go swimming. He took the kite in hand and let it pull him around by wind power while he floated all the way across the pond—today we call this activity windsailing.

Ben had little formal schooling but was in the famed Boston Latin School for a year and then received tutoring in arithmetic and writing. His formal education was over by the time he was ten years of age. Nonetheless, he had a thirst for knowledge, was curious, and definitely had intellectual gifts. Additionally, he was continually reading books and scripture, and he had a love for learning. He was exposed to all sorts of reading material as he was apprenticed to his brother James's printing business when he was twelve. Ben began writing poetry and was permitted to publish his own work.

Five years into the apprenticeship Ben moved to Philadelphia to serve as a printer's assistant. In 1732 he published the first edition of *Poor Richard's Almanac* and five years after that he was appointed the Philadelphia postmaster. Benjamin Franklin's contributions to the colonies include his becoming postmaster of them some thirty-five years following his apprenticeship to his brother.

Some major accomplishments of Benjamin Franklin include flying a kite with his son William in 1752 and this experiment linking lighting to electricity; proposal of a plan to join the colonies together when in 1754 the French and Indian War began; inventing the glass harmonica, a musical instrument, in 1762; being elected to the Second Continental Congress in 1775 and proposing the first Articles of Confederation; helping to draft the Declaration of Independence in 1776; signing treaties of alliance, amity, and commerce with France in 1778; and in 1782, with John Adams and John Jay, negotiating a peace treaty with Britain.

Franklin died in 1790 at the age of eighty-four and in his lifetime witnessed the first manned balloon flight and was instrumental in the establishment of the great compromise with the creation of a United States House of Representatives and Senate. For a man from humble beginnings, he contributed widely to the ideas held by our present government with freedom and representation of the people in a democracy.

Questions for Team Learning: Benjamin Franklin

1. In what year and century was Ben Franklin born?
2. What do you suppose is meant by the term *founding father* of the United States, and what events established Ben as such?
3. What type of person was Ben Franklin?
4. In what year did Benjamin Franklin become an apprentice to his brother James, and what was this apprenticeship?
5. How did being an apprentice to James Franklin help Benjamin with respect to reading and writing?
6. What were two interests of Ben's during his childhood?
7. Benjamin Franklin went to work when he was twelve years of age. How do you think you'd feel about doing that today? (Your answers may vary, but record them all.)
8. What were three major accomplishments during the life of Benjamin Franklin in which he was directly involved?
9. How does the schooling you experience differ from that of Ben Franklin? List five differences at a minimum.
10. This is the creative portion of team learning. Select one of the following to present to the class. You will have approximately forty minutes to complete this portion of the team learning.

    a. Create a poem (acrostic, rhyming, or free verse) that conveys at least five accomplishments of Ben Franklin.
    b. Illustrate five things for which Benjamin Franklin is noted (cartoon, mural, storyboard).
    c. Using the computer, create five slides depicting important events in Ben's life.
    d. Write and present a scripted role play about two important events in the life of Ben Franklin.
    e. Create a comparison chart of Ben's life between ages six and twelve and your own lives during those years. There need to be at least five events mentioned.

f. Create a travel brochure or poster to entice people to visit the newly formed "Benjamin Franklin History Museum." Highlight important events in his life, and feel free to conduct further research about Franklin using the Internet.
g. Create a song with a minimum of five stanzas about the accomplishments of Ben Franklin.

Circle of Knowledge

This is a small-group activity with three to four groups competing in a timed-response situation (see example below). The scoring of correct answers is recorded on chart paper or a board. Each group provides answers to a basic question and receives one point for each correct answer. However, if one group provides an answer that another group has on its list, but has not given, then that answer may not be repeated.

If a group is concerned that an incorrect response has been given, this group may challenge that answer. If the group cannot provide substantial verification for their answer, then the point is given to the challenging group. If they can provide the information, then that group receives the point without penalty to the challenging group. The group with the most points is declared the winner of the Circle of Knowledge activity.

Example: In one minute, make a list of all the words you can think of that relate to ecosystems.

Possible responses: Environments, ecosystems, succession, climax stage, forests, inanimate objects, living objects, plants, animals, mammals, predator, prey, plains, niche, habitat, and so forth.

Topic 4: The Art of Storytelling

An Overview of Storytelling (Schiering, Hayes, and Marino, 2005)

Storytelling is the communication of a happening or connected series of happenings, whether true or fictitious, an accounting or narration, an anecdote, a tale, a report, or a rumor, which is historically based, personal, and sometimes biographical. Its presentation may be loosely organized or structured, but complies with the concept of a giving of information that serves to entertain and/or motivate the listener and add insight, through introspection, to the storyteller. Storytelling creates a compelling social literacy component in a classroom by bringing students together as they realize the effect of life events on each individual. Pellowski (1977, pp. 9–15) defines storytelling as "the art or craft or narration of stories in verse and/or prose, as performed or led by one person before a live audience: the stories narrated may be spoken, chanted or sung with or without musical, pictorial, and/or other accompaniment, and may be learned from oral, printed, or mechanically recorded sources; one of its purposes must be that of entertainment."

Price (1978, p. 13) relates that "little is known of the origins of storytelling, however 'tales' and the art of storytelling predates the 'written' records found scratched on bones and stones in regions of Africa, caves in France and other parts of Europe. In fact, some paleoanthropologists believe our oldest known samples of this 'written' record may well be thirty-five thousand years old." Since Homo erectus lived one million years ago, storytelling predates the written word by almost nine hundred thousand years.

The purpose of telling a story, aside from playful entertainment, includes the following: "Man's *need* for entertainment, attempts to explain the physical and metaphysical world around them: to spread and enforce common beliefs, fulfilling the need for communication between humans including their aesthetic need for beauty and form, passing on the mores and enculturation of the society; encouraging family solidarity, and preserving history; through narrations that chronicle events" (Pellowski, 1977, p. 19).

Lynch-Brown and Tomlinson (2005, p. 255) and Toale (1985/2005), in courses taught at the high school level in the Brooklyn Diocese and at Molloy College, related that stories provoke curiosity and compelling repetition; unite us in a holistic way to nature; bridge one's culture and one's roots and promote memory; bind us to the universal family; and provide escape, as well as a basis for hope, morality, and healing.

Marino mentioned storytelling being utilized as an icebreaker, establishing empathy in a team environment, introducing class participants and stimulating conversation, and assisting in early decision-making activities. And Schiering relates that storytelling stimulates memory acquisition depending on the relevance of the story to individuals' belief systems and/or connection to the topic being presented.

Schiering explains that "the beauty of storytelling is that anyone can tell a story, whether it is fiction, fantasy, or a real-life experience relating to a specific topic. Some people require more practice at perfecting the art but others are naturally born to it. It does not really matter to the listener. Listening to a voice that can excite, calm, make us laugh, cry, or ponder something is a wonderful thing" (Schiering, Hayes, and Marino, 2005, p. 5).

Hayes (Schiering, Hayes, and Marino, 2005) adds to the above: "Companion animals enjoy hearing the sound of their owner's voice. Their reactions are similar to humans" (Hayes, 2000, p. 10). In short, storytelling provides a means for information conveyance that stimulates the learner and provides for knowledge acquisition, as well as learning about *who* one is in relation to the characters being discussed, by noting personal similarities and differences, and analyzing these for present "in" action or later "on" action reflection.

Storytelling also serves a purpose in implementing an experientialist teaching philosophy. This is with comprehension regarding the necessity of students and teachers actually being actively engaged in the learning experience. Sharing one's learning process is important for ascertaining *who* one is as a learner.

In so doing a comfort zone for learning and teaching cross-culturally and interdisciplinarily serves as the mainstay. Classroom comfort zones may be created through practical applications of objectives that attune to life experiences having an international commonality. These serve as vehicles for students coming together to know their capabilities and build self-esteem for self-efficacy.

Feeling comfortable in the learning environment allows progressive and positive learning to occur, because first a learner needs to feel at ease and relaxed to be an active recipient for gaining knowledge. In some respect, as the educational gaming and storytelling teaching method is practiced, knowledge acquisition is achieved through osmosis.

The mind does not necessarily have an overt awareness of learning being the main objective, but a subliminal one just beneath conscious thought. School comes to be viewed as a place where the classroom is metacognitively charged, with an exchange of daily living experiences that connect to the past through lessons presented in order to bring one to the present.

Storytelling may be viewed as a *connective* tool for the organization of curriculum within any classroom setting, regardless of the age level of the learners or teachers. The authors relate that when an individual listens to or shares a story the result is most often a gaining of information that may then be shared with others.

If the story is humorous, the chances of repeating and/or retaining it appear to be greater than if the story is a recitation of facts. Nonetheless, storytelling, as opposed to a lecture, provides a connective means for information transference along with serving to provide interest, whether the topic is in reference to a character in history, or a fictionalized piece that provides relevancy to current events and circumstances.

Utilizing this information from storytelling regarding learning, Blank (1997) reported that this leads to "knowledge acquisition," which is constructed when students restructure or replace existing conceptions. Students revealing and reflecting upon the status of their conceptions, how they know what they know, is the demonstration of comprehension of what they've learned. This includes "generalizations, facts, terms, dates, and names" (Glatthorn, 1995).

Storytelling causes listeners to think, have ideas, and form opinions through "feelings" that correspond to what is being related. "The reaction or thought-process-reciprocity, resulting from telling a story then serves as the motivational component and subsequently fosters learning, which leads to knowledge" (Schiering, Hayes, and Marino, 2005, p. 2; Hayes, 2005, p. 12).

Directions for a Storytelling Assignment (Schiering, 2000–2010)

The following is an explanation of the steps to be taken for storytelling, the Reciprocal Thinking Phases Identification Chart for developing cognitive and metacognitive awareness, and application of knowing what one is thinking (Schiering, 2000–2010).

Step 1: Before telling the story, the storyteller:

a. Writes a narrative of the story for a several-weeks-later oral presentation to the class.

b. Fills in a Reciprocal Thinking Phases Identification Chart to address which specific cognitive skills are being applied in the story.

c. Creates convergent and divergent questions for cognitive/meta-cognitive skill development and literal, applied, and implied comprehension, which may be later added to by the whole class. These questions should involve deductive and inductive reasoning.

Step 2: The story is told, but not read, in the classroom setting. Feelings are expressed through the use of facial expressions, gesturing, and words that connote the emotions involved regarding the scope and sequence of story events. The printed story is distributed to the class for review. Additionally, a Reciprocal Thinking Phases Identification Chart, which the storyteller has filled in, is given to classmates for review and collaboration on cognitive skill applications.

Step 3: During the telling of the story, there's audience awareness through identification of when and how the cognitive skills are being applied to the story events, problem, and solution in the storyteller's opinion and one's own viewpoint.

Step 4: Following the storytelling, in small-group format and using the Reciprocal Thinking Phases Identification Chart filled in and distributed by the storyteller, the audience and storyteller discuss their reflections on these. Comparisons and contrasts of one another's opinions about the thinking skills applied and when and how these were utilized are shared. Convergent and divergent questions to extend and develop comprehension skills are initially addressed at this time and in step 5.

Step 5: Together, as a whole class, there is conversation connoting a consciousness and responsiveness concerning the story topic; realization of story events that may be in or out of sequence, depending on flashbacks; and then reactions to these occurrences with analysis of story information and comparison and contrast to individuals' personal life experiences.

This happens with recognition and discernment of whether the storyteller was and/or the listener is a thoughtful cautionary-type person, a risk-taker, and an analytic or holistic thinker. One's perception becomes the *key* element in deciphering the beginning, during, or following portions of using the thinking phases.

Step 6: Whole-class discussion provides further information regarding step 5. Consensus is reached on the use of the story in relation to the cognitive skills presented. Additions and/or deletions on the Reciprocal Thinking Phases Identification Chart may be done at this time.

Step 7: A tally sheet is provided for polling the class members regarding the information from step 6. A graphic representation is constructed for future reference.

One Teacher Candidate's Story

The following three sections of topic 3, "One Teacher Candidate's Story," "Questions to Extend the Story," and "Reciprocal Thinking Phases Identification Chart," have all been contributed by Molloy College teacher candidate Kathleen Carter (2009).

The Trip to the Land of Pencils

It was 1972 and it was a warm, quiet evening. The familiar sounds of crickets and cicadas filled the air. We sat on the rounded brick steps of the front patio, waiting for the car to come get us. We all agreed not to say a word about anything. It had been a long day of waiting for the answer we so desperately needed to know. It was nearing the end of August and we'd soon have to go back to school. Our family, all eleven children and our parents, had always taken a trip during August, and there was not much time left to find out about this summer.

Suddenly, we heard a car turn the corner. Out from just around the bend was the familiar white, four-door Torino. Our Dad, looking like a giant, emerged from the driver's side door and into the dusky night light. We all ran to him and were greeted with open arms. Together, we walked up the long driveway, anxiously filing into the house one by one, trailing behind him.

As we sat patiently and waited for dinner to be served, we took turns reporting on the day's activities. Some of us went to the pool, while others mowed the lawn or rode our bikes or skateboards with friends. No one would dare give an answer of having been bored unless you wanted to have more chores added under your name on the job list that hung on the wall next to the telephone.

After dinner, we enjoyed the most delicious dessert in the world, Grandma's ice box cake. My Grandma lived with us and she was like a second mother to us all. Actually, it was like living with both saint and angel. She cooked, cleaned, sewed, drove, cared for, listened to, and inspired us. It was a surprise to have been served her famous ice box cake that evening, because it was usually made to celebrate a special occasion. Perhaps we would be told the answer about the trip.

As he smacked his lips, Dad said, "This was the best cake I have ever eaten."

We all sat and stared at him, wondering what would be said next.

"Mmmmmm. I wonder if they serve a cake this good at the Holiday Inn in Pennsylvania?" he said.

No way. He did not just say Pennsylvania, "the land of pencils"?

We jumped right up from the kitchen benches, hugging and high-fiving each other for what seemed to be an eternity! We ran to Dad and hugged him too, thanking him over and over again for being the best dad ever in the whole, wide world.

"We will leave this Friday morning. Everyone must pack one suitcase and bring all of the things you'll need to have fun," he said.

Since we only had three nights left to pack, my three younger siblings and I decided we should get started right away. However, that was a problem because it meant we would have to work our way through the older boys' rooms in order to get to the attic where the suitcases were stored. While they loved us, they did not like us, the four little ones, being up in their rooms. Yet, that night, they were just as excited as we were to go on the trip and had actually invited us to walk through their rooms freely!

Shocked, we approached the attic door and opened it slowly. We were a bit suspicious of the older boys, since they had been so nice to us to and permitted us to pass. We definitely thought they would turn off the lights and lock the door behind us. Much to our surprise, they did not make such an attempt. In a way, it was almost disappointing!

Our attic was large, very hot in the summer and freezing in the winter. This was not an ordinary attic. It was our huge family's treasury of all things past. There you could find everything from books to hand-me-downs, Halloween costumes, boxes of holiday decorations, memory boxes, knickknacks, baby furniture, and more. Unsteadily, we carefully walked around boxes and items that were neatly stacked alongside the walls and walked up a few steps. There, under the shelves in the corner, were the suitcases, just waiting to be taken away for the next great escape.

We decided to pack our very "best" play clothes, those favorites that were somewhat of our "summer uniform." That meant we had to wear our "unfavorites" for the next few days. Those were the clothes that never made it to the top of the pile in the dresser drawers! It was worth wearing old clothes for a few days, because that meant you would look great and cool in the "land of pencils."

We all agreed that we should take our favorite and most important games too. Naturally, Monopoly, checkers and chess, Trouble, and Welcome Back, Kotter topped the list. And despite the fact that we could all swim very well, we felt compelled to bring along our pool safety equipment. Full-size, standard regulation life jackets, swim fins, blow-up beach balls, goggles, masks, nose plugs, and coins for diving made it into bags. All of this for a two-night, three-day stay in the "land of pencils." One never knows when the need will arise for any of these "swim things"! As Mom used to say to us all, "It's always better to be safe than sorry."

Naturally, the next three days passed by at a snail's pace. But finally it was early Friday morning and the Holiday Inn in the "land of pencils" was waiting for our arrival. We each carried our suitcase to the family wagon and watched as Dad and the older boys hoisted up and tied down all of our belongings to the top roof rack, methodically covering our bags with bright, orange tarpaulins. Everyone in the neighborhood knew that we were going on vacation when the tarps came out of the garage. Yes, sir. The world travelers we were, Peggy and Ken (Mom and Dad), three little angels, and eight little men!

The outbound trip always seemed to take so much longer than the trip coming home. All thirteen us of traveled in the one station wagon in an organized seating arrangement. We sat in assigned seats by age. In the front sat Mom, Dad, and the youngest child. Five children sat in the middle seat and five more sat among two seats that faced each other in the rear and on the car "hump." This seat was where it often got very hot.

There were no car seats or seat belt laws in 1972, so we practically sat on top of each other. There was definitely little room to move around, but we didn't care. We were used to living and traveling in close quarters, so there was not much about which to complain.

We would look out the narrow, rear, triangular windows and watch the landscape change as we traveled from Nassau County through Queens and the Bronx to the outlying rural areas. Instead of looking up at tall concrete buildings, we were looking up at the plethora of green, top-heavy pine trees shooting up from the ground like oversized number-two pencils; trunks looking like slender, wooden barrels and tops like erasers.

After passing the trees, we finally saw the large, rectangular, blue sign along the thruway that to us seemed like a personal invitation, which said, "Smile. You're in Pennsylvania." This meant we would finally be free to get out, use a bathroom, and stretch our crunched-up, stiff bodies. Before long, within our limited view we saw the Holiday Inn sign. When we saw that sign, we thought it was what a traveler must have felt when seeing a mirage while crossing the desert. The only difference was this sign was for real. At last, we had arrived in the "land of pencils."

One of the significant elements of this annual adventure was who would be selected to accompany Dad to the lobby desk to register the clan. We had never all gone in to register. Dad told us that he would base his selection upon who had behaved the best while in the car. As we approached the hotel entrance, Dad called out four names: John, Greg, Mary, and Kevin. (I think John was picked just so he could not cause any more trouble in the car!)

The rest of us were instructed to sit close to one another and quietly as we drove through the main registration area. I loathed having to do this. It always stirred controversial arguments like "get off of me" and "stop leaning on me" or "you're in my spot."

My dad always had a well-thought-out plan in his pocket for every occasion. He requested a room in the back of the hotel, on the upper floor, on the same side as and in view of the pool. Although we belonged to the village pool back home, going to this pool was the biggest highlight of our summer vacation because it was private and we felt like we "owned" it.

Dad returned to the car with two keys on large diamond-shaped plastic key tags emblazoned with the same familiar logo we saw on everything that was Holiday Inn. We drove around the building and parked. We listened to the homily outlining the expected weekend behaviors. Prior to arriving at any locale, whether filing into church pews, visiting relatives, or shopping in a store, rules were given like orders and we responded like a small army—missionlike, well behaved, and quietly devious.

We waited as Dad supervised the older boys, who removed the orange tarps and ropes from the top of the wagon and unloaded the suitcases one by one to their rightful owners. Together, we hurriedly walked down hallways and into elevators with our suitcases dragging behind us to the room that would become Grand Central Station for the next three days.

When the door to *our* room was opened, our mouths hung open in utter amazement. Oh, look! The main room had two double beds covered with shiny, flowery bedspreads. The outer bathroom area had double sinks, plastic-covered cups, and a huge mirror. The shower section a rack with perfectly folded, stark white towels. The bathtub was dressed in a thick, magnetic shower curtain and on its edge sat small soaps and tiny shampoo bottles.

In the closet hung an iron, an ironing board, cool wooden hangers, and a free shoeshine bag. The desk drawer contained a Bible, some stationery, and a pen! Why not a pencil? After all, we were in the "land of pencils"! We all thought this room to be a fine example of complete luxury. It must have cost Dad a fortune, because we only have *one* room for *all* of us. We *must* be rich.

In a large family, real estate was always at its prime no matter where you went. Once room inspection was satisfactorily completed, you had to quickly claim a dresser drawer into which you would unpack your favorite clothes. Otherwise, you would have to live the next three days out of your suitcase.

Once we settled in, we were asked to briefly sit down. Again, we received another round of codes of conduct and housekeeping rules before we could venture outside. Dad said, "You shall not yell, scream, argue, or fight while at the pool."

"You shall not run in the hallways."

"You shall not play on the elevator."

"You shall not play knock and run.

"You shall not jump on the beds."

"You shall not leave clothing or wet suits on the floor."

"You shall not take overly long showers."

Interestingly, shortly after, this request followed: "You shall, however, discreetly 'borrow' from any maid's cart any extra soaps, towels, cups, and garbage bags and bring them back to our room!"

Finally, we put on our suits, grabbed all the necessary pool safety devices we had packed, and headed down to the pool. Mom put my oldest sister Peggy Anne in charge of us and we were all assigned a buddy. In small groups, we walked down the hall and into the elevator, very quietly, until we all arrived at the pool. It was at that moment that the family registered with four children nearly tripled in size! Amazing! Year after year, the hotel manager never said a word. I imagine it was because we were so very well behaved.

Upon returning from the trip to the local supermarket for food, drinks, snacks, and necessities, my parents joined us all at the pool. It was then I knew I was definitely on vacation. It was a bonus to hold the attention of both parents simultaneously as we perfected dives, performed tricks, or held swim contests. They even came in to swim with us!

Mom and Dad were always working. Dad worked in the city and had a private law practice at home, for which Mom was his trusty secretary. They worked long days and nights together. The visit to the "land of pencils" was really more for us than it was for them, as Mom packed her Smith-Corona electric typewriter and Dad his briefcase, so they could steal a few hours of work here and there, even at the poolside under an umbrella. They were self-sacrificing and hardworking parents. We respected and fully appreciated anything we did together, especially the trip to the "land of pencils."

As the lifeguard blew her whistle at 6:00 p.m. sharp, we collected and packed up our belongings and walked back to our room, looking for a random maid cart along the way from which to "borrow" some necessary items. We were hungry, but never too tired to continue having fun throughout the evening.

One may wonder how a family of our size could eat out while on vacation. "It must cost you a fortune!" people would comment. Well, let's just say our meals were always served "family style."

No matter where we were, my parents were very resourceful and always found practical ways to solve problems both big and small. Prior to dinner, the two lovely queen-size beds were transformed at once into two tables for six. The orange tarps that had once covered our suitcases atop the car became tablecloths, protecting the slippery and shiny bedspreads covering the beds.

We "set" the tables with paper plates, plastic cutlery, and cups as Mom and Dad worked side by side in the "kitchen." No, this was not an efficiency kitchen. The double sink served as a counter where Mom's pots, filled with water, sat on the Coleman stove, cooking Banquet boil-in-a-bag meals and fresh corn on the cob. Hot, tasty food was served plate by plate to the eleven guests kneeling around the beds anxiously waiting to eat. We were actually permitted to watch the television as we ate our meal, making us feel like we were in a five-star, luxury hotel.

After dinner, we were instructed to crawl on hands and knees to pick up crumbs and fuzz from the carpet. The boys took out the day's garbage to the Dumpster in the parking lot. No maid was ever going to get past the "Do Not Disturb" sign that hung on the door all weekend long. Once we completed our chores, we were permitted to walk around the hotel together in small groups. Perhaps we would find an adventure or two or visit the game room.

Once we returned to our room, the boys usually made a joint run down the hall to fill the ice bucket at the ice machine for the sodas we would come to enjoy later. Since we were on vacation, we were allowed to stay up beyond our normal bedtimes and watch TV in bed, play board games, and eat *real* Hostess cupcakes and Oreos.

The bedtime routine was another fine example of quick-witted planning. In addition to the cot (which our oldest sister always had reserved for herself), our room comfortably accommodated thirteen sleeping people. The two big queen-size beds that had once been tables, for fine dining earlier, were now converted into four deluxe beds. By simply separating mattresses from box springs, each makeshift bed slept four, three, three, and two.

This sleeping arrangement resulted in overall greater tolerance and understanding of each other as we slept side by side, putting up with unusual sleeping behaviors and fighting for covers and shared resting space. By and large, we all enjoyed the feelings of security, peace and togetherness as they abundantly filled the once unoccupied room at the Holiday Inn.

One by one, we drifted off to sleep with the sounds of our luxury vacation room all around us. As I lay, I listened to the television flickering as it aired late-night programming I had never before heard. The air conditioning unit rattled, blowing the heavy drapes up into a gentle wave as it circulated cool air throughout the room. The "trip to the land of pencils" resulted in more than just a family vacation. That which was normal and ordinary became incredible and extraordinary. The "land of pencils" unified those who were often divided because of busy schedules and activities. We were one, big, remarkable family.

Questions for Extending the Story

Extending the Story with Convergent and Divergent Questions for the Story about the Trip to the Land of Pencils

1. For what reason is the title of the story "The Trip to the Land of Pencils"?
2. What was the name of the cake that Grandma baked for dessert?
3. In what season of the year did the story take place? Give some details from the story that gave you some clues.
4. Where were all of the suitcases stored, and was it easy for the children to get to them?
5. What do you think did the narrator meant by, "The next three days passed by at a snail's pace"?
6. How many girls and boys were there in the family?
7. Why do you suppose Dad requested a room in the back of the hotel?
8. What type of job did Dad do for a living, and how did Mom help him? Also, what details in the story told you that they were very busy?
9. Why do you think Dad reserved one room at the Holiday Inn? Do you think he did so for a specific reason?
10. What does it mean to be resourceful? What are two examples of someone being this in the story?

11. What does the phrase "it's better to be safe than sorry" mean to you? Have you ever had such an experience?
12. What is a tarpaulin? In what ways was it used during the vacation?
13. What is the meaning of tolerance? How were the children in the story tolerant of each other? Have you had show tolerance to someone or in a situation?
14. What do you think are some things to be learned from this author's experience?

Reciprocal Thinking Phases Identification Chart

Table B.1. Identifying Thinking "Phases" Chart for "The Trip to the Land of Pencils"

COGNITVE SKILLS	*APPLICATION OF COGNITIVE SKILLS*
Phase 1	*Portion of Story When Cognitive Term Was Addressed: What Was I Thinking*
Recognizing and Realizing	As we sat on the stoop, we realized that summer vacation was almost over and our annual trip had not yet been taken.
Classifying	We knew it was the end of summer and the start of school year was near.
Comparing	I compared having ice box cake and receiving good news or having a celebration.
Contrasting	Dad was the best dad in contrast to the whole wide world of other dads.
Phase 2	*Portion of Story When Cognitive Term Was Addressed: What Was I Thinking*
Prioritizing	The priority was the agreement made not to say a word when Dad pulled up in his car.
Communicating	We communicated when we reported and shared our daily activities at the dinner table.
Inferring	We inferred that since we are having ice box cake, good news must be coming.
Initial Problem-Solving	We can solve our problem and get the answer we need by showing good behavior and acting patiently.
Generalizing	In general, we take this trip every year so we must be taking it again this year.
Predicting	Since we are having ice box cake, we predicted that good news was forthcoming.
Active Listening	We listened closely as Dad spoke while eating his piece of cake.

(continued)

APPENDIX B

COGNITVE SKILLS	*APPLICATION OF COGNITIVE SKILLS*
Initial Deciding and Problem-Solving	Our problem was initially solved as we were told of Dad's decision that the trip would take place in three days.
Phase 3	*Portion of Story When Cognitive Term Was Addressed: What Was I Thinking*
Evaluating	We judged the decision as an excellent one by jumping up and down and hugging each other.
Organizing	Realizing there are only three nights to pack, we organized our suitcases, favorite clothes, and games.
Critiquing	Even though we were relieved, we actually felt disappointed that the older boys did not lock us in the attic.
Risk-Taking	It was a risk having to walk through the boys' rooms to get to the attic. It was even a bigger risk when all eleven children showed up at the swimming pool.
Tolerating and Collaborating	Much tolerance and collaboration took place among us as we worked together to pack and unpack the car and keep our room clean.
Advanced Problem-Solving	Our biggest problem was how to feed and sleep thirteen people staying in one room.
Inventing	We had to devise a way eat and sleep by taking beds apart and using the bathroom as a convenience kitchen.
Synthesizing	We came together as we knelt around the beds to eat and slept in small groups on makeshift beds.
Analyzing	We carefully examined every amenity available in the room.
Recalling and Reflecting	I used recall when I thought we "must have been rich" for only getting one room. I also reflected on how my parents had been so resourceful and implemented plans that worked so well.
Self-actualizing	At the end of the day, I went to bed thinking and praying how thankful I was to belong to and be a part of such a wonderful family. I realized that I was truly blessed!

APPENDIX C

This appendix addresses evaluations of students' work with samples of four teacher candidate's assignments. In many cases the assessment of students' work, at whatever grade level, may well be a fearful experience. This is the result of one being concerned about meeting one's personal expectations or those of family members, teacher, and peers. Why this happens is often a conundrum, but when examined we realize that it's part of our common social and societal realities.

Tests bring a sense of the unknown, and the unknown may be frightening. What questions will be asked, what is anticipated, how will one perform, and will the results affect one's social position in the class, friendships, any relationships? Or will the assessment results yield a positive affect? Overall, tests may be feared by the evaluator as much as by the one being rated. This is because social norms find that many perceive the students' test results have a proportionate effect on the teacher's recognized ability to teach. It's thought if the students do well, then the teacher must be good, and if not, well, then the opposite may be true.

The teacher wants his/her students to do well and the students also want to do well. This is possible with a few things kept in mind. First is that you are teaching the whole student. This is the thinking and feeling one who is in your classroom. He/she has a set of predispositions about being tested and has realized that the word *failure* is more than just a word.

Failure is a label. It is a way of identifying those who will be expected to do well and those who will not. Failure, when attached to a person, means all the negatives one can conjure up that denote that individual as being less than others, and inadequate. This is something the student feels and thinks and comes to believe as being true about himself or herself.

Secondly, concerning students wanting to do well when it comes to testing, evaluations must be designed to meet the needs of the student, not just content-wise, but success- and intent-wise as well. The third thing for you to address when testing is whether the comments you make will encourage or discourage students' future learning endeavors. With these three things in mind, here are several dos and one don't regarding assessments.

Topic 1: Suggestions for Evaluating Students' Work

Dos:

1. Prepare the students for the test by covering the material in such a way that it addresses their learning needs. This facilitates a sense of ease when test taking occurs, as the student is prepared. And encourage pretest classmate collaboration and cooperative learning of material that will be on the test.
2. Be positive about administering the test and make encouraging statements like "We've prepared for this evaluation. You will do well on it, and if not then we'll revisit the material and try again."
3. Or make a potential negative experience into a positive one. You may do this by reducing the anxiety level of students with assurance that an in-class test may be given in his/her perceptual preferences and/or retaken after academic intervention, additional study, or assisted study is conducted.

   (An example of preferred perceptual preference is to give a student who learns best by listening the test in oral format. Read the questions and record the answers the student provides.)
4. Make positive comments when grading the test. And, when you make positive comments, state in detail why you've said that by explaining your reasoning. Sometimes teachers write words like *good work, nice job, excellent, exemplary,* and *out-*

standing, but refrain from stating why this was interpreted as such by the teacher.

Also, if the work is not up to your expectations and your comment reflects this, then *soften it* with an explanation so the statement is without hostility. Be *compassionate* when evaluating students' work, at whatever grade level (K–16+), because this feedback information is important for students to know for their growth. See examples A–C presented later in this appendix.

5. Try grading the test, for elementary-level students, with errors marked by dots and correct answers with a large letter *C*. In case anyone is looking to see how a classmate did on the test, they'll be drawn to the *C*, as opposed to the dot noting the incorrect answer. Doing this assists in having test results only known by you and the student.

6. Consider having a pretest on subject matter that does not count as a grade. This allows the student to know the content of the posttest, which will be graded. Arrange the posttest in a different format than the pretest. While the topics addressed are the same on both tests, their order of presentation is not identical. This thwarts rote memorization and helps the student gain content conceptualizations.

7. Assure the students that the tests are not the "end all" of this study area, but serve as a marker as to what needs to be either retaught by the teacher or reexamined by the student.

8. Appreciate your own ability to be clear and encouraging in evaluating by adhering to the concept of not putting anyone down, including yourself, when assessments are addressed.

9. Realize you will receive more of a learning effort from a student who feels good about himself or herself than you will from one who finds the classroom stressful due to tests and the potential negative outcomes of these. And it's important to realize that although you might have done well when taking tests, your students' experiences may be different. So be helpful with follow-through that supports the learning and teaching situation.

10. Use alternative means of assessment which do not involve pen-and-paper tests, such as fill-in-the-blank, multiple-choice, true/false, and short-answer types. Alternative means of assessment may include a student producing a project or conducting a performance-based activity, creating a brochure to demonstrate content knowledge, doing a drawing, making an audiotape, inventing a way to demonstrate comprehension such as making a board game, or doing a demonstration lesson for the class.
11. A final "do" thought is something heard time and again during growing-up years: "You'll receive more with sugar than you will with salt" (After, 1953). What this meant was that having a pleasant (sweet) attitude and demeanor by being proactive and/or being complimentary will reap, or has the strong potential of providing, others being positive or showing kindness in return.

The one don't is under no circumstances pit one student against another. *Overall, you need to be "for" your students!*

It's hoped that a look at these following samples of assessments and accompanying comments will provide you with the idea that the concept of being positive will result in the student feeling good about himself or herself. In turn this provides a favorable learning environment regarding attitude and self-acceptance, due in part to you being upbeat, encouraging, affirmative, and constructive.

Topic 2: Samples of Rubric Criteria and Evaluation Comments

Storytelling: Kathleen Carter

You may recall that in appendix B there was an example of storytelling with the written story, questions to extend the story, and a Reciprocal Thinking Identification Chart on "A Trip to the Land of Pencils." The rubric criteria for evaluation of these three components, as well as the fourth one, oral presentation, are presented along with comments.

Rubric Criteria: Oral Presentation: Level 3
The presenter demonstrated all the components of an oral presentation with excellent body posture and movement, voice stress, juncture, modulation, and articulation. There were appropriate gestures, eye contact, and facial expressions, connoting the presenter's interest in the topic. Artifacts were included. (Levels 2 and 1 relate that the presenter had "most" of these components or few to none of them, respectively.)

Rubric Criteria: Written Story: Level 3
The story had appropriate paragraphing and good sentence structure, scope, and sequence. There was a good amount of pertinent information provided. The punctuation and grammar were excellent. (Levels 2 and 1 relate that the story usually had these components and they were satisfactory, or that what was written was incorrect and/or of poor quality, respectively.)

Rubric Criteria: Questions to Extend the Story: Level 3
The questions continuously extended the story to other theme-related topics and/or personal comparison and contrast to events in the story. (Levels 2 and 1 related that the questions partially extended the story with minimal comparisons made, and the questions did not address the story topic or theme with lack of extension and personal comparisons, respectively.)

Rubric Criteria: Reciprocal Thinking Phases Identification: Level 3
Each cognitive and metacognitive skill in each phase was addressed in a relevant manner with appropriate excerpts from the story provided when applicable. (Levels 2 and 1 related some of these skills being addressed in a relevant manner and then few of these being present, respectively.)

Comments
Kathy, from the beginning of your storytelling about "the land of pencils," the audience was captivated by your animated delivery of the story content. That you took extra time to dress up in swim goggles, flippers, and snorkel only added to this unique and fascinating presentation! Each of the criteria on this rubric were met with excellence!

Your expressive visual imagery was exemplary, and this applied to the written story as well. I'm thinking that if you could condense the story, you might have a children's book in the making. Also, in the written format you have anticipatory set, ascending, and descending action, with main ideas followed by detail sentences to create intrigue.

In both the written and oral versions of the story, when you referenced "treasury of things past," I found myself actually envisioning childhood events, as you applied perfect grammar, paragraphing, and sentence structure. The comparison to life experiences continued throughout the story, which made it all the more compelling as you selected situations many of us may have experienced. At the close of the story you mention a "remarkable family." To that I add that you are a remarkable person!

Questions: I thought that questions 5, 7, 9, 10, and 13 were outstanding and these, along with the others, were exemplary and erudite as representations of literal, applied, and implied comprehension. Actually, question number 13 had all three of these types of comprehension required for the answer. Lastly, the Reciprocal Thinking Phases Identification Chart was of particular interest, as you provided fine detail and were "right on the mark" when addressing each cognitive and metacognitive skill. Thank you for the excellence of your work in this four-tier assignment. Grade: A

Story Map Graphic Organizer Followed by Evaluation: Laura Hefele (2008)

In chapter 11, there was an example given of a story map graphic organizer. The evaluation of this story map follows, with rubric criteria and professor comments.

Rubric Criteria: Story Map Design and Format: Level 3
The design of the graphic organizer clearly showed the use of good color contrast. There was appropriate bordering and labeling when necessary. The flow, scope, and sequence were clear, with either lines or arrows showing the connection from one section to the other. The material fit on the display board in the correct format style, as presented on the example handout in class. The spacing of sections was such that the appearance of the graphic organizer was exemplary, as the font was large and easily read-

able. (Levels 2 and 1 reported some of these components being provided and a severe lack of them, respectively.)

Rubric Criteria: Content: Level 3
Each section contained a clear explanation that met the criteria of each labeled section. The material was an excellent representation of the book's events. These events were well presented on the graphic organizer. The overt and subliminal intent of the author(s) were not the same and clearly represented the in-depth reflection of the board's designer.

A positive message was conveyed for elementary readers with the selection of this literature. Story scope and sequence were exceptional. (Level 2 remarked on the criteria being somewhat met, presenting inconsistency of reflection without a positive message being conveyed, and scope and sequence only partially represented. Level 1 noted an overall lack of clarity and little to no reflection being evident with no positivity of message and scope and sequence.)

Rubric Criteria: Grammar: Level 3
The punctuation and sentence structure were completely correct. There were no grammatical errors. (Levels 2 and 1 noted some errors and numerous errors, respectively.)

Rubric Criteria: Oral Presentation: Level 3
The presentation demonstrated appropriate body stance, voice modulation, stress, and juncture, with good articulation. An interest in the story content topic was obvious and the presenter was able to address questions concerning his/her story map theme. The presenter was affable and had a pleasant demeanor that connoted exceptional interest in the assignment presentation. (Levels 2 and 1 explained that the criteria in this area lacked some of the components and an overall inability to meet the criteria, respectively.)

Comments
Laura, the graphic organizer story map you constructed on the book *Chrysanthemum* is extraordinarily well designed! You selected a topic that addresses the need for friendship and help to stop bullying, which is very viable. From the "mouse" shapes for the elements to the hand-drawn flower in the middle, this work is simply beautiful!

The connecting lines done in arch shapes with the color coordination all over the board, as well as the color contrast being profound, make this story map one of exemplary and exceptional design. Even the title being on the flower stem is fantastic, with the accompanying book's author placed on the leaf, which demonstrates you being clever, imaginative, and creatively ingenious!

The story elements are well addressed, although I'd suggest having a personality trait or relationship connection for the characters in the story. This is especially true when it comes to the events section, and one wonders, "Who is Mrs. Twinkle?" I realize the persons using the story map will have read the book, and you explained each character in your presentation, but having this information is helpful for others to encourage them to read the book, or be keenly aware of the interconnection of the characters.

The setting, moods, events, problem, and solution are well represented. And the ideas regarding bullying being acceptable may be thwarted by help from a friend. In this case, Mrs. Twinkle is well represented on the final portions of the graphic organizer. The grammar and punctuation are perfect, with sentence structure, where appropriate, well configured.

Your oral presentation was superb with excellent voice modulation, stress, and juncture, with gesturing facial expressions connoting interest in the book, and all were generally exemplary! Thank you for your attention to the components of this assignment and congratulations on such profoundly exceptional work on it. Grade: A

EDU 504A: Partnership-Written Lesson Plan and Teaching Performance Demonstration Lesson Evaluation: Rachele Campisi and Colleen Freehill

The following is an example of an evaluation of a partnership teacher candidates' written and teaching performance lesson. With respect to grading this assignment, the professor addresses each area of the lesson plan parts with positive comments. Suggestions of other ways to address the lesson's individual sections, when applicable, are also provided.

Feedback from teacher candidates has been most positive because of the detail of the evaluation being such that a comment is supported with information as to why this was evaluated in the stated manner. Doing this type of evaluation with respect to detail, length, and positive statements enables teacher candidates to be open to alternative suggestions and consider remediation or other ways to address the lesson topic in the future if necessary.

Teacher Candidates: Rachele Campisi and Colleen Freehill (Spring 2010)

Lesson Plan Topic: Ecosystems

Heading: This section was written correctly, but the word *vocabulary* might best be removed and just the word *rainforest* applied to the topic section.

Objective: This section is exceptionally well written, with the students having seen a video clip addressing ecosystems and then identifying ten vocabulary words relating to ecosystems. The addition of illustrating these is good, with the students making science notebook entries of these and the definitions of the selected words. The reason for stating this as being such is because you have students involved in using their visual and tactile modalities in more than one discipline.

Standards and Indicators: The learning standards you chose are correct, with English/language arts and the arts, as well as science, New York State learning standards. However, most impressive is the indicator section. This is because you have the wording from the objective in the appropriate places as evidence, and the exact phrasing in place.

Motivation: The details you provided with the scenarios are superb! The students are not left to question what is expected of them with regard to this serving as a catalyst for the upcoming lesson/developmental procedures activities. Additionally, what you've written affords the students with opportunities to collaborate, which prepares them for the lesson.

Materials: Excellent! You have a thorough listing of the items needed for the later activities section (developmental procedures).

Strategies: Kindly omit the strategies of kinesthetic and technology and this section will be excellent. Kinesthetic is not a strategy, but a perceptual preference. The same applies to technology. These are means for differentiation in a lesson plan or making an adaptation.

Adaptations: Having the words to be addressed in the lesson being on an audiotape for the visually impaired is a viable idea. Also, you may want to have the student with this visual disability supplied with the vocabulary words on an overhead projector, or since you have the technology component, these words may be presented on a slide or series of slides in large font.

Differentiation of instruction: One could not ask for a better written differentiation of instruction, with students separated by interest groups. The first and third ideas you have presented are similar, as they involve tactile and kinesthetic involvement. However, it seems reasonable to have each represented to address varied interests of the students.

Developmental procedures: This section of your lesson plan is well configured with questions to match the activities you plan to implement. The first activity with the review of information from the video clip on ecosystems is excellent. This is because it provides the students with an opportunity to recall and reflect on the vocabulary words.

Having these ten words placed on the bulletin board serves as an anticipatory set for the remaining activities you've selected. Overall, by doing this you are preparing the students for success in comprehending the scope and sequence for the lesson. The questions that you've selected address the cognitive skills of recalling, comparing and contrasting, realizing the term *word wall*, evaluating, risk-taking, analyzing, and communicating to make this bulletin board.

The next activity addresses the students working in small groups to define the selected vocabulary words, which is excellent. This assists in developing students' communication while working in a collaborative manner. The cognitive skills you employ are comparing and contrasting, collaborating, realizing, recognizing, prioritizing with the words not matching the definition when placed on the board, analyzing when you ask about matching words and definitions, and synthesizing as well.

(The suggestion I would make is that you have this activity, or the following one, being where the students separate into teams or work individually to match the words with their corresponding definitions. You relate that this is the purpose of the mismatch equals matching words and definitions, but not having students play this matching game.)

The third activity with the students placing their ecosystem vocabulary words in their science notebooks with an illustration of each word is outstanding, as this meets your lesson objective and addresses a varied modality format, as well as a creative means for identification of to lesson vocabulary through visualization of key words. The questions you wrote definitely apply to the lesson, with the students discerning what it means to illustrate the words and determining how this is to be accomplished.

Then comparing and contrasting while evaluating which parts of an ecosystem are most liked is interesting in that it calls for discernment, analyzing, risk-taking, evaluating, and self-actuating with the entries in their science notebooks. You have excellent application of cognitive and metacognitive skills for this lesson!

Perhaps what I liked best about this activity is when you ask about other types of ecosystems and address the classroom as possibly being an ecosystem. Certainly it is! But that question has the students making transferences of information and conceptualizations regarding an ecosystem by imagining and expanding their present definitions to include a comprehensive understanding of the ecosystem term. This is outstanding, as you allow for students' transfer of concepts to specific categories and application in their real environment.

The final activity with the students creating an acrostic poem using one of the ten vocabulary words is excellent. I think this because you allow for reentrance into the English/language arts discipline in a new manner with the creation of the poem. Additionally, you give the students the opportunity to examine their creativity and apply what has been learned about the format/requirements of this type of poem.

Having these presented to the class reinforces their work and allows for whole-class participation, as well as an opportunity to demonstrate their content knowledge. Components of a formal oral presentation are other considerations met with this activity. The developmental procedures and corresponding questions for each activity are very, very well conceived and applied in this lesson plan.

Assessment: Having a teacher checklist to ascertain if the students have the ten ecosystem words and corresponding definitions is excellent, as it represents your organization of criteria being met!

Independent practice: The idea of the students creating a mock ecosystem at home is certainly an engaging concept. That you have a reporting alternative is excellent. I'd add that this is the type of homework that truly applies the concepts taught in class being reinforced at home and in a student-friendly manner. Also, you have a reporting alternative to demonstrate that the students completed the homework assignment with them sharing the work with the class the following day.

Academic intervention: Brilliant idea! The words and definitions being provided as well as the illustrations of each of the vocabulary words is an outstanding idea. This is because these give the students something to refer to when trying to meet the lesson objectives. And a suggestion is that you might mention teacher assistance is available.

Academic Enrichment: Oh my, a Weave around! What a great idea for these students who've met the objective and for those who later will enjoy playing the Weave around with tactile involvement being used to engage them!

References: Perfect! All three were excellent examples of where you obtained material for this lesson.

Teaching Performance: Demonstration Lesson

Dear Rachele and Colleen,

Your lesson on ecosystem vocabulary words was both engaging and well planned with respect to students being involved in learning about ecosystems. The motivation you provided really had the class collaborating and enjoying the activity, with laughter abounding when illustrations were created and shared. This was also fun! Then each of you went to the groups to praise the students and offer prompts for creating the illustrations in a teacher-student friendly manner. This allowed for the students being prepared to be successful in completing the forthcoming assignments in the developmental procedures section of the lesson plan.

The use of praising vocabulary and your overall demeanor was of the highest caliber. The results of the first group, with the illustrations of the water, plants, greenhouse, and questions you asked about consumers were outstanding for lesson comprehension being evidenced. The same may be said for the second group's farm, water, rain, animals, and hybrid "dog-cow," then eggs and milk.

Certainly, this participation was enjoyable in the motivation section of your plan.

Then there needs to be mention of the excellent voice modulation and articulation, clarity of presented ideas, and scope and sequence of the lesson, which was outstanding. The students were asked what words go on the wall with reference to the previous lesson, and here you provided opportunity for recall and reflection with reinforcement of what was previously learned. Rachele, I would have liked you to address the class more, but when you did this it was fine, you were calm and encouraging, and you appeared interested.

Colleen, you have an energetic way of presenting material, which is definitely good. And you diverted Laura exceptionally well when she wanted to write a sentence instead of the word's definition. That you gave each student a turn to participate was excellent! The overall kinesthetic involvement was at a high level, which provided ample engagement in the lesson objectives. This is to your credit. Giving examples of what was to be accomplished either through prompts or actually showing examples made this lesson all the more sensational.

The use of gesturing by both of you was good. This is because of your facial expressions and personal attention to students' needs. Perhaps most enthralling was the way you provided, through questions as well as the activities, the use of student imagination and creativity components. Thank you for the excellence of your work on this partnership lesson demonstration and written lesson plan.

Grade: Written Lesson Plan: A

Demonstration Lesson on Ecosystems: A

Decision-Making Graphic Organizer Rubric

Rubric Level 3

Design: This section is the same as that presented on the story map.

Content: The "problem" was clearly stated with a minimum of three choices. Each choice had three possible positive and three possible negative outcomes for the stated option. There was a "final decision," which clearly and exceptionally stated the reason(s) for that decision. The scope and sequence were exemplary.

Grammar: This section is the same as that presented on the story map.

Oral Presentation: This section is the same as that presented on the story map. However, "An interest in the topic was obvious and the presenter was able to aptly address questions concerning his/her presentation topic. There was a willingness to accept other alternative problem solutions, or other possible choices and/or decisions" were additions to this section. (The level 2 and 1 criteria for content refer to these components being partially or somewhat being met, and lack of clarity or attention to reasoning being evident, respectively.)

Comments: Kathy, your Decision-Making Graphic Organizer with the three choices of whether to "Buy a Puppy," "Not Buy One Now," and "Get a Kitten/Cat" was quite well formatted. All the criteria for design, content, grammar, and oral presentation were met very well. The color contrast of the deep yellow and dark bordered areas, as well as doggie-type stickers, made the board attractive. And your exceptional presentation followed all the components of the formal oral presentation criteria. The grammar was perfect.

You clearly presented the three choices. Each possible negative and possible positive for the choices demonstrated a good deal of cognitive and metacognitive skill application. I noted that you addressed the beliefs and values of your children, husband, and mother with equal interest and concern. Also, in several areas you demonstrated motherhood experience and intuition guiding you.

The possible negative of nonaffordability concerning a puppy purchase was certainly brought forward. However, it was surpassed by questioning who would be caring for any family pet that was bought now or later. With your children being rather young and your husband being away at work, you taking on this responsibility was definitely a worry.

Then you mentioned there being kenneling fees when you went on vacations; upkeep of a family pet; impact on your mom, who lives with you; keeping the pet on your property; possible jealousy between children regarding sense of ownership; possible allergies; what if the puppy got sick; and cost of upkeep.

Other possible negatives for other choices included some family members not really liking kittens/cats. The disappointment of your children if you didn't get a pet seemed to deter you from waiting until a later time. Evidence of you thinking seriously about each option included your husband not really wanting a puppy or a kitten/cat; thoughts about the size of the pup when fully grown; the breed being an issue, with lack of agreement in this area; cats being too independent; furniture scratching; and possible damage to carpets due to accidents.

The positives for getting the puppy were heartwarming. This was with extensive consideration of your children's feelings and desires being foremost in your "weighing" what's of most importance to the family in general.

The liveliness of a puppy was addressed, with this impacting the children in positive ways. Also, there was your mention of having a family dining-room table discussion as a positive for puppy purchasing. This discussion possibly leading to acceptance of responsibilities for puppy care was another component. While you had positives for waiting, and the benefits of owning a kitten/cat were compelling, in comparison to the puppy purchase, these seemed less formidable.

The final decision to buy a puppy, with the children's desires being most important and everyone accepting the responsibility for walking and training the pup, was most generous, I thought. I will be interested in learning how this decision works for you and your family. And I wish you the best of luck with the training and caregiving. From what you've shared in class about your children and husband being compassionate and generally accountable persons, I think you've a good chance of this decision working out very nicely!

BIBLIOGRAPHY

Abbot, J. (1994). *Learning makes sense: Recreating education for a changing future.* London: Education 2000.

Abedi, J., and O'Neil, Jr., H. F. (1996). Reliability and validity of a state metacognitive inventory: Potential for alternative assessment. *Journal of Educational Research, 89*(4), 234–45.

Affholder, L. P. (2003). *Differentiated instruction in inclusive elementary classrooms* (published EdD thesis). University of Kansas.

After, M. (1953). *Advice from my mom: Conversations on ways to behave.* Presentations in Rochester, NY, and Columbus, OH.

Allport, G. W. (1937). *Personality: A psychological interpretation.* New York: Rinehart and Winston.

Angelou, M. (June 2007). Quote in *Villager Voice.* Clemmens, NC: PK and Co.

Bandura, A. (1977). *Social learning theory.* Englewood Cliffs, NJ: Prentice-Hall.

———. (1997). *Self-efficacy: The exercise of control.* New York: Freeman.

———. (2003). On the psychosocial impact and mechanisms of spiritual modeling. *International Journal for the Psychology of Religion, 13,* 167–73.

Bauer, E. (1993). *The relationship between and among learning style perceptual preferences, instructional strategies, mathematics achievement, and attitude toward mathematics of learning disabled and emotionally handicapped students in a suburban junior high school* (EdD thesis). St. John's University.

Beane, A. L. (2004). *Together we can be bully free: A mini-guide for parents.* Minneapolis, MN: Free Spirit.

Blank, L. M. (1997). *Metacognition and the facilitation of conceptual and status change in students' concepts of ecology (learning and middle school students)* (PhD dissertation). Indiana University.

Bogner, D. (1990). *John Dewey's theory of adult education and adult development* (PhD dissertation). University of Kansas.

———. (2007). *The process of memorization* (unpublished). Molloy College, Rockville Centre, NY.

———. (2008). *Conversations and unpublished narrative on a synthesis of Dewey's learning theory and personal reflections on teaching and learning* (unpublished). Molloy College, Rockville Centre, NY.

Bogner, D., and Schiering, M. (2007). *Conversations on the effect of external factors on belief and value systems.* Molloy College, Rockville Centre, NY.

Borish, G. D. (2007). *Effective teaching methods: Research-based practice* (6th ed.). Boston: Pearson.

Borkowski, J. G. (April 1992). Metacognitive theory: A framework for teaching literacy, writing, and math skills. *Journal of Learning Disabilities, 25*(4), 253–57.

Borkowski, J. G., Estrada, T. M., Milstead, M., and Hale, C. A. (1989). General problem solving skills: Relations between metacognitive and strategic processing. *Learning Disability Quarterly, 12,* 57–70.

Boudah, D. J., and Weiss, M. P. (2002). Learning disabilities overview: Update 2002. *ERIC Digest.* ED4628080.

Brandt, R. (1999). Educators need to know about the human brain. *Phi Delta Kappan, 81*(3), 235–38.

Brazil, M. (2004). Parents ponder academics vs. character. *USA Today Magazine* (The Society for the Advancement of Education). www.usatodaymagazine.org.

Bretherton, J. (1985). Attachment theory: Retrospect and prospect. In J. Bretherton and E. Waters (Eds.), *Growing points of attachment theory and research* (32–35). Society for Research in Child Development Monographs 50 (serial 209). Chicago: University of Chicago Press.

Britzman, M., and Hanson, W. (2005). *What every educator and youth must know.* Bloomington, IN: Unlimited Publishing.

Bronfenbrenner, U. (1979). *The Ecology of Human Development.* New Haven, CT: Harvard University Press.

Brooks, B. D., and Goble, F. (1997). *A case for character education.* Northridge, CA: Studio 4 Productions.

Bruer, J. (1993). *Schools for thought: A science of learning in the classroom.* Cambridge, MA: Massachusetts Institute of Technology Press.

Buli-Holmberg, J., and Ekeberg, T. R. (2009). *Equal and inclusive education.* Oslo: Universitetsforlaget.

Buli-Holmberg, J., Guldahl, T., and Jensen, R. (2007). *Reflections about learning in a learning style perspective.* Oslo: Damm.

Cafferty, E. (1980). *An analysis of student performance based upon the degree of match between the educational cognitive style of the teachers and the educational cognitive styles of the students* (PhD dissertation). Nebraska University.

Campisi, R., and Freehill, C. (Spring 2010). *Professor evaluation of a written lesson plan.* Presented at Molloy College, Rockville Centre, NY.

Carter, K. (Fall 2009). *The land of pencils.* Storytelling, reciprocal thinking chart, and questions to extend the story. Presentation to fulfill assignment for integrated English language arts and reading/EDU 506A, at Molloy College, Rockville Centre, NY.

Cates, A. W. (1992). Considerations in evaluating metacognition in interactive hypermedia/multimedia instruction. Paper presented at the Annual Conference of the American Educational Research Association, San Francisco, CA. (ERIC Document Reproduction Services No. IR015705).

Damasio, A. (1994/2007). *Decartes' error: emotion, reason, and the human brain.* New York: Putnam Berkley Group.

———. (2008). The neuroscience of the brain. Fourth International Brain World Conference, Ellenville, NY.

Deighton, L. C. (1969). Instructional games. In *Encyclopedia of Education* (Vol. 4, pp. 106–10).

Dewey, John. (1893/1972). *Self realization as the moral idea. John Dewey: The early works, 1882–1898.* (Vol. 4). Carbondale: Southern Illinois Press.

———. (1916/1980). *Democracy and education. John Dewey: The middle works, 1899–1924.* (Vol. 9). Jo Ann Boydston (Ed.). Carbondale: Southern Illinois Press.

———. (1933/1986). *How we think: a restatement of the relation of reflective thinking to the educative process. John Dewey: The later works, 1925–1955.* (Vol. 8, pp. 105–352). Jo Ann Boydston (Ed.). Carbondale: Southern Illinois Press.

———. (1934). *How we think.* Boston: Heath.

———. (1937). *From absolutism to experimentalism.* In *Contemporary American Philosophy,* 13–27. New York: Macmillan.

———. (1938). *Experience and education.* New York: Collier Books.

———. (1938/1988). *Experience and education. John Dewey: The later works 1925–1953.* (Vol. 13, pp. 1–62). Carbondale: Southern Illinois Press.

Dunn, R. (Winter 1984). Learning styles: State of the science. *Theory into practice, 23*(1), Matching teaching and learning styles, 10–19.

———. (1997). Teaching students to teach themselves. *International Education, 23*(75), 4–6, 14.

Dunn, R., and Blake, B. (2008). *Teaching every child to read.* Lanham, MD: Rowman and Littlefield Publishers.

Dunn, R., and Dunn, K. (1978). *Teaching students through their learning styles: A practical approach.* Englewood Cliffs, NJ: Prentice Hall.

———. (1992). *Teaching elementary students through their individual learning styles.* Boston: Allyn and Bacon.

———. (1993). *Teaching secondary students through their individual learning styles: Practical approaches for grades 7–12.* Boston: Allyn and Bacon.

Dunst, C., Trivette, C., and Deal, A. (1994). Enabling and empowering families. In C. Dunst, C. Trivette, and A. Deal (Eds.), *Supporting and strengthening families* (2–11). Cambridge, MA: Brookline.

Eisner, E. (1997). Cognition and representation: A way to pursue the American dream. *Phi Delta Kappan, 78*(5), 349–53.

Ennis, R. H. (1985). A logical basis for measuring critical thinking skills. *Educational Leadership, 43*(2), 44–48.

Fine, E. (1997). The sharing tree: Children learn to share. *Teaching Exceptional Children, 28*(3), 76–77.

Fogarty, R., and McTighe, J. (1993). Educating teachers for higher order thinking: The three-story intellect. *Theory Into Practice, 32*(3), 161–69.

Freire, P. (1998). *Pedagogy of freedom, ethics, democracy and civic courage.* Lanham, MD: Rowman and Littlefield Publishers.

Freire, P., and Macedo, D. (1995). A dialogue: Culture, language, and race. *Harvard Educational Review, 66*(3), 377–88.

Gagne, R. M. (1977). *Conditions of learning* (3rd ed.). New York: Holt, Rinehart, and Wilson.

Gardner, H. (1993). *Multiple intelligences: The theory in practice.* New York: Basic Books.

Gaul, C. (2010). Bullying survey reports 50% of high school students admit to violence. *USA Live Headlines.* www.usaliveheadlines.com.

Gazzaniga, M. S. (1998). *The mind's past.* Berkeley: University of California Press.

Glass, A., and Holyoak, K. J. (1986). *Cognition* (2nd ed.). New York: Random House.

Glatthorn, A. (1995). *Developing the classroom curriculum: Developing a quality curriculum.* Alexandria, VA: Association for Supervision and Curriculum Development.

Hayes, B. (2000). *Critical examinations and issues.* In Molloy Course Syllabus (Ed.), *Molloy College Undergraduate Education.* Molloy College, Rockville, Centre, NY.

———. (2005). *Literacy in the content area for childhood teachers and reading language arts.* Molloy Course Syllabus (Ed.), *Molloy College Undergraduate Education.* Molloy College, Rockville, Centre, NY.

Hall, T. (2002). *Differentiated instruction: Effective classroom practices* (report). National Center on Accessing the General Curriculum (NCAC). U.S. Department of Education, Office of Special Education Programs: Ideas that Work. Washington, DC.

Haugsbakk, G., and Nordkvelle, Y. (2007). The rhetoric of ICT and the new language of learning: A critical analysis of the use of ICT in the curricular field, *European Educational Research Journal, 6*(1), 1–12.

Hefele, L. (Spring 2008). *The Story Map Graphic Organizer.* Evaluation for Interdisciplinary methods for the diverse learning in the inclusion classroom (EDU 504) at Molloy College, Rockville Centre, NY.

Hilgard, E. R., and Bower, G. H. (1975). *Theories of learning* (4th ed.). Englewood Cliffs, NJ: Prentice Hall.

Honigsfeld, A., and Schiering, M. (2004). Diverse approaches to the diversity of learning styles in teacher education. *Journal of Educational Psychology, 24*(4), 487–507.

Idol, L., Jones, B., and Mayer, R. (1991). *The teaching of thinking, educational values and cognitive instruction: Implications for reform* (32–54). Hillsdale, NJ: Erlbaum.

Illeris, K. (1978). Quoted in Hausstatter and Nordkvelle (2007). Perspectives on Group Work in Distance Learning. *Journal of Distance Education* (Oslo, Norway), *8*(1).

———. (2007). *How we learn: Learning and non-learning in school and beyond.* London and New York: Routledge.

Jensen, E. (2008). *Brain-based learning: The new paradigm in teaching*. Thousand Oaks, CA: Corwin Press.

Josephson, M. (2002). *The six pillars of character: Character counts.* Los Angeles, CA: Josephson Institute, Center for Youth Ethics.

Keefe, J. W. (Ed.). (1979). Learning styles: An overview. In *Student learning styles: diagnosing and prescribing programs* (1–17). Reston, VA: National Association of Secondary School Principals.

Keefe, J. W., and Languis, M. (1983). Description of the learning style profile. In J. W. Keefe and J. S. Monk (Eds.), *NASSP Bulletin* (43–53). Reston, VA: National Association of Secondary School Principals.

King, M. L. (1947). *The maroon tiger.* Student paper, Morehouse College, Atlanta, GA.

Koestler, A. (1978). *Janus: A summing up*. New York: Random House.

Kolb, D. A. (1984). *Experiential learning theory: Experience as the source of learning and development.* Englewood Cliffs, NJ: Prentice Hall.

Koster, R. (2005). *A theory of fun for game design*. Phoenix, AZ: Paraglyph Press.

Lau Tzu. (2500 BC). *In the path of virtue: The illustrated Tao Te Ching Lao Tzu* (James Legge, Trans.). With illustrations from the Cleveland Museum of Art. New York: Abrams.

Li, M. (1996). *Empowering learners through metacognitive thinking, instruction, and design.* Proceedings of Selected Research and Development Presentations at the Convention of the Association for Educational Communications and Technology Sponsored by the Research and Theory Division, New Orleans, LA, January 13–17, 1993. (ERIC Document Reproduction Services No. ED 362108).

Lynch-Brown, C., and Tomlinson, C. M. (2005). *Essentials of children's literature* (6th ed.). Boston: Allyn and Bacon.

McLean, S. V. (1999). Becoming a teacher: The person in the process. In R. P. Lipka and T. M. Brinthaupt (Eds.), *The role of self in teacher development* (55–91). Albany: State University of New York Press.

McNamara, J. K., and Wong, B. Y. L. (2003). Memory for everyday information in students with learning disabilities. *Journal of Learning Disabilities, 36*(5), 394–406.

McTighe, J., and Lyman, F. (1988). Cueing thinking in the classroom: the promise of theory-embedded tools. *Educational Leadership, 45*(7), 18–24.

Million, J. (2007–2008). *Conversations with J. Million on psycho-social drama and the work of Koestler on "holons"* (unpublished). Port Charlotte, FL, and Stony Point, NY.

Mulroy, H., and Eddinger, K. (2003). Differentiation and literacy. Paper presented at the Institute on Inclusive Education, Rochester, NY.

Murray, C. L., and Keeves, J. L. (1994). Students' learning processes and progress in higher education. *ERIC Document Reproduction Services.* ED 3703.

O'Connor-Petruso, S., and M. Schiering. (2005). *Linking learning styles, character development, service learning, and pedagogy for empirical application.* Tenth Annual Learning Style Conference CD. Surrey, UK: Unis.

Olsen, D. G. (1995). "Less" can be "more" in the promotion of thinking. *Social Education, 59*(3), 130–38.

O'Neil, J. (1996). On emotional intelligence: A conversation with Daniel Goleman. *Educational Leadership, 54*(1), 6–11.

Ormond, J. E. (1999). *Human learning* (3rd ed.). Upper Saddle River, NJ: Prentice Hall.

Pellowski, A. (1977). *The world of storytelling.* New York: R. R. Bowker Co.

Piaget, J. (1936/1963). *The origins of intelligence in children.* New York: W. W. Norton and Company.

———. (1968). *Play, dreams and imitation in childhood.* New York: W. W. Norton and Company.

Price, R. (1978). *A palpable god.* New York: Atheneum.

Rosenberg, M. (2004). Feelings. New York Council for Nonviolent Communication. www.nycnvc.org.

Salend, S. J. (2004). *Creating inclusive classrooms: Effective and reflective practices for all students* (5th ed.). Columbus, OH: Merrill/Prentice Hall.

Schiering, M. (1965). *The four kinds of sentences.* Hubbard Avenue School, Columbus, OH.

———. (1974). *A comparison of teacher made educational games and traditional reading methods in visual perception, visual discrimination, reading achievements and reading attitudes among slow primary students* (published master's thesis). College of New Rochelle, New Rochelle, NY.

———. (1999). *The effects of learning-style instructional resources on fifth grade suburban students' metacognition, achievement, attitudes, and ability to teach themselves* (PhD dissertation). St. John's University.

———. (2000–2010). Course syllabi for Integrated ELA and reading (EDU 506A) and Interdisciplinary methods for the diverse learning in the inclusion classroom (EDU 504). Molloy College, Rockville Centre, NY.

———. (2000a). *Character development in the classroom.* New York State Project SAVE. Course syllabus. Division of Education, Molloy College, Rockville Centre, NY.

———. (2000b). *The Thinking Phases Identification Chart.* Molloy College, Rockville Centre, NY.

———. (2002).The phases of thinking: Evolving from cognition to metacognition. In Raynor and Armstrong, et al. (Eds.), ELSIN 7th International European Learning Style Conference. Ghent, Belgium.

———. (2003). The "how" and "who" of teaching and learning. In Raynor and Armstrong, et al. (Eds.), *Bridging Theory and Practice.* ELSIN 8th International European Learning Styles Conference. Hull, England: ELSIN.

———. (2005). *The equanimity of SOW and REAP (Sociology of the world with reasoned reflection, economics, academics and politics): Using interactive tri-fold boards, the interactive book report, and storytelling, as an interdisciplinary approach to teaching.* Presentation at the University of Oslo and the teacher centers in Oslo, Nesodden, Asker, and Skein, Norway.

———. (2007). What if we knew the cause of school violence and how to prevent it? Chapter 14 in R. Dunn and S. A. Griggs (Eds.), *What If? Promising Practices for Improving Schools* (79–83). Rowman & Littlefield Publishers: Lanham, MD.

———. (January 2008). Learning styles methods, resources for creative and talent development: Teaching and learning with learning styles. International Program from the University of Buffalo in Medellin, Colombia.

———. (Spring 2009a). *Self acceptance and influences on teaching and learning*. Eleventh Annual Summer Institute for Faculty and Staff for the Molloy College Faculty Professional Center, Rockville Centre, NY.

———. (Winter 2009b). Character development and the brain. *Brain World*, *2*(1), 28–29, 68–69.

———. (March 2010a). *Science and Technology and Arts and Humanities: Two Cultures; Real or Perceived . . . We're Human Beings . . . Humans in the Act of Being*. Oxford, England: Oxford Round Table.

———. (2010b). A teacher's journey: A personal account of how women's rights and education have progressed hand in hand. *Brain World*, *3*(1), 53–57.

Schiering, M., and Bogner, D. (2007). *Conversations on the effect of external factors on belief and value systems*. Molloy College, Rockville Centre, NY.

Schiering, M., Buli-Holmberg, J., and Bogner, D. (2008). *A model for developing academic and social cognition, character development and the interactive book report*. Presentation at the University of Oslo and Teacher's College at the University of Bergen, Norway.

Schiering, M. S., and Dunn, K. (2001). Student empowerment: from cognition to metacognition. In R. Dunn (Ed.), *The art of significantly increasing science achievement test scores: Research and practical applications*. New York: St. John's University Press, Center for the Study of Learning and Teaching Styles.

Schiering, M., Hayes, B., and Marino, A. (2005). Storytelling as a learning style motivational technique and within class identifier of cognition and metacognition thought processes. In Raynor and Armstrong, et al. (Eds.), *Learning styles in education and training: problems, politisation and potential*. Surrey, UK: Proceedings of the Tenth Annual European Learning Style Conference.

Schiering, M., and Taylor, R. (1998). In R. Dunn (Ed.), *Practical approaches to individualizing staff development for adults*. Westport, CT: Praeger Publications.

Schiering, S. D. (2006). *Tri-fold board for an interactive learning center*. EDU 341: Social Studies Methods of R. Iovino. Molloy College, Rockville Centre, New York.

Schön, D. (1983). *The reflective practitioner: How professionals think in action*. London: Temple Smith.

———. (1997). Reflective practice and professional development. *ERIC Digest*.

Shenk, D. (2000). *The forgetting: Alzheimer's: Portrait of an epidemic*. New York: Random House.

Takata, N. (1969). The play history. *American Journal of Occupational Therapy, 23*, 314–18.

Toale, V. (1985/2005). *Storytelling for hope, morality and healing*. Course syllabus, Diocese of New York and Molloy College.

Tobias, S., and Everson, H. (1995). *Development and validation of and objective measure of metacognition.* In W. E. Montague, *Issues in metacognitive research and assessment.* Symposium conducted at the annual meeting of the American Education Research Association, San Francisco, CA.

Tomlinson, C.A. (2000). Differentiation of instruction in the elementary grades. *ERIC Clearinghouse on Elementary and Early Childhood Education* (pp. 2–7). Champaign, Illinois.

———. (2001). *How to differentiate instruction in mixed ability classrooms* (2nd ed.). Alexandria, VA: Association for Supervision and Curriculum Development (ASCD).

Trigwell, K., and M. Prosser. (1997). Towards an understanding of individual acts of teaching and learning: Phenomenographic perspective. *Higher Education Research and Development, 16*(2), 241–52.

USA Today. (2004). Together we can be bully free: A mini-guide for parents (by A. L. Beane). Minneapolis: Free Spirit.

Vygotsky, L. S. (1978). *Mind in society.* Cambridge, MA: Harvard University Press.

———. (1986). *Thought and language* (A. Kozin, Trans.). Cambridge, MA: MIT Press.

Weiss, M. P., and Boudah, D. J. (2002). Professional development schools and special education: How can we help each other meet our goals? In I. Guadarrama, J. Ramsey, and J. L. Nath (Eds.), *Forging alliances in communities and thought: Research in professional development schools* (105–24). Greenwich, CT: Information Publishing.

Wenger, E. (1998). *Communities of practice: learning, meaning and identity.* Cambridge, MA: Cambridge University Press.

———. (June 2006). *Communities of practice: A brief introduction.* http://ewenger.com/theory/index.htm.

Wilbur, K. (2000). *A theory of everything: An integral vision for business, politics, science, and spirituality.* Boston: Shambhala Publications.

Wilen, W., and Phillips, J. (1995). Teaching critical thinking: A metacognitive approach. *Social Education, 59,* 135–38.

Yount, W. R. (1996). *Created to Learn.* Nashville, TN: Broadman and Halman Publishers.

ABOUT THE AUTHORS

Reverend Dr. Marjorie Schiering's doctoral work has been concentrated on developing cognition and metacognition in a social context. She has thirty-one years of experience teaching in elementary and middle school. The following fourteen years of teaching have been at the postgraduate level, first at St. John's University as an adjunct professor, and then in the Division of Education at Molloy College, where she's presently a full professor. Also, since 2003 she has taught children's literature in the undergraduate program for the English department at Molloy.

She received her bachelor's degree in childhood education from Ohio State University in 1965 and earned her master's degree in reading from the College of New Rochelle in 1974. A Dunn and Dunn Learning Styles Model certified Learning Styles trainer and practitioner, she began Molloy College's International Learning Styles Network (ILSN) Center in 2004. Newsletter coeditor for the European International Learning Style Network (ELSIN) from 2002 to 2008, she became an international presenter on how to adapt teaching to the way children learn.

She's a member of the Oxford Round Table and a published author on the topics of children's literature, developing cognitive and metacognitive skills in individuals, and brain-based education. She is internationally recognized for her innovative approaches to teaching creativity, critical thinking, motivating teachers and students, inspiring learning and building classroom community, and providing safe school environments by instruction regarding the six international traits of being a person of good character. Dr. Schiering became an ordained interfaith minister in 2008 and volunteers nearly six hundred hours a year as a chaplain at Westchester Medical Center in Valhalla, New York.

Dr. Drew Bogner, whose doctoral work and research has been focused on John Dewey and metacognition applied to experiential teaching, currently serves as president and professor of education at Molloy College in Rockville Centre, New York, posts he has held for twelve years. Previously, he was provost and director of the Institute for Teacher Education at Newman University in Wichita, Kansas, for twelve years.

Professor Jorun Buli-Holmberg is an active researcher on inclusive education and metacognition with numerous publications in Norway and other European countries. She has over twenty years of experience teaching at different levels from preschool to high school, with fifteen years at the university level in Oslo, Norway.

We are educators working on the topic of metacognition and its connection to teaching and learning. We collaborated on this book because we believe that education would be improved if both students and teachers know how thinking and feelings, as well as emotions, impact learning and teaching. Aspects of the model and its accompanying pedagogy have been presented at numerous workshops across the globe. Presentations of the model for academic and social cognition were well received at the universities of Hull and Surrey in England in the early 2000s.

These were followed by magazine and journal publications and simultaneous presentations of the model at Leuven University, Ghent, Belgium; the divisions of education at the universities of Oslo and Bergen; the teacher centers of Asker, Nessoden, and Skein, Norway; as well as for the University of Buffalo, New York, in Medellin, Colombia, South America; University of Iceland, Reykjavik; Molloy College on Long Island, New York; the New York City school system numerous times; and New York State's and the International Council for Exceptional Children's conferences in Niagara Falls and Saratoga Springs, New York; as well as Riga, Latvia. The success of these presentations gives credence to the concept that there is a wide audience for the book both internationally and within the United States.

28457272R00186

Made in the USA
Middletown, DE
15 January 2016